InDesign Essentials

The Fast Track to Mastering Adobe's Revolutionary Page Layout Application

InDesign Essentials

The Fast Track to Mastering Adobe's Revolutionary Page Layout Application

Alistair Dabbs   Ken McMahon   Keith Martin   Anne-Marie Concepción

ILEX

Contents

INDESIGN ESSENTIALS

Copyright © 2006 The Ilex Press Limited

First published in the United Kingdom in 2006 by:

I L·E X

The Old Candlemakers,
West Street, Lewes,
East Sussex, BN7 2NZ

Publisher: *Alastair Campbell*
Managing Director: *Stephen Paul*
Creative Director: *Peter Bridgewater*
Managing Editor: *Tom Mugridge*
Editor: *Ben Renow-Clarke*
Art Director: *Julie Weir*
Designer: *Ginny Zeal*
Junior Designer: *Kate Haynes*

I L E X is an imprint of the Ilex Press Ltd
Visit us on the Web at:

www.ilex-press.com

This book was conceived by:

I L·E X , Cambridge, England

British Library Cataloguing-in-publication data.
A catalogue record for this book is available from the British Library.

ISBN 10 – 1-904705-70-7
ISBN 13 – 978-1-904705-70-3

Printed and bound in the UK by Butler and Tanner

For more information on this title please visit:

www.web-linked.com/stqiuk

INTRODUCTION

Adobe InDesign is the biggest thing to hit the design and production world for well over a decade. It has turned the old concept of basic digital galleys on its head and ushered in a new way of approaching page design. From its flexible layout features to its unprecedented levels of typographic control and professional output features, InDesign CS2 shows the way forward for high-end digital design and production.

This book is an in-depth and comprehensive guide to getting the most from this industry-leading software. Whether you're a seasoned print professional or are fresh to the world of page layout, you'll find recipes

and tips for every task you could want to tackle, created by experts with real-world experience in using InDesign. This book is intended to be used as both a high-speed learning tool for those getting started with InDesign, and a complete reference for designers using the software in a professional environment. Think of the authors as experienced InDesign chefs right at your elbow, ready to lend you a hand. Pick a topic and find the task you want to do, then work through the recipe and expert tips to complete it quickly and professionally.

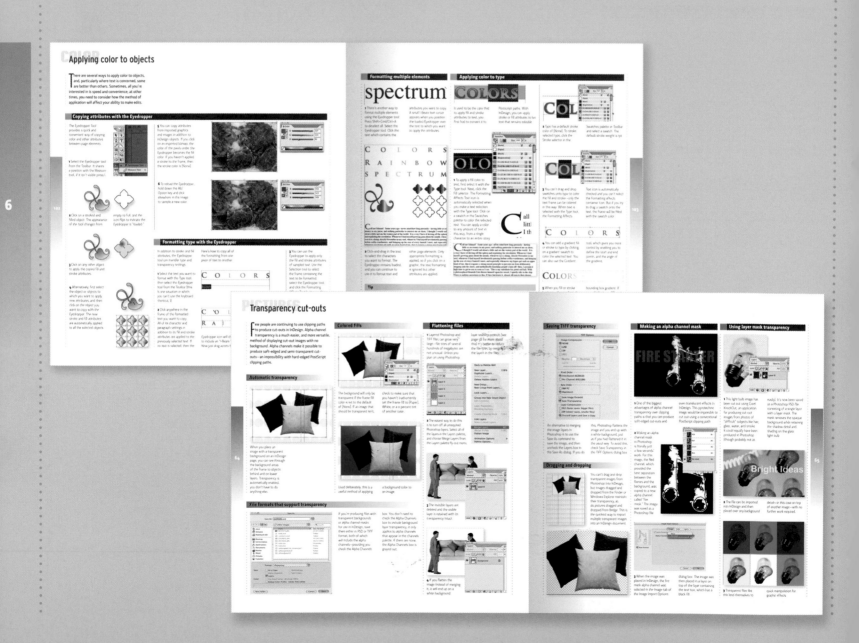

This book begins with the real secrets of working with text: importing and flowing content from different sources, handling multilingual documents and foreign-language spellchecking, and getting the most from InDesign's Story Editor. You'll learn how to work with multiple baseline grids and layers, and how to take advantage of the dynamic links offered by InDesign's master pages.

One of this application's hidden strengths is its extensive use of styles. Not just simple character and paragraph styles, although these important basics are certainly covered. InDesign's styles can be nested and can switch settings intelligently depending on what's being formatted. So, with a little experimenting and the cookbook recipes on pages 10–53, you'll be able to style complete, complex layouts—including detailed, multi-part tables, nested references and quotes, and even object style settings—with a few simple clicks. Similarly, InDesign style tags help control text from the moment it enters your layout. Master InDesign's intelligent style sheets and you'll have acquired a key ingredient for efficient, professional results.

When you're ready to try something else, InDesign has a slew of creative features waiting for your direction. Type on paths, Illustrator-style drawing tools, and support for object transparency open up whole new vistas of creative possibilities. In order to achieve professional-level results, all of these features need to be properly applied. The book covers the full gamut of production topics, including color management, packaging layouts for output, testing separations, and producing tailored PDF files to ensure that your work is reproduced to the most exacting standards. And, for those heading into interactive media production, InDesign's support for hyperlinking and rollovers, as well as embedded audio and video, brings ease of use and high-level design control to an area that was once the sole preserve of high-tech geeks.

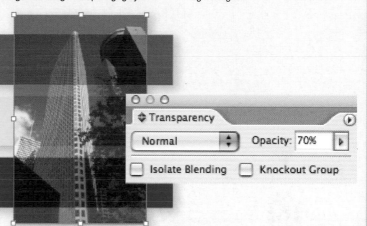

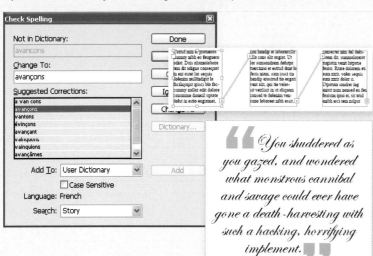

> *You shuddered as you gazed, and wondered what monstrous cannibal and savage could ever have gone a death-harvesting with such a hacking, horrifying implement.*

If you're feeling daunted at the thought of tackling these high-end topics, relax. Find the sections and recipes that cover what you want to know and you'll be brought up to speed in next to no time. And if you're a QuarkXPress user feeling nervous about making the switch, turn to page 178. The final section is written specifically to keep you productive while you learn where all the most important equivalent features and controls are found and, equally importantly, where they differ.

InDesign CS2 provides the user with immense creative and productive power, spread across myriad different options and controls. The best way to harness it and turn it to your advantage is to get insider help from the experts, and that's exactly what you get in the secrets, tips, and tutorials in this book.

As well as formatting more efficiently, you'll be free to push your typography to new heights: InDesign's full support for OpenType is like having the abilities of a skilled typesetter just a mouse-click away. In addition, optical type alignment, hanging punctuation, and other typographic touches that are standard in CS2 are fully covered here, along with lots of other useful tricks and techniques.

7

TEXT

Text frames and columns

Text layout is a fundamental feature of InDesign. InDesign is a very flexible program, and provides a number of different methods for putting words on the page. It is worth familiarizing yourself with the pros and cons of each method.

Adding text

1 The most basic method for adding text is to click on the Type tool in the Toolbar, and then click-and-drag a rectangular frame onto your page.

When you let go of the mouse button, you can immediately begin typing. The text will appear within the text frame that you have drawn, and will be set in the default style unless otherwise specified.

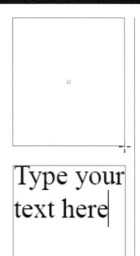

Type your text here

2 Another way of adding text to your page is to import it from an external text file (including those saved in Microsoft Word doc and Excel xls formats). Then, in InDesign, choose **File > Place**, locate the text file you prepared, and double-click on the file or click OK at the bottom of the dialog window.

3 InDesign loads the text, but waits for you to decide how it should be placed. The mouse cursor changes to show that it is "loaded" with text. You can then place the text by either clicking in an existing frame, or clicking on an empty part of the layout and allowing InDesign to create a frame for you. The frame you click on does not need

to be empty—the placed text replaces the previous content—nor does it need to be a text frame. InDesign converts any kind of frame into a text frame as soon as you try to place text in it.

Digital cameras

Cheaper, better quality, more functions. It's the same old story every time we bring together the latest digital still cameras for a lab test, and this occasion is certainly no exception.

4 Another alternative is to click-and-drag to draw a text frame with the loaded cursor—the text will flow into it automatically.

Instead of choosing a text file first and then drawing a text frame for it, you can work the other way around, QuarkXPress-style, drawing a text frame first, leaving the text cursor in the frame, then going to **File > Place** and picking a text file to flow into it.

Running text in columns

1 Running text that flows across multiple columns can be constructed in two ways. One is to draw several text frames and link them together using the in and out ports (see page 11).

2 The other option is to draw one big text frame that contains multiple columns. Any text frame can be given multiple columns by choosing **Object > Text Frame Options** and editing the Columns attributes in the General tab of the dialog window.

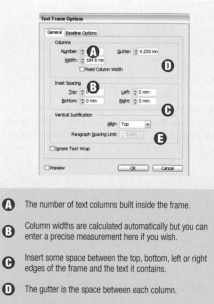

A The number of text columns built inside the frame.

B Column widths are calculated automatically but you can enter a precise measurement here if you wish.

C Insert some space between the top, bottom, left or right edges of the frame and the text it contains.

D The gutter is the space between each column.

E Choose whether to align text with the top or bottom of the frame, centre it vertically between top and bottom, or justify it vertically to fill the whole space from top to bottom.

In ports and out ports

Every text frame has an "in" port and an "out" port, visible when it is selected with the Selection tool. These are used to link text frames together across columns and pages.

When the out port shows a red "+" symbol, the text has run into overmatter—that is, the frame is too small to show all the text it contains. You can resize the frame by dragging on its handles with the Selection tool, or click once in the out port to load the cursor with the overmatter text, then click-and-drag to draw a new frame linked to the first one.

(A) perat, sequis dionsed delis acidunt praesto conse modio dipis nulla facipsu scipis exer sumsan ulputpat. Cil dui ea feugait adions alit, susto ero commodionsed endre vulla alis augiatie mod etuero elit prat. **(B)**

(A) In port

(B) Out port

Text threads

To see the order in which linked text frames flow, go to **View > Show Text Threads**. The links are shown as blue lines between the out and in ports of each text frame in the story.

Usrud min er pranueros ummy nibh eu feuguero odiat. Duis alismolobore tem dit adigna consequat in ent autet lor sequis dolenin nullundipit la faciliquipit ipisci bla fac-cummy mullut adit dolore comummo dionull uptate riduit in estio eugiamet,

con hendip er loborercilit illa cons alit augiat. Ut lor sumsandrem dolutpa tuercinisi et estrud dunt la feuis niam, sum iusci tin hendip erostrud tio eugnit vent alit, qui tie veles-sit verilisit in ut aliquam consed te dolenim ven-ismo loboreet nibh essit.

consecter nim del doiu-item dit, summolorerat augiatin venit lurpatie feuisi. Riure dolorem ex eum zzrit, volor sequis eum zzrit dolor si. Utpatum sandrer ing enisit num nonsed eu feu feuisim ipisi et, sit wisl enibh erci tem mulput

Tip

SELECTING TEXT

When using the Selection or Direct Selection tools, double-click on any text frame to automatically activate the Type tool instead.

RESIZING TEXT FRAMES

While using the Type tool, hold down the Ctrl/Cmd key to toggle temporarily to the Selection tool. You can then resize the frame (but not the text inside it) by dragging its handles.

Using advanced text flow options

1 If your page layout has been set up with multiple column guides, InDesign can use them to semi-automate the creation of text frames within these columns. For more on setting column guides for page layouts, see page 130. Go to **File > Place** and choose a text file, then click once within any pair of empty column guides. InDesign draws a new text frame to fill the column area starting from the point at which you clicked. You can link more text frames to it using the out port technique explained above.

Before clicking the mouse to place the text, hold down one of the following keyboard modifiers to alter the appearance of the loaded text cursor and change the way you create multiple columns:

2 With the Alt/Option key pressed down, you don't have to link text frames using the out port technique. Just create each frame in turn and they are linked automatically.

3 With the Alt/Option + Shift keys pressed down, click once inside a column guide to instantly fill all the columns on the page (and on any subsequent pages) with linked text frames.

4 Hold down the Shift key and click once inside any column guide to fill all the column guides instantly with linked text frames, adding more pages automatically as necessary until there is no more overmatter.

5 When you have a loaded text cursor, bringing it close to a column guide changes its appearance to an "empty" arrow rather than a black-filled one. When you click, the text frame snaps to that guide.

Baseline grids

A baseline is the invisible horizontal line along which characters sit, aligned side-by-side. A baseline grid is a stack of baselines used to ensure that text is aligned correctly throughout a page or document. Every InDesign document has a default baseline grid. To toggle the baseline grid visibility on and off, go to View > Grids & Guides > Show/Hide Baseline Grid.

Grid preferences

This default baseline grid is customized in the Preferences dialog window, accessible by going to **InDesign** > **Preferences** > **Grids** (Mac) or **Edit** > **Preferences** > **Grids** (Win).

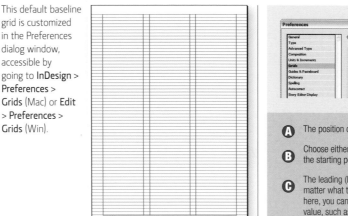

A The position of the first baseline, relative to the starting point.

B Choose either "Top of page" or "Top of margin" as the starting point.

C The leading (line spacing) of the baseline grid. No matter what type of measurement is currently used here, you can type over it with a conventional point value, such as 12 pt.

Aligning text to the baseline

12

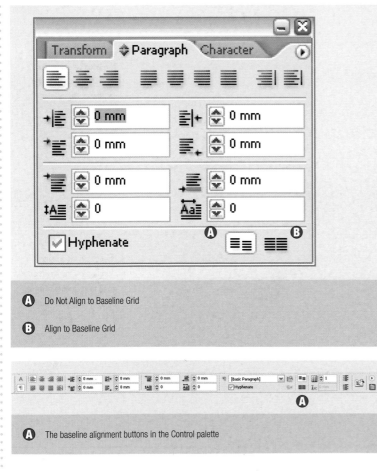

A Do Not Align to Baseline Grid

B Align to Baseline Grid

A The baseline alignment buttons in the Control palette

Baseline alignment is a paragraph attribute, so the baseline buttons are found in the Paragraph palette and in the Paragraph mode of the Control palette.

Bont? Ocreo Catu inam nonsulictur aperio, cae et; nihi, ublicullessi pertus effrestis. Foremus tam morbita strarbensil tillabes etrei ferio utera conver-vir ia consimihic rehem Roma, Palabis recri tan-tierei popostr acchic ipse crit iam fat Catis, culartem obse, consum quam et Catra aut videt; nori se in pro achucie fuissa vasta, adem, Catum vigiternihi, nondum tantra rehem,

consin Etrunu mere ceporte ridiente abus ausperet L. Vivividit. Firi publica; noximus caticaut fenatque norum hil vit, quam hebatudam fatifecris horus tas cotine fere, que inatum die con-sili caeque vissen Etris? in hortistortus perfenatis Nihili ta L. Bis hi, nosula vignati enatquam dienato ditrae ta ius acchilinum in derfecitre possit, te, C. Po-tilici ia in nes orbis pat, con vagiti, senaris simius, ut

Bont? Ocreo Catu inam nonsulictur aperio, cae et; hi, ubicullessi pertus frestis. Foremus tam orbita strarbensil tillabes ei ferio utera conver-r ia consimihic rehem oma, Palabis recri tan-rei popostr acchic ipse it iam fat Catis, culartem se, consum quam et tra aut videt; nori se in pro achucie fuissa vasta, adem, Catum vigiternihi, nondum tantra rehem,

consin Etrunu mere ceporte ridiente abus ausperet L. Vivividit. Firi publica; noximus caticaut fenatque norum in hil vit, quam hebatudam fatifecris horus tas cotiner-fere, que inatum die con-sili caeque vissen Etris? Ir in hortistortus perfenatis. Nihili ta L. Bis hi, nosula vignati enatquam dienato ditrae ta ius acchilinum in derfecitre possit, te, C. Po-tilici ia in nes orbis pat, con

1 Let's say you have a text story running over a couple of frames. Unless the frames themselves are perfectly aligned, their baselines will not match. When you select the text with the Type tool, the Do Not Align To Baseline Grid button is active.

2 Click on the Align To Baseline Grid button to fix the selected text to the document's baseline grid.

Baseline shift

Baseline shift pushes the selected text above or below the baseline of the other characters in the line, regardless of whether it is aligned to the baseline grid or not. It is a character attribute, so the setting is found in the Character palette and in the Character mode of the Control palette.

Ⓐ Baseline Shift

Ⓐ The baseline shift option in the Control palette

Select some text with the Type tool and increase the Baseline Shift value above 0 (zero) to push it upward, or reduce it below 0 to push it downward.

base**line** shift

Frame-level baseline grids

In addition to the document-level baseline grid, you can set up custom baseline grids for each frame independently. Select a text frame and go to **Object > Text Frame Options**, then click on the Baseline Options tab and check the Use Custom Baseline Grid option.

Ⓐ Choose how the first line of text is offset from the top of the frame.

Ⓑ The starting point of the frame-level baseline grid.

Ⓒ The position of the first line of the frame-level baseline grid relative to the starting point. Choose from the options shown.

Ⓓ The leading (line spacing) of the frame-level baseline grid. Just type over the existing values with a conventional point value.

Let's say you want to create a logotype using live text instead of outline shapes.

1 Using the Type tool, select some characters and increase the Baseline Shift value to push them upwards.

2 Insert the text cursor between the shifted characters and the initial capital, then reduce the kerning value (see page 16).

3 Complete the logo with fill and stroke colors (see page 80) and a drop shadow effect (see page 120).

Tip

BASELINE OBJECT STYLE
Another way to apply frame-level baseline grids is to set them up within an object style. Open the Object Styles palette and Alt/Option + click on the Create New Style button at the bottom or choose New Object Style from the palette menu. In the Object Style Options window, click on Text Frame Baseline Options in the left-hand list and enter your preferred baseline settings.

Click on the new object style, and your custom frame-level baseline grid settings are applied.

Tip

MULTI-COLUMN GRID
There are several ways to apply a frame-level baseline grid across multiple threaded columns. The easiest is to use a single text frame containing multiple columns, as explained on pages 10–11.

If the story runs across non-aligned, non-adjacent, or irregular columns, this method is not practical. Instead, select the text frames using the Selection tool by Shift-clicking each one, or by dragging a selection marquee over them, then go to Object > Text Frame Options. The settings you enter under the Baseline Options tab will then apply to all the selected frames.

An easier way is to use the Type tool to select the text before going to the Text Frame Options and customizing the Baseline. If you add another text frame to the story, it won't automatically take on the baseline setting of the previous frames.

13

Spelling

pellchecking is easy in InDesign: just go to Edit > Spelling > Check Spelling to open the Check Spelling palette (or use the Ctrl/Cmd+I keyboard shortcut) and click on the Start button.

Using the Check Spelling palette

1 Whenever the program finds a word that is not in its built-in dictionary, it stops and prompts you with suggested corrections. Select one, and then click the Change or Change All button.

3 If the queried word is not incorrect, you can click the Ignore All button to continue the spellcheck. If you want to add the word to your user dictionary, do not select any of the Suggested Corrections—click on the Add button instead.

2 The Search pop-up at the bottom of the palette lets you decide which text to check. For example, to spellcheck multiple InDesign documents at once, open them all and choose All Documents from the pop-up.

4 Your user dictionary is activated by default—there is no need to look for it on your hard disk. You can manage multiple user dictionaries if you want by going to **InDesign** > **Preferences** > **Dictionary** (Mac) or **Edit** > **Preferences** > **Dictionary** (Win).

If you have multiple user dictionaries, you can choose which one to add new words to by choosing its name from the Add To pop-up next to the Add button in the Check Spelling palette. To look at a user dictionary, click on the Dictionary button.

5 A user dictionary is actually just a list of additional word preferences that is linked to the built-in dictionary. The built-in dictionary itself cannot be edited. To specify Added

Words, Removed Words, or Ignored Words for future spellchecks, pick your preference from the Dictionary List pop-up, type a word into the Word field, and click the Add button.

Tip

DYNAMIC SPELLING

To view spelling errors without having to run a spellcheck, go to Edit > Spelling > Dynamic Spelling or choose InDesign > Preferences > Spelling (Mac) or Edit > Preferences > Spelling (Win). This enables on-screen underline highlights for the same errors that the spellchecker looks for. The Preferences window also lets you choose the colors with which each kind of error is underlined.

Fixing typos

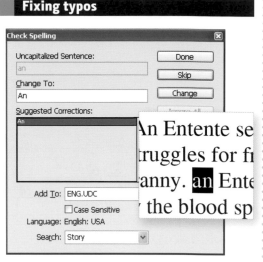

1 By default, InDesign will also check for capitalization typos such as sentences that don't begin with a capital letter. Choose one of the Suggested Corrections or enter your own and click Change.

2 InDesign also checks for duplicated words. These errors can be fixed in the same way.

3 Go to **InDesign** > **Preferences** > **Spelling** (Mac) or **Edit** > **Preferences** > **Spelling** (Win) to tell InDesign what to look for when spellchecking.

14

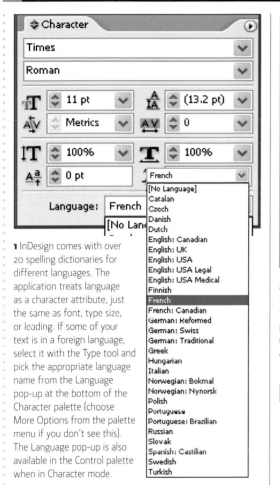

1 InDesign comes with over 20 spelling dictionaries for different languages. The application treats language as a character attribute, just the same as font, type size, or leading. If some of your text is in a foreign language, select it with the Type tool and pick the appropriate language name from the Language pop-up at the bottom of the Character palette (choose More Options from the palette menu if you don't see this). The Language pop-up is also available in the Control palette when in Character mode.

2 If you've assigned a foreign language attribute to specific words or passages, the next time you run a spellcheck, InDesign automatically switches from one language dictionary to another as it moves through the text It will even spot missing accents in those languages.

3 If a particular foreign word or phrase crops up several times throughout a document, assign the language attribute to it globally using the Find/Change window. Go to **Edit > Find/Change** and type in the word or phrase in both the Find What and Change To fields.

Tip

CUSTOM SPELLCHECK

In addition to adding new words to your user dictionary, use the Removed Words list in the Dictionary window (Edit > Spelling > Dictionary) to deal with problem words, such as homophones, or those that need attention in your editorial house style. For example, by adding "council" and "counsel" or "its" and "it's" to your Removed Words list, every spellcheck in that language will stop at both spellings and prompt you to choose which is correct in that instance.

Tip

AUTOCORRECT

InDesign can automatically correct spelling errors as you type, word processor-style. Enable the feature by choosing Edit > Spelling > Autocorrect or go to InDesign > Preferences > Autocorrect (Mac) or Edit > Preferences > Autocorrect (Win). The Preferences window also lets you add and remove the kinds of errors you want InDesign to correct.

4 Then click on the Format button next to Change Format Settings at the bottom of the Find/Change palette. In the Change Format Settings window, click on Advanced Character Formats in the left-hand list pane and choose the appropriate language from the Language pop-up.

Click OK, and then click Find Next in the Find/Change palette. At the first instance, click Change All. Remember to tell InDesign where to look in the Search pop-up.

15

Characters

Character attributes are set using the Character palette. The same functions (and a few more) are also available in the Control palette when it's set to Character mode. Many of the same functions can also be found under the Type menu.

The Character palette

A Font family
The pop-up reveals visual previews and icons indicating whether a font is TrueType, OpenType, or Adobe Type 1.

○	Stencil Std	**SAMPLE**	
a	Symbol	Σαμπλε	
○	Tahoma	Sample	▶
ᴛᴛ	Techno	**Sample**	
ᴛᴛ	Textile	*Sample*	
✓ ᴛᴛ	Times	Sample	▶
ᴛᴛ	Times New Roman	Sample	▶
○	Trade Gothic LT Std	Sample	▶
○	Trajan Pro	SAMPLE	▶
ᴛᴛ	Trebuchet MS	Sample	▶

B Type style
This pop-up shows the individual fonts within the currently selected family. Some fonts may have only one face.

✓	Regular	**Sample**
	Italic	*Sample*
	Bold	**Sample**
	Bold Italic	***Sample***

C Type size
Use the pop-up or enter a value to set the size of selected text, measured in points.

6 pt
8 pt
9 pt
10 pt
11 pt
✓ 12 pt
14 pt
18 pt
24 pt
30 pt
36 pt
48 pt

D Leading
Use the pop-up or enter a value to set the vertical spacing of selected text, measured in points. Note that leading is a character, not paragraph, attribute in InDesign.

✓ Auto
6 pt
8 pt
9 pt
10 pt
11 pt
12 pt
14 pt
18 pt
24 pt
30 pt
36 pt
48 pt
60 pt
72 pt

E Kerning

Optical
✓ Metrics
-100
-75
-50
-25
-10
-5
0
5
10
25
50
75
100
200

First, place the text cursor between the two characters you wish to kern. To increase the space between letters, use a positive value; to decrease the space between the letters, use a negative value.

InDesign also gives you an option called Optical, which automatically calculates the optimum kerning between all selected characters based on the actual font and current type size. You can still alter individual kern values after applying the Optical setting.

Tip

PALETTE VALUES

Instead of clicking inside a field, click on the little icon label next to it—this activates the relevant field and selects its contents in one click. You can then type new values and tap the Tab or Return key to apply them instantly. Alternatively, while a field's contents are selected, you can press the Up and Down Arrow keys to increase and decrease the values in gradual increments, or use these in combination with the Shift key for large increments. This tip works with field name labels in many dialog windows as well.

Tip

FRAME-LEVEL ATTRIBUTES

To edit the character attributes for the entire contents of a text frame, select the frame using the Selection tool and make your changes in the Character or Control palette as normal.

16

F Tracking
Use the pop-up or enter a value to adjust the spacing uniformly between characters in text selections, measured in 1/1000 em units. For example, here is some text with increased tracking...

-100
-75
-50
-25
-10
-5
✓ 0
5
10
25
50
75
100
200

Incip eu facip eliqu
ipisiscing esenit
num velisi te feum
dolutpat, conse eu
feum velenisi.

... and the same text again with the tracking reduced to minus values.

Incip eu facip eliquat
ipisiscing esenit num
velisi te feum dolutpat,
conse eu feum velenisi.

G H Vertical and Horizontal Scale
Use the pop-up or enter a value to stretch and compress selected text, measured as a percentage of the original size. Vertical Scale preserves the existing text width while adjusting the height; Horizontal Scale preserves the existing text height while changing its width.

200%
175%
150%
125%
110%
✓ 100%
90%
75%
50%
25%

150% Vertical Scale

150% Horizontal Scale

I Baseline shift
Raises selected text above, or lowers it below, its nominal baseline. For more details on baseline shift, see page 13.

J Skew
When a font family does not include an italic face (many display fonts lack them), enter a Skew angle to fake it. Positive values slant to the right, negative values slant backward to the left. 12° is often used as the angle to emulate an italic face.

Beware of using Skew with serif fonts, because sometimes the serif tips on the extreme left and right of the selection can be sliced off at output. If in doubt, convert Skewed text to outlines (see page 92).

K Fly-out menu
This provides access to further character styling functions.

Hide Options	
OpenType	▶
All Caps	⇧⌘K
Small Caps	⇧⌘H
Superscript	⇧⌘=
Subscript	⌥⇧⌘=
Underline	⇧⌘U
Strikethrough	⇧⌘/
✓ Ligatures	
Underline Options....	
Strikethrough Options...	
No Break	

Choose All Caps (or click the All Caps button in the Control palette) to do this:

ALL CAPS

Choose Small Caps (or click the Small Caps button in the Control palette) to do this:

SMALL CAPS

Choose Superscript (or click the Superscript button in the Control palette) to do this:

32nd

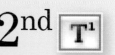

Choose Subscript (or click the Subscript button in the Control palette) to do this:

32$_{10}$

gregarious

The Underline and Strikethrough functions are explained on page 18.

Changing case

In addition to the All Caps and Small Caps functions, InDesign provides a set of letter case conversion commands in the main menus and contextual menus. Note that these are not styling attributes, but actual conversions.

1 Choose **Type > Change Case** and pick from four submenu options:

UPPER CASE

2 Upper Case sets all of the type in upper case.

lower case

3 Lower Case sets all of the type in lower case.

Title Case

4 Title Case gives each word an initial cap.

Sentence case

5 Sentence Case gives only the first word in each sentence an initial cap.

Characters, continued

Underline Options

gregarious

Choose Underline from the Character palette menu (or click the Underline button in the Control palette) to add an underline to selected text.

gregarious

For a different effect, turn off the underline for characters that have descenders.

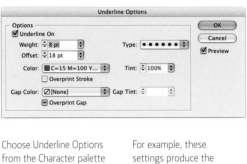

Choose Underline Options from the Character palette menu. The Underline Options window lets you edit the weight, color, and style of the line, and adjust its offset (the distance from the text baseline).

For example, these settings produce the following result on large display text.

gregarious

Strikethrough Options

Choose Strikethrough from the Character palette menu (or click the Strikethrough button in the Control palette) to pass a line through selected text. Admittedly, this does not have a great deal of practical use, but try this

pen highlighter effect. First select some text and choose Strikethrough Options from the Character palette menu.

Check the Strikethrough On and the Preview options, then increase the Weight to thicken the line into a

band big enough to obscure the characters completely. You may need to adjust the Offset values. Choose a color from the pop-up, and check the Overprint Stroke option. Click OK and go to **View > Overprint Preview.**

It may be helpful to strike through sections of this text to give the impression it has been marked with a highlighter pen.

Inserting special characters

Auto Page Number	⌥⇧⌘N
Next Page Number	
Previous Page Number	
Section Marker	
Footnote Number	
Bullet Character	
Copyright Symbol	
Ellipsis	
Paragraph Symbol	
Registered Trademark Symbol	
Section Symbol	
Trademark Symbol	
Em Dash	
En Dash	
Discretionary Hyphen	⇧⌘-
Nonbreaking Hyphen	⌥⌘-
Double Left Quotation Mark	
Double Right Quotation Mark	
Single Left Quotation Mark	
Single Right Quotation Mark	
Tab	
Right Indent Tab	⇧→
Indent to Here	⌘\
End Nested Style Here	

1 While editing text with the Type tool, go to **Type > Insert Special Character.** This calls up a submenu of commands for inserting a variety of commonly used characters at the cursor position. The submenu is also available in the contextual menu when you Right/Ctrl+click in a text frame.

Clowns were entertaining the kids all day.

3 Insert a discretionary hyphen before the final "ing" to allow a natural hyphenation break. If the text reflows so that

"entertaining" is no longer at the end of the line, the word returns to its full form and the hyphen vanishes.

The police spoke to a passer-by at the scene.

4 The Nonbreaking Hyphen command prevents a hyphenated word or expression from being split

at the end of a line. Here, the word "passer-by" has been broken across two lines.

Philip: *(stage left)* Hello there! It's a lovely day outside. Anyone for tennis?

6 The Tab commands are self-explanatory too, but you may find Indent To Here useful on many occasions.

In the text below, we have inserted the text cursor immediately before the opening parenthesis.

Philip: *(stage left)* Hello there! It's a lovely day outside. Anyone for tennis?

7 The Indent To Here command forces all lines below to indent, aligning with that position in the first line.

Clowns were entertaining the kids all day.

2 For details on using the page-numbering commands at the top of the submenu, see page 134. The symbol characters underneath are self-explanatory, as are the Em Dash (—) and En Dash (–), and the quotation marks. The Discretionary Hyphen

command inserts invisible hyphenation points into words, only coming into play when the word hits the end of a line. Take this instance, where the word "entertaining" has no automatic hyphenation points.

The police spoke to a passer-by at the scene.

5 Replace the standard hyphen with a nonbreaking hyphen to prevent the break, forcing the complete word to move to the next line.

Inserting white space

Em Space	⇧⌘M
En Space	⇧⌘N
Flush Space	
Hair Space	
Nonbreaking Space	⌥⌘X
Thin Space	⌥⇧⌘M
Figure Space	
Punctuation Space	

1 While editing text with the Type tool, go to **Type > Insert White Space**. This calls up a submenu of commands for inserting at the cursor position a variety of alternative word spaces. The submenu is also available in the contextual menu.

The flush space character only works with paragraphs that have been set to Justify All Lines in the Paragraph palette (or the Control palette when it's in Paragraph mode). Normally, the word spacing in the last line of such a paragraph would be spread out evenly, but the flush space character grabs all that space for itself. It is particularly useful when ending a full-justified story with a graphic end mark. It may also alter the typography of the whole paragraph. ■

---

2 Use the Flush Space on the last line of a final paragraph in a story that has been set to Justify All Lines (see page 20), just before a final end mark. This saves you from having to align tabs, and it automatically adjusts if the text reflows or the column width changes.

"My full name is John Smith," he said.

3 A Nonbreaking Space works just like a nonbreaking hyphen, preventing a fixed expression from being broken across two lines. Take this proper name, for example.

"My full name is John Smith," he said.

4 Adding a nonbreaking space has prevented it from being split at the end of a line.

Inserting break characters

Column Break	✂
Frame Break	⇧✂
Page Break	⌘✂
Odd Page Break	
Even Page Break	
Forced Line Break	⇧↵
Paragraph Return	

1 While editing text with the Type tool, go to **Type > Insert Break Character**. This calls up a submenu of commands for forcing a story to jump to the next line, column, frame, or page. The submenu is also available in the contextual menu.

2 The Column Break and Frame Break commands are useful for balancing columns of text without having to insert blank lines or change the height of the columns. The untidy three-column text frame (above) has been more attractively balanced by inserting a Column Break in front of each heading (below).

Creating glyph sets

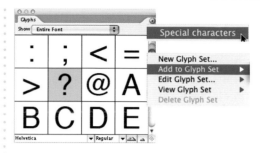

1 Go to **Type > Glyphs**, or **Window > Type & Tables > Glyphs** to open the Glyphs palette. You can use it to browse all the characters in any font on your system, and double click on them to insert them at the cursor position in your current text frame. If you use the same special characters repeatedly, build a custom glyph set for them. To do this, choose New Glyph Set from the palette menu and give it a name such as "Special Characters." Then use the Glyphs palette to browse to a particular character you use often, click on it to select it, and choose **Add to Glyph Set > Special Characters** from the palette menu.

Special characters
✓ Alternates for Selection
Entire Font

2 To view your Special Characters glyph set, choose it from the Show pop-up at the top of the palette.

Who is it?
Who is it?

3 You can then use the glyph set to insert your special characters. For example, if you don't like the squiggly question mark in Futura, you can replace it by double-clicking on your preferred alternative.

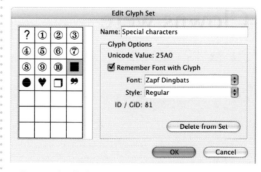

4 Choose **Edit Glyph Set > Special Characters** from the palette menu to further customize the characters you have added to your set. Ensure the Remember Font with Glyph option is selected if you want to insert the character in its particular font. This is especially handy for inserting Dingbat characters.

Paragraphs

Type attributes that apply to entire paragraphs rather than just to selected characters are set using the Paragraph palette. The same functions are also available in the Control palette. Remember that you may need to click on either the Character mode or the Paragraph mode button on the left of the Control palette in order to view the appropriate settings.

Tip

HYPHENS IN WORDS

InDesign's built-in dictionaries include word-by-word hyphenation preferences. To see how a word has been predesigned to hyphenate, go to Edit > Spelling > Dictionary, type the word in the Word field, and click the Hyphenate button. The hyphens are represented as "~" (tilde) characters.

~ represents the preferred (or only) hyphenation point.

~~ represents a second-choice hyphenation point.

~~~ represents a third-choice hyphenation point.

You can override these built-in settings for any word by editing the hyphenation points and clicking on Add to add it to your user dictionary. For example, InDesign's hyphenation points for the word "analysis" are "anal~y~~sis." If you think that ending a line with "anal-" is undesirable, use the Dictionary window to change it to "analy~sis" or "ana~~ly~~sis."

The Paragraph palette

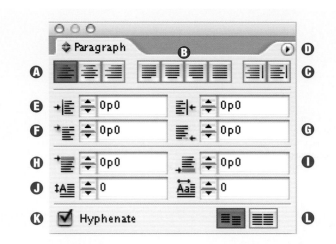

A Alignment
Standard left, center, and right alignment of selected paragraphs.

B Justify
Four options for justified text (aligned to both the left and right edges of the frame or column). Each option determines what to do with the last line at the bottom of a justified paragraph: align left, align center, align right, or justify.

C Spine alignment
Make selected paragraphs always align towards or away from the spine in spread layouts (see Chapter 6). This can be handy if it's part of your visual design and you move text frames from page to page, or if a layout shifts from a left-hand page to a right-hand page.

> Show Options
>
> ✓ Adobe Paragraph Composer
>   Adobe Single-line Composer
>
>   Only Align First Line to Grid
>   Balance Ragged Lines
>
>   Justification...   ⌥⇧⌘J
>   Keep Options...   ⌥⌘K
>   Hyphenation...
>   Drop Caps and Nested Styles... ⌥⌘R
>   Paragraph Rules...   ⌥⌘J
>   Bullets and Numbering...
>   Convert Bullets and Numbering to Text

D Fly-out menu
For details on the Composer and Balance Ragged Lines commands, see pages 36–37. For more information on baseline grids, see page 12. The other commands in this menu are dealt with here and overleaf.

Lendignim euipis aciduis nonsequis dolore mincin henim iliscil iquat. Pat, quat. Ut niamet irit amet, quisi ea feu facilit lam zzriuscin heniat.

Ut er am niat nonse magna feuisis num dolore modiam vel dignim at, consectem ea faccumm odignibh euisis auguerci ex se diat.

Ut iniate feugait, senit ulput lam dolent nim er sum qui tem dunt amet, sequatis eniam iure adipit pratie dolore faci tat nulput alit nibh et ea henis am quate faccumsan.

E Left and right indent
Indent all the text in selected paragraphs from the left-hand or right-hand edge of a frame or column. You can use these for short passages such as extended quotations (above).

Paragraph indents and spacing can be set using the Paragraph palette or the Control palette in Paragraph mode.
You can also assign these settings to paragraph styles so they can be applied across longer passages in a choice of automated ways.
Further paragraph settings can be edited using commands found inside the Paragraph palette pop-up menu.

F First line left indent
This adds a conventional indent to the first line at the top of each selected paragraph.

Paragraph indents and spacing can be set using the Paragraph palette or the Control palette in Paragraph mode.
You can also assign these settings to paragraph styles so they can be applied across longer passages in a choice of automated ways.
Further paragraph settings can be edited using commands found inside the Paragraph palette pop-up menu.

G **Last line right indent**
This forces a right-hand indent to the last line at the bottom of a selected paragraph that has been justified with the All Lines setting. If the paragraph is aligned in any other way, InDesign ignores this indent attribute.

Paragraph indents and spacing can be set using the Paragraph palette or the Control palette in Paragraph mode.

You can also assign these settings to paragraph styles so they can be applied across longer passages in a choice of automated ways.

Further paragraph settings can be edited using commands found inside the Paragraph palette pop-up menu.

H **Space before**
Insert a vertical gap above a selected paragraph.

Paragraph indents and spacing can be set using the Paragraph palette or the Control palette in Paragraph mode.
You can also assign these settings to paragraph styles so they can be applied across longer passages in a choice of automated ways.

Further paragraph settings can be edited using commands found inside the Paragraph palette pop-up menu.

I **Space after**
Insert a vertical gap below a selected paragraph.

J **Drop cap**
Produce an automated dropped capital effect using the first characters at the beginning of a paragraph. The left-hand control determines how many lines deep the drop cap should be. The right-hand control enables you to apply the effect to multiple characters.

K **Hyphenate**
Enable or disable hyphenation for selected paragraphs by checking or unchecking this option.

L **Baseline grid alignment**
Use these two buttons to align selected paragraphs to or release them from a baseline grid. For more details on working with baseline grids, see page 12.

Hyphenation Settings

To customize the way in which long words at the end of each line in a paragraph are split when the Hyphenate option is ticked, choose Hyphenation from the Paragraph palette menu. This opens the Hyphenation Settings window in which you can set standard preferences for minimum word lengths and the minimum number of characters allowed before and after a hyphen.

The Hyphenation Limit determines the maximum number of consecutive lines allowed to hyphenate in a paragraph. For unlimited hyphens, set this to zero.

The Hyphenation Zone value sets the amount of white space allowed at the end of a non-justified line in Single-Line Composer mode (see page 36) before hyphenation kicks in.

If the settings seem fiddly, just use the slider instead to choose between Better Spacing and Fewer Hyphens.

Using Drop Caps

1 To adjust the spacing between an automated drop cap and the text next to it, insert the flashing text editing cursor immediately after the drop cap.

2 Then use the Character palette to change the kern value at this point (see page 16). Positive kerning adds more space, negative kerning reduces it.

3 If you set a whole word as drop caps, include the trailing word space in the drop cap character count. Then select the last character and the space with the Type tool and use the Character palette to change their Track value (see page 16).

4 Another way to set drop caps is to choose Drop Caps and Nested Styles from the Paragraph palette menu. Simply enter a preferred line depth and character count for the drop cap in the Drop Caps and Nested Styles window and click OK.

5 Note that this window also lets you apply a character style to the drop cap at the same time, for example giving it a different font (see page 26 for more on character styles).

More paragraph options

The Paragraph palette menu (see page 20) provides several more features for customizing typography and formatting design and editorial effects automatically.

Changing Justification

Thus we were weaving and weaving away when I started at a sound so strange, long drawn, and musically wild and unearthly, that the ball of free will dropped from my hand, and I stood gazing up at the clouds wh[...] voice dropped like

1 Choose Justification from the Paragraph palette menu to fine-tune the visual appearance of selected paragraphs that have been set to one of the Justify alignments. The default settings produce this typical appearance.

Justification	Minimum	Desired	Maximum	
Word Spacing:	80%	100%	133%	OK
Letter Spacing:	0%	0%	0%	Cancel
Glyph Scaling:	100%	100%	100%	☑ Preview

Auto Leading: 120%
Single Word Justification: Full Justify
Composer: Adobe Paragraph Composer

Thus we were weaving and weaving away when I started at a sound so strange, long drawn, and musically wild and unearthly, that the ball of free will dropped from my hand, and I stood gazing up at the clouds whe[...] voice dropped like

2 Increase the Word Spacing and decrease the Letter Spacing percentages to produce a less dotty visual effect while allowing more space between words to maintain readability.

Justification	Minimum	Desired	Maximum	
Word Spacing:	200%	250%	300%	OK
Letter Spacing:	–25%	–20%	–10%	Cancel
Glyph Scaling:	100%	100%	100%	☑ Preview

Auto Leading: 120%
Single Word Justification: Full Justify
Composer: Adobe Paragraph Composer

3 Changing the Glyph Scaling values to anything but 100% varies the horizontal width of characters, which is generally undesirable. Similarly, for conventional typography, leave the Single Word Justification at its default Full Justify. For details on the Composer pop-up options, see page 36.

Using Keep Options

1 Choose Keep Options from the Paragraph palette menu to prevent selected paragraphs from being broken from others immediately before or after them, at the top or bottom of a column or frame. This is useful for keeping a crosshead with the first paragraph that follows it. For example, if a crosshead falls at the bottom of a column or frame...

It may be but an idle whim, but it has always seemed to me, that the extraordinary vacillations of movement displayed by some whales when beset by three or four boats; the timidity and liability to queer frights, so common to such whales; I think that all this indirectly proceeds from the helpless perplexity of volition, in which their divided and diametrically opposite powers of vision must involve them.

Ear of the whale

But the ear of the whale is full as curious as the eye. If you are an entire stranger to their race, you might hunt over these two heads for hours, and never discover that organ. The ear has no external leaf whatever; and into the hole itself you can hardly insert a quill, so wondrously minute is it. It is lodged a little behind the eye. With respect to their ears, this important difference is to be observed between the sperm whale and the right. While the ears of the former has an

2 ... select the crosshead, open the Keep Options window, and enter 1 in the Keep With Next field.

Keep Options		
Keep with Next: 1 lines		OK
☐ Keep Lines Together		Cancel
⦿ All Lines in Paragraph		☐ Preview
○ At Start/End of Paragraph		
Start: 2 lines		
End: 2 lines		
Start Paragraph: Anywhere		

It may be but an idle whim, but it has always seemed to me, that the extraordinary vacillations of movement displayed by some whales when beset by three or four boats; the timidity and liability to queer frights, so common to such whales; I think that all this indirectly proceeds from the helpless perplexity of volition, in which their divided and diametrically opposite powers of vision must involve them.

Ear of the whale

But the ear of the whale is full as curious as the eye. If you are an entire stranger to their race, you might hunt over these two heads for hours, and never discover that organ. The ear has no external leaf whatever; and into the hole itself you can hardly insert a quill, so wondrously minute is it. It is lodged a little behind the eye. With respect to their ears, this important difference is to be observed between the sperm whale and the right.

3 This ensures the crosshead stays with the next line, effectively forcing it over to the next column.

4 Check the Keep Lines Together option to establish more specific settings. The settings here, for example, prevent widows and orphans for selected paragraphs from appearing at the top and bottom of columns.

Keep Options		
Keep with Next: 0 lines		OK
☑ Keep Lines Together		Cancel
○ All Lines in Paragraph		☐ Preview
⦿ At Start/End of Paragraph		
Start: 2 lines		
End: 2 lines		
Start Paragraph: Anywhere		

✓ **Anywhere**
In Next Column
In Next Frame
On Next Page
On Next Odd Page
On Next Even Page

5 The Start Paragraph drop-down menu lets you determine where the text will go to when Keep Options forces it over.

Paragraph Rules

Choose Paragraph Rules from the Paragraph palette menu to add a single rule (a horizontal line) above and/or below selected paragraphs. These rules then stay with their paragraphs whenever text is edited or reflowed. The Rule Above and Rule Below options are switched on and edited independently, choosing the one you want from the drop-down at the top of the Paragraph Rules window.

> **Rule Above**
> ✓ **Rule Below**

[Paragraph Rules dialog box: Rule Above ☑ Rule On; Weight: 1 pt; Type: (solid); Color: ■ (Text Color); Tint; ☐ Overprint Stroke; Gap Color: ☑ [None]; Gap Tint; ☐ Overprint Gap; Width: Column; Offset: 0 mm; Left Indent: 0 mm; Right Indent: 0 mm; ☑ Preview; OK; Cancel]

[Paragraph Rules dialog box: Rule Above ☑ Rule On; Weight: 8 pt; Type: (wavy); Color: ☐ C=0 M=0 Y=10...; Tint: 100%; ☐ Overprint Stroke; Gap Color: ☐ C=100 M=0 Y=...; Gap Tint: 70%; ☐ Overprint Gap; Width: Column; Offset: 12 mm; Left Indent: 0 mm; Right Indent: 0 mm; ☑ Preview; OK; Cancel]

The options in the window are similar to those in the Stroke palette (see page 80), letting you set weight (thickness), type, color (chosen from your current swatches—see page 98), tint, and gap color for dotted and dashed stroke types. Most important is the Offset value, which lets you position the rule vertically in relation to the paragraph.

> *"The boat! the boat!"*
> *cried Starbuck,*
> *"Look at thy boat,*
> *old man!"*

The pull-quote effect here is created with thick rules above and below, choosing the wavy stroke type, colored yellow with a blue tint gap.

Using bullet points and numbered lists

Choose Bullets and Numbering from the Paragraph palette menu to convert selected paragraphs into a bulleted or numbered list.

[Bullets and Numbering dialog box: List Type: Bullets; Bullet Character grid; Add...; Delete; Font Family: (Times); Size: (12 pt); Font Style: (Regular); Color: ■ (Text Color); Bullet or Number Position; Position: Flush Left; Left Indent: 0p0; First Line Indent: 0p0; Tab Position: 1p6; ☑ Preview; Cancel; OK]

1 The default offering of bullet characters is not terribly interesting, so click on the Add button, choose a symbol font from the Font Family drop-down, and pick a new bullet character. Make sure the Remember Font with Bullet option is checked.

[Add Bullets dialog box: character grid; OK; Cancel; Add; Font Family: Zapf Dingbats; Font Style: Regular; ☑ Remember Font with Bullet]

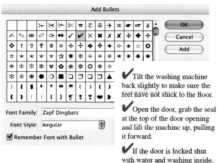

✔ Tilt the washing machine back slightly to make sure the feet have not stuck to the floor.

✔ Open the door, grab the seal at the top of the door opening and lift the machine up, pulling it forward.

✔ If the door is locked shut with water and washing inside, try syphoning out the water from the drain hose round the back. Then take out the soap drawer and use the hole to grasp the machine and pull it forward.

2 Click OK, and OK again to apply the new bullet to your selected paragraphs.

3 You can adjust the distance between the bullet and the first word in each paragraph by editing the Tab Position value at the bottom of the Bullets and Numbering window. The Position drop-down also lets you switch to a Hanging indent if you prefer.

✔ Tilt the washing machine back slightly to make sure the feet have not stuck to the floor.

✔ Open the door, grab the seal at the top of the door opening and lift the machine up, pulling it forward.

✔ If the door is locked shut with water and washing inside, try syphoning out the water from the drain hose round the back. Then take out the soap drawer and use the hole to grasp the machine and pull it forward.

> ✓ **Hanging**
> **Flush Left**

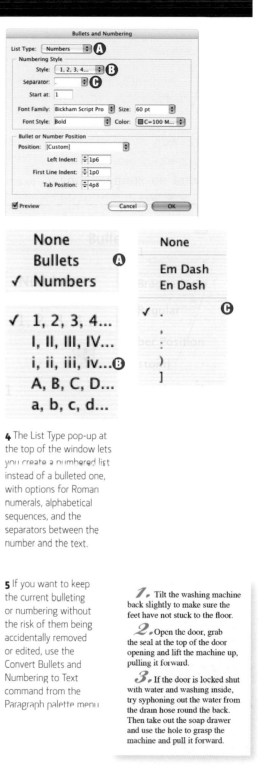

[Bullets and Numbering dialog box: List Type: Numbers Ⓐ; Numbering Style; Style: 1, 2, 3, 4... Ⓑ; Separator: . Ⓒ; Start at: 1; Font Family: Bickham Script Pro; Size: 60 pt; Font Style: Bold; Color: ■ C=100 M...; Bullet or Number Position; Position: [Custom]; Left Indent: 1p6; First Line Indent: 1p0; Tab Position: 4p8; ☑ Preview; Cancel; OK]

None	
Bullets	
✓ Numbers	Ⓐ

None	
Em Dash	
En Dash	

✓ 1, 2, 3, 4...	
I, II, III, IV...	
i, ii, iii, iv...	Ⓑ
A, B, C, D...	
a, b, c, d...	

Ⓒ (separator options: ✓ . , ;)])

4 The List Type pop-up at the top of the window lets you create a numbered list instead of a bulleted one, with options for Roman numerals, alphabetical sequences, and the separators between the number and the text.

5 If you want to keep the current bulleting or numbering without the risk of them being accidentally removed or edited, use the Convert Bullets and Numbering to Text command from the Paragraph palette menu.

1. Tilt the washing machine back slightly to make sure the feet have not stuck to the floor.

2. Open the door, grab the seal at the top of the door opening and lift the machine up, pulling it forward.

3. If the door is locked shut with water and washing inside, try syphoning out the water from the drain hose round the back. Then take out the soap drawer and use the hole to grasp the machine and pull it forward.

OpenType

OpenType is a font format that combines the best features of the TrueType and Adobe Type 1 font formats. Like TrueType, OpenType fonts are single, self-contained files (i.e. no separate printer and screen fonts). Like Adobe Type 1, OpenType can be based on PostScript font data. Additionally, OpenType expands the number of glyphs per font, giving you more typographical options with a choice of alternatives for each character. Also, OpenType fonts are compatible across Mac and Windows platforms without conversion.

OpenType fonts are marked with this symbol: *O* in InDesign's font menus. When using an OpenType font, special features are enabled for selected text in the OpenType submenu, accessible through the Character palette menu.

Commands enclosed in square brackets are not available for the current font—not all OpenType fonts support all features. This submenu is also available in the Control palette when it's in Character mode.

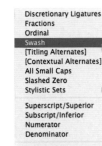

Discretionary ligatures

Standard ligatures built into modern fonts, such as those that apply to "fi" and "ff," are enabled by default. You can enable or disable ligatures for selected text by checking or unchecking Ligatures in the Character palette menu. Discretionary ligatures, on the other hand, are only available for OpenType fonts. These are additional, non-standard ligatures which you may wish to enable for typographical effect. The "fi" here is a standard ligature, but the "ct" and "st" are discretionary.

a fictional story

Fractions

Enabling the Fractions feature in the OpenType submenu allows InDesign to recognize sequences such as "1/2," and automatically matches them to fraction glyphs in the font, if available.

1/2	½
2/3	⅔
3/4	¾
7/8	⅞

Ordinals

InDesign recognizes number order abbreviations such as "1st" and "2nd." Enabling the Ordinal option automatically matches them to the ordinal glyphs in the font, if available.

1st	2nd	3rd	79th
1st	2nd	3rd	79th

Swashes

Some OpenType fonts contain alternative glyphs for certain characters that feature typographical flourishes, called swashes. They are most often found in stylized serif and script fonts, especially for capitals and characters at the beginning and end of a word. Here's a script font before and after checking the Swash option.

The Quick Brown Fox Jumped Over the Lazy Dog

The Quick Brown Fox Jumped Over the Lazy Dog

Titling alternatives

When a serif body text font is used for a headline or title, it may appear oddly thick and chunky. Some OpenType fonts include alternative glyphs for use as titles, enabled using the Titling Alternates option. The upper title here is set as Titling Alternates—the effect is very subtle.

Titling

Titling

Contextual alternates

This feature is enabled by default for OpenType fonts. Some OpenType fonts provide alternative glyphs for a particular character depending upon context, such as whether it begins or ends a word, or what other characters are next to it. This is particularly noticeable in script fonts since the swashes need to match up. Watch as we type the word "thereby" in Bickham Script Pro.

All Small Caps

The Small Caps command in the Character and Control palettes only applies to lower-case characters. The All Small Caps option in the OpenType submenu converts all selected characters, including capitals, to special small cap glyphs rather than merely shrinking standard capitals.

All Small Caps

ALL SMALL CAPS

Slashed zero

Tick this option to have all zero characters set with slashed zero glyphs, if they are available in the font.

100 100

Stylistic sets

In addition to dynamic contextual alternative glyphs for individual characters, some OpenType fonts have been prepared with complete sets of style alternatives. Just pick the sets you want to enable from the Stylistic Sets submenu.

player league in gym
player league in gym

Super/subscript and manual fractions

The Superscript/Superior and Subscript/Inferior commands work just like those in the main Character palette menu and Control palette, except that they apply specifically designed super/subscript glyphs rather than just shrinking the selected text. The Numerator and Denominator options enable you to format any selected numbers as fractions—including those not supported as standalone glyphs, in one easy step.

79/130

Figure style

Many OpenType fonts include modern lining and oldstyle alternatives for numbers. Lining numbers have a consistent height and sit on the baseline, while oldstyle numbers have varying heights and some characters have descenders. Choose your preference from the following:

1234567890
1234567890

Tabular Lining or Tabular Oldstyle

1234567890
1234567890

Proportional Oldstyle or Proportional Lining

$$137 + 364 = 501 \qquad 137 + 364 = 501$$

Tabular numbers occupy a fixed width, making it easy to align them vertically. Proportional numbers act like ordinary typeset text, with varying character widths. The example here shows a math book sum set as proportional (left) and as tabular.

Character styles

A character style is a set of type attributes that have been collected together and given a name. You can then apply those attributes to selected text quickly by applying the character style; you do not have to set all the attributes one by one using the Character or Control palettes.

Using character styles

The purpose of character styles is to help you apply the same specific type attributes in multiple places.

In <u>this sentence</u>, I will use a character style to *give emphasis* to selected words and characters. These character styles can exist independently of or in conjunction with paragraph styles.

1 Here, we've created a document containing two character styles.

In <u>this sentence</u>, I will use a character style to *give emphasis* to selected words and characters. These <u>character styles</u> can exist independently of or in conjunction with ***paragraph styles***.

2 The styles can be applied again and again to other selected text with just one click or keyboard shortcut.

In *this sentence,* I will use a character style to **give emphasis** to selected words and characters. These *character styles* can exist independently of or in conjunction with **paragraph styles**.

3 If you then re-edit the character styles with different type attributes, all the text in your document which uses those styles is updated automatically.

The Character Styles palette

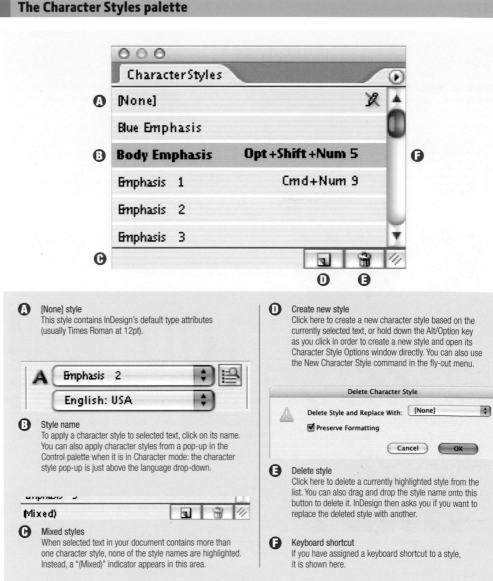

A **[None] style**
This style contains InDesign's default type attributes (usually Times Roman at 12pt).

B **Style name**
To apply a character style to selected text, click on its name. You can also apply character styles from a pop-up in the Control palette when it is in Character mode: the character style pop-up is just above the language drop-down.

C **Mixed styles**
When selected text in your document contains more than one character style, none of the style names are highlighted. Instead, a "(Mixed)" indicator appears in this area.

D **Create new style**
Click here to create a new character style based on the currently selected text, or hold down the Alt/Option key as you click in order to create a new style and open its Character Style Options window directly. You can also use the New Character Style command in the fly-out menu.

E **Delete style**
Click here to delete a currently highlighted style from the list. You can also drag and drop the style name onto this button to delete it. InDesign then asks you if you want to replace the deleted style with another.

F **Keyboard shortcut**
If you have assigned a keyboard shortcut to a style, it is shown here.

Tip

UNDEFINED ATTRIBUTES
Unlike QuarkXPress, InDesign's character and paragraph styles do not need to define all type attributes, but only those that need changing. For example, a character style might define a font but not its type size, letting you apply the style to any text whether it is 12pt or 200pt. In other words, existing text attributes that are not defined by the style are preserved.

To remove an attribute setting from the Character Style Options window, either use the Backspace key or pick "(Ignore)" from the relevant pop-up. To remove text color from a style, go to the Character Color section and locate the named color in the list.

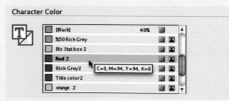

Character Style Options

Choose the Style Options command from the Character palette fly-out menu to open this window for setting the type attributes for a style. You can also open this window by holding down Ctrl/Cmd+Alt/Option+Shift and double-clicking on a style name.

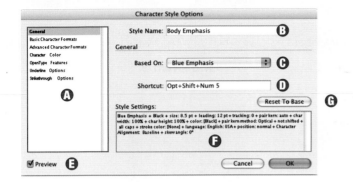

A Type attributes
These attributes correspond to those in the Character and Control palettes (see pages 16-19). There is also a Character Color attribute (see Chapter 4).

B Style Name
Give your character style a helpful name, or change it, here.

C Based On
Character styles can be based on other character styles. For example, to set up several alternative colors for a style, first create the basic character style and then create further styles based upon it, giving each one a different Character Color attribute. If you subsequently edit the first style, all other styles based upon it will update automatically.

D Shortcut
You can assign a keyboard shortcut to the style using a combination of the numeric keypad and the Ctrl/Cmd, Alt/Option, and Shift keys. InDesign will warn you if you try to set a keyboard shortcut that has already been assigned to another style.

E Preview
Tick the Preview option to see the effect of your changes in the document without having to close the window.

F Style settings
This is a summary of the type attributes of the style you are editing.

G Reset to base
Click on this button to reset all type attributes to default values (typically Times Roman 12pt).

Hold down the Command (Mac) or Ctrl (Win) key and click on the named color. This deselects it, leaving the text color icon grayed out and surrounded by question marks. From now on, applying this character style to text will leave its existing color unchanged.

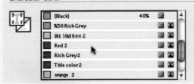

Overriding character styles

If you change the type attributes of your text after applying a character style, it is said to be "overridden" and a plus symbol (+) appears next to its name in the Character Styles palette.

1 To re-apply the original character style to selected text, getting rid of any overrides, just click on the highlighted style name in the palette.

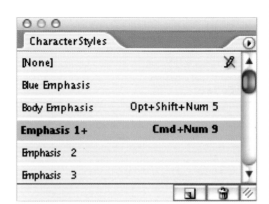

2 To incorporate any overrides from selected text back into the character style, choose Redefine Style from the palette menu. You can also use the keyboard shortcut Ctrl/Cmd+Alt/Option+Shift+C. This will update all instances in the document where you have used this style.

New Character Style...
Duplicate Style...
Delete Style

Redefine Style   ⌥⇧⌘C

Style Options...

Break Link to Style

Load Character Styles...
Load All Styles...

Select All Unused

Small Palette Rows

3 To leave all type attributes of the selected text as they are, but dissociate them from its character style (whether overridden or not), choose Break Link to Style from the palette menu. If you subsequently edit the original character style, this selected text will not change.

New Character Style...
Duplicate Style...
Delete Style

Redefine Style   ⌥⇧⌘C

Style Options...

Break Link to Style

Load Character Styles...
Load All Styles...

Select All Unused

Small Palette Rows

27

Paragraph styles

A paragraph style is a set of paragraph attributes that you can apply to selected text quickly without having to edit settings in the Paragraph or Control palettes. As with character styles, the great advantage of using paragraph styles is that they can format text throughout a document with just a few clicks. When you edit a style, your document updates automatically wherever that style has been applied.

Tip

QUICK APPLY

When a document contains a lot of styles—character styles, paragraph styles and object styles (see page 32)—use the Quick Apply feature to make it easier to find the styles you want to use without having to keep their palettes on-screen all the time.

To call up Quick Apply, click on its button in the Control palette or use the keyboard shortcut, Ctrl/Cmd+Return. Quick Apply appears as a pop-up scrolling list at the top right-hand corner of your InDesign window.

Type part of the style name you want to use, whereupon styles with matching names are displayed in the list.

Then just click on the style you want to apply to the selected text in your document, or scroll down to it using the cursor keys and tap Return.

The Paragraph Styles palette

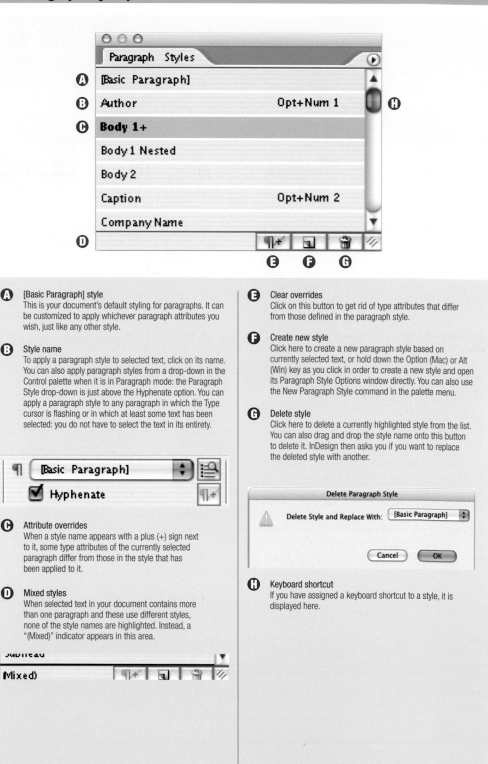

A [Basic Paragraph] style
This is your document's default styling for paragraphs. It can be customized to apply whichever paragraph attributes you wish, just like any other style.

B Style name
To apply a paragraph style to selected text, click on its name. You can also apply paragraph styles from a drop-down in the Control palette when it is in Paragraph mode: the Paragraph Style drop-down is just above the Hyphenate option. You can apply a paragraph style to any paragraph in which the Type cursor is flashing or in which at least some text has been selected: you do not have to select the text in its entirety.

C Attribute overrides
When a style name appears with a plus (+) sign next to it, some type attributes of the currently selected paragraph differ from those in the style that has been applied to it.

D Mixed styles
When selected text in your document contains more than one paragraph and these use different styles, none of the style names are highlighted. Instead, a "(Mixed)" indicator appears in this area.

E Clear overrides
Click on this button to get rid of type attributes that differ from those defined in the paragraph style.

F Create new style
Click here to create a new paragraph style based on currently selected text, or hold down the Option (Mac) or Alt (Win) key as you click in order to create a new style and open its Paragraph Style Options window directly. You can also use the New Paragraph Style command in the palette menu.

G Delete style
Click here to delete a currently highlighted style from the list. You can also drag and drop the style name onto this button to delete it. InDesign then asks you if you want to replace the deleted style with another.

H Keyboard shortcut
If you have assigned a keyboard shortcut to a style, it is displayed here.

28

Paragraph Style Options

Choose the Style Options command in the palette menu to open this window for setting the type attributes for a style. You can also open this window by holding down Ctrl/Cmd+Alt/Option+Shift and double-clicking on a style name.

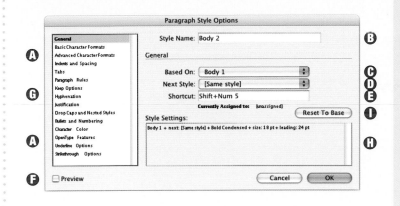

(A) Character attributes
These attributes correspond to those in the Character Styles palette (see page 26) and the Character and Control palettes (see pages 16-19).

(B) Style Name
Give your paragraph style a helpful name, or change it, here.

(C) Based On
Paragraph styles can be based on other paragraph styles. For example, various treatments of the body text in a book or magazine can be based on one central style.

(D) Next Style
This tells InDesign which paragraph style is expected to follow the current style. See below for tips on using this feature.

(E) Shortcut
As with character styles, you can assign a keyboard shortcut to paragraph styles using a combination of the numeric keypad and the Ctrl/Cmd, Alt/Option, and Shift keys. InDesign will warn you if you try to set a keyboard shortcut that has already been assigned to another style.

(F) Preview
Tick the Preview option to see the effect of your changes in the document without having to close the window.

(G) Paragraph attributes
These attributes correspond to those in the Paragraph and Control palettes (see pages 20-23).

(H) Style settings
This is a summary of the type attributes of the style you are editing.

(I) Reset to base
Click on this button to reset all type attributes to default values.

Using the Next Style command

1 Once you have created paragraph styles for a document, build them into a logical sequence. For example, headings are normally followed by subheads, which are followed by bylines, which are followed by body text, and so on. To do this, open the Paragraph Style Options for the first style (such as one for headings) and, in the General section of the window, use the Next Style pop-up choose which style to apply to the paragraph that will immediately follow it (such as one for subheads).

2 Repeat this process for each paragraph style in turn. When your style sequence is complete, you can apply it to any plain text story.

3 Select all the text and Right/Ctrl+click on the first style you want to apply, which will normally be one for headings. In the contextual menu that appears, click on Apply "STYLENAME" then Next Style.

4 The Next Style sequence is applied across the selected paragraphs beginning at the top, effectively formatting your entire story in one go.

Dealing with paragraph style overrides

When a plus (+) symbol appears next to a paragraph style name, you have several options for dealing with it.

1 To reapply the original paragraph style to selected text, removing any character or paragraph-level overrides, click on the Clear Overrides button at the bottom of the Paragraph Styles palette.

2 To get rid of character-level overrides only, hold down the Ctrl/Cmd key and click on the Clear Overrides button.

3 To get rid of paragraph-level overrides only, hold down Ctrl/Cmd+Shift and click on the Clear Overrides button.

4 To incorporate any overrides from selected text back into the paragraph style, choose Redefine Style from the palette menu. You can also use the keyboard shortcut Ctrl/Cmd+Alt/Option+Shift+R. This will update all instances in the document where you have used this style.

5 To leave all type attributes of selected paragraphs as they are but dissociate them from their paragraph styles (whether overridden or not), choose Break Link to Style from the fly-out menu. If you subsequently edit the original paragraph style, these paragraphs will not change.

Nested styles

A nested style is a character style that is applied to specific text ranges as part of a paragraph style. In other words, you can set up a paragraph style so that it applies one or more character styles in sequence to the first words, sentences, or other ranges in each paragraph.

Styling simple stories

Entering that gable-ended Spouter-Inn, you found yourself in a wide, low, straggling entry with old-fashioned wainscots, reminding one of the bulwarks of some condemned old craft. On one side hung a very large oil painting so thoroughly besmoked, and every way defaced, that in the unequal crosslights by which you viewed it, it was only by diligent study and a series of systematic visits to it, and careful inquiry of the neighbors, that you could any way arrive at an understanding of its purpose.

This story starts with a drop cap and three words in a different font from the rest of the text. This formatting can be automated easily with nested styles.

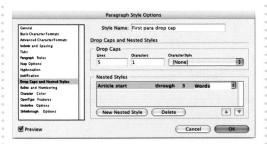

1 Begin by creating a new character style. Give it a useful name (such as "Article start") and choose a bold or heavy font style in the Basic Character Formats section of the Character Style Options window.

2 Now create a new paragraph style based on your normal body text style, but name it something like "First para drop cap." In the Drop Caps and Nested Styles section of the Paragraph Style Options window, set up a single-character drop cap that's five lines deep. Click on the New Nested Style button.

3 Choose your "Article start" character style and apply it to the first three words of the paragraph.

This applies the nested character style to the first three words before reverting to the paragraph style's own text format settings. You can choose a different font for the drop cap (see pages 20–23) if you wish.

Nested style options

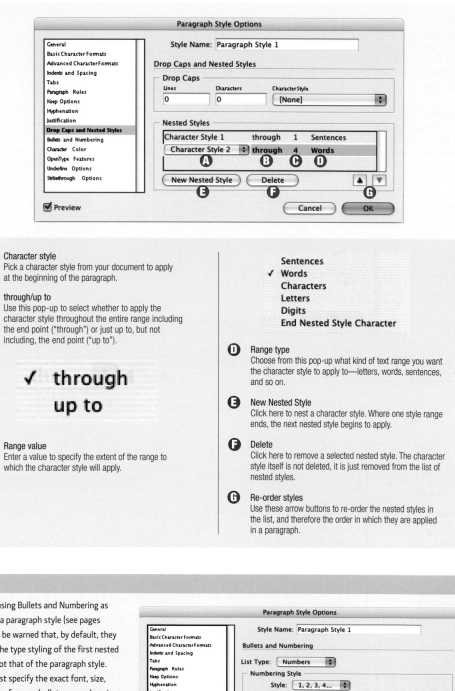

A Character style
Pick a character style from your document to apply at the beginning of the paragraph.

B through/up to
Use this pop-up to select whether to apply the character style throughout the entire range including the end point ("through") or just up to, but not including, the end point ("up to").

✓ through
   up to

C Range value
Enter a value to specify the extent of the range to which the character style will apply.

Sentences
✓ Words
Characters
Letters
Digits
End Nested Style Character

D Range type
Choose from this pop-up what kind of text range you want the character style to apply to—letters, words, sentences, and so on.

E New Nested Style
Click here to nest a character style. Where one style range ends, the next nested style begins to apply.

F Delete
Click here to remove a selected nested style. The character style itself is not deleted, it is just removed from the list of nested styles.

G Re-order styles
Use these arrow buttons to re-order the nested styles in the list, and therefore the order in which they are applied in a paragraph.

Tip

When using Bullets and Numbering as part of a paragraph style (see pages 20–23), be warned that, by default, they adopt the type styling of the first nested style, not that of the paragraph style. You must specify the exact font, size, and color for your bullets or numbers in the Paragraph Style Options window in order to override the nested style at the beginning of the paragraph.

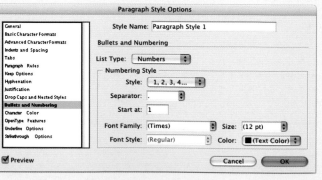

A pull-quote that contains multiple fonts and formatting can be styled with one click. Take this example, which puts a script font between two giant, colored, sans serif quote marks.

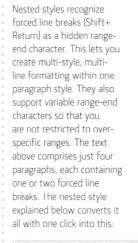

You shuddered as you gazed, and wondered what monstrous cannibal and savage could ever have gone a death-harvesting with such a hacking, horrifying implement.

1 First create a character style for the quote marks, determining their font, size, baseline shift, and color. In our example, the opening and closing quotes needed different measurements for baseline shift, so we created a separate character style for each of them.

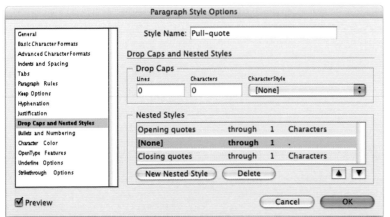

2 Go to the Drop Caps and Nested Styles section of the Paragraph Style Options window. Click on the New Nested Style button, and apply the "Opening quotes" character style to the first character of the paragraph ("through 1 Characters").

3 Add a second nested style, choosing "[None]" as the character style, so reverting back to the paragraph style's own formatting. Again, pick "through 1 Characters" but in place of the word "Characters", type a full point. This tells InDesign to apply the "[None]" character style up to and including the first full point it finds (at the end of the quotation).

4 Add a third nested style, applying the "Closing quotes" character style "through 1 Character" as before, which applies to the closing quote mark after the full point.

Nested styles recognize forced line breaks (Shift+ Return) as a hidden range-end character. This lets you create multi-style, multi-line formatting within one paragraph style. They also support variable range-end characters so that you are not restricted to over-specific ranges. The text above comprises just four paragraphs, each containing one or two forced line breaks. The nested style explained below converts it all with one click into this:

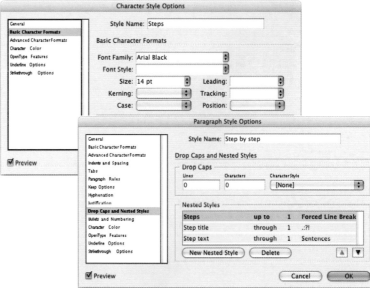

Step 1
Find yourself a pen. You'll need something to write with or nothing will get written.
After all, it is supposed to be mightier than the sword.

Step 2
Do you have any paper? Without paper, you will have big trouble getting your words down.

Step 3
Ink is important too: your pen won't work without any ink inside it.
You don't want to end up scratching away in the dust.

Step 4
Begin writing! You can now put pen to paper and begin writing your first novel.

Note how the red headings do not conform to the same word length, nor do they all end with a full point. Here's what to do.

1 Create character styles for each of the text formats you want—in our case, that's sans serif blue for the step numbers ("Steps"), red script for the step titles ("Step title"), and bold sans serif for the subheadings ("Step text"). Ignore the roman font because it will be defined as the default formatting in the paragraph style.

2 Create a new paragraph style and go to the Drop Caps and Nested Styles section of the Paragraph Style Options window. For the first nested style, apply the "Steps" character style "up to 1 Forced Line Break". For the second nested style, apply the "Step title" character style "through 1 Character," but replace "Character" with "..?!". This tells InDesign to apply the character style until it finds the first full point, colon, question mark, or exclamation point. For the third nested style, apply the "Step text" character style "through 1 Sentences" After this sentence, the formatting for any further text in the paragraph reverts to the default settings of the paragraph style.

3 Note that only the "Characters" range allows you to enter specific characters as alternative range-end indicators for nested styles. To apply a nested style to a number of letters not including punctuation, white space, digits, or symbols, use the "Letters" range instead.

31

Object styles

An object style is a set of shape, frame, or open path attributes that have been collected together and given a name. You can then apply all those attributes to other objects quickly by applying the object style. For more information on drawing paths and shapes, see Chapter 3.

Object style options

The window for creating or editing an object style differs from those for character and paragraph styles. Attributes are listed in the left-hand pane. Click on an attribute name to view its options, and use the checkboxes to add or remove an attribute from the object style definition. Leaving an attribute unchecked simply means you customize those object settings on the page without overriding the style. You can, of course, customize an object's style-defined attributes just the same, but it is then considered to

be "overriding" the style, and a plus symbol (+) appears

next to the style name in the Object Styles palette.

Using styled strokes

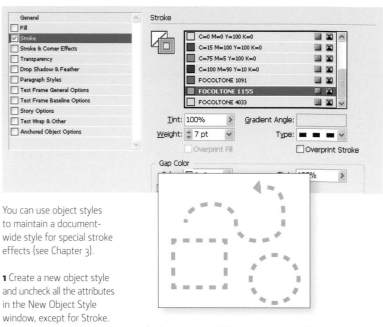

You can use object styles to maintain a document-wide style for special stroke effects (see Chapter 3).

1 Create a new object style and uncheck all the attributes in the New Object Style window, except for Stroke.

2 Click on the Stroke attribute to select it, then choose a stroke color, weight and type. If you

picked a stripe or a dotted or dashed stroke from the Type pop-up, you can also pick a Gap Color. Click OK.

Every object you apply this

style to will have the same stroke appearance. If you edit the object style later, all instances on the page will be updated automatically.

The Object Styles palette

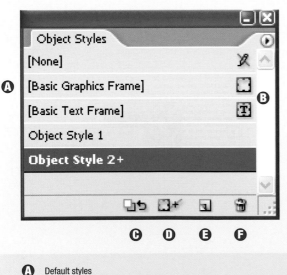

Ⓐ Default styles
By default, when you draw a new path or shape, it is assigned the "[Basic Graphics Frame]" object style. New text frames are assigned the "[Basic Text Frame]" style. Image placeholder frames and placed images are assigned the "[None]" style.

Ⓑ Custom defaults
These icons indicate the default graphic and text object styles for any new objects you add to a page. To set custom object styles as the default for new objects, drag the two icons to other style names in the list.

Ⓒ Clear attributes not defined by style
Click here to remove any attributes that you have applied manually to an object, which are not defined within its object style.

Ⓓ Clear overrides
Click here to reset any attributes you have applied manually to an object that override those defined in its object style.

Ⓔ Create new style
Click here to create a new object style, or Alt/Option+click to create a new style and open its Options window immediately.

Ⓕ Delete
Click here to remove a selected object style, or drag and drop a style onto this button. If an object style is in use in your document, you will be prompted to replace all instances with another style.

To apply an object style, select one or more objects on the page and click on the style name in the Object Styles palette. Alternatively, drag and drop a style name from the palette onto any object on the page, even if it is not currently selected. Object styles can also be applied from the Control palette when the selection and drawing tools are active.

Commands for clearing undefined attributes and overrides, and for redefining an object style based on a currently selected object, are also available in the palette fly-out menu.

New Object Style...
Duplicate Object Style...
Delete Object Style...

Redefine Object Style

Object Style Options...

Clear Overrides
Clear Attributes Not Defined by Style

Break Link To Style

Default Text Frame Style   ▶
Default Graphic Frame Style   ▶

Load Object Styles...

Select All Unused

Sort By Name

Small Palette Rows

Box-outs and sidebars are usually taken from a library (see page 154) or an old document, and the new text content pasted in bit by bit so as not to interfere with the type formatting. With object styles, however, you can place the new text onto your page and turn it into a finished sidebar in an instant.

1 Here's the starting text placed onto an InDesign page. Note how the text from "Price" to "www.capson.com" is just one paragraph separated with forced line turns (Shift+Return). This will allow you to apply nested styles (see page 30).

Inkjet printers
Capson PhotoPAX 700
An inkjet that combines the best in image quality with the best in output performance, even on glossy stock.
Price
£170
Warranty
One year, return to base
Contact
Capson 0800 012345
Internet
www.capson.com
Specifications
2400 x 4800 dpi; 150-sheet input tray, 50-sheet photo paper tray; USB 2.0 Hi-Speed

2 Create character styles for the headings (bold sans serif) and the Web address (blue, underlined). Then create paragraph styles for each paragraph in the text—product name, verdict, specifications, and so on.

3 Set up each paragraph style with a Next Style (see page 29), building an automated sequence of styles to apply.

4 Create a new object style. Activate the Paragraph Styles attribute, select the first paragraph style from your sequence, and check the Apply Next Style option.

5 In paragraph style for the product details (between "Price" and "www.capson.com"), set up a nested style that applies the Product details headings character style to alternate lines, ending with the Web address character style.

6 Edit the Fill and Stroke attributes to add color to the object itself (see page 80). Edit the Drop Shadow & Filter attribute to give the object a drop shadow (see page 120). Click OK.

INKJET PRINTERS

Capson PhotoPAX 700

An inkjet that combines the best in image quality with the best in output performance, even on glossy stock.
Price
£170
Warranty
One year, return to base
Contact
Capson 0800 012345
Internet
www.capson.com
★ ★ ★ ★
Specifications
2400 x 4800 dpi; 150-sheet input tray, 50-sheet photo paper tray; USB 2.0 Hi-Speed and USB 2.0 Full-Speed interfaces (separate ports), PictBridge digital camera interface; drivers for Windows 98/Me/2000/XP.

7 Drag the new object style from the Object Styles palette and drop it onto the plain text frame. The box appearance and the sequence of Next and Nested styles are instantly applied.

Usually, a design style dictates how images should appear—for example, whether they have a keyline around the frame, and how far runaround text should be pushed away from the picture's edges. Here's how to automate these settings using object styles.

1 Create a new object style, and select Text Wrap & Other in the New Object Style window. Click on a text wrap icon and enter an offset value (see page 46).

2 Select the Stroke attribute and choose a 0.25pt black, plain stroke. Click OK.

3 Using this object style, you can now assign these multiple settings—text wrap and keyline—with one click.

33

Story Editor

Editing small text on a page layout is often difficult unless you zoom in close to the area you are working on. This, however, is usually inconvenient when editing a story that flows across multiple columns or pages, because it forces you to scroll back and forth. InDesign's answer to this problem is the Story Editor.

Story Editor is a window that presents the current story in simple text-editor fashion. Open it at any time by choosing **Edit > Edit in Story Editor**. This command is also available from InDesign's contextual menu whenever a text frame is selected, regardless of which tool is currently active in the Tools palette. The easiest way to open Story Editor is to use its keyboard shortcut: Ctrl/Cmd+Y.

The left-hand column in the editor window indicates paragraph styles and a rough guide to "galley" depth according to the text frame size and your current unit of measurement. Click-and-drag on the vertical

divider line to adjust its position. As you edit the text in the Story Editor

window, your page layout is updated instantly.

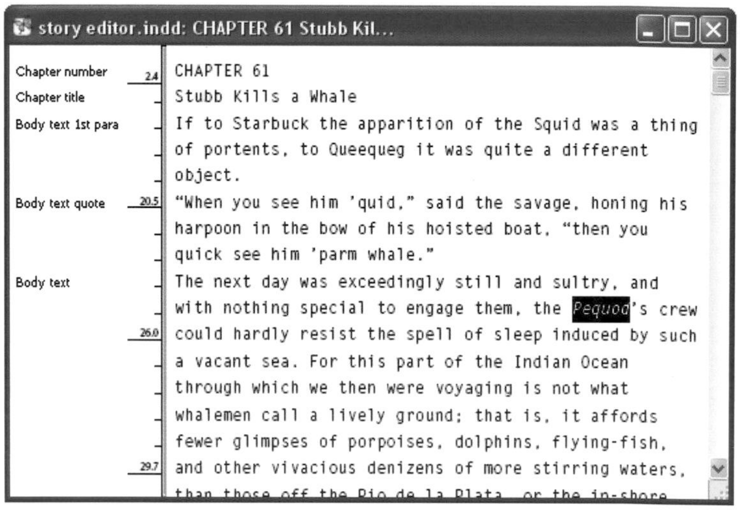

Overset text

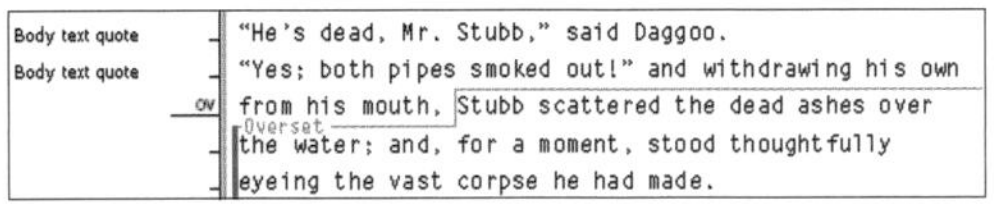

Text that continues beyond the boundaries of the final frame in a threaded story is called "overmatter." Story Editor graphically highlights this text at the end with a vertical red bar and a black division line labeled "Overset." You can continue to edit this overset text here even though you can't see it in your page layout.

Text in tables

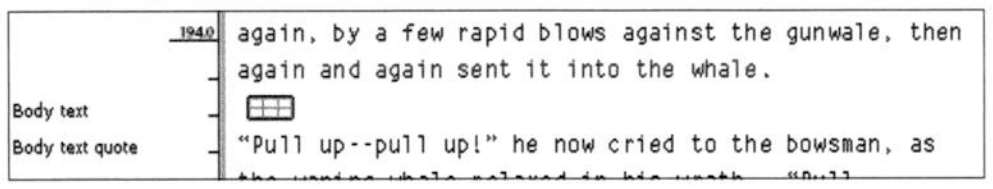

Although Story Editor cannot edit content within tables (see page 40), it does at least indicate the location of tables in a story using the icon shown above.

Footnotes

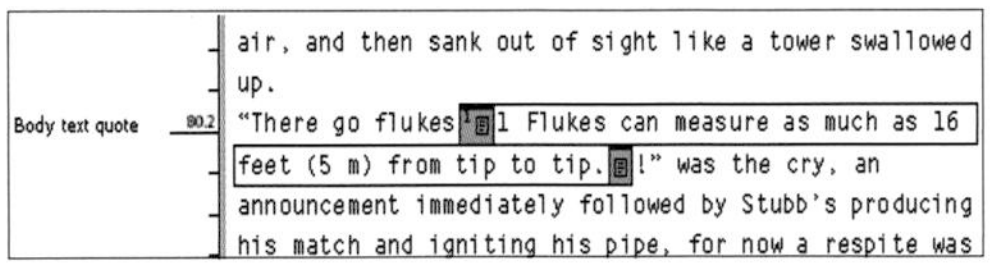

Although it is easy to insert and edit footnotes in a layout (see page 52), locating their tiny reference points in the story can be very tricky. Story Editor, on the other hand, ensures their locations are unmissable. The colored blocks at either end of a footnote also act as clickable toggles for showing or hiding the footnote text.

Inline objects

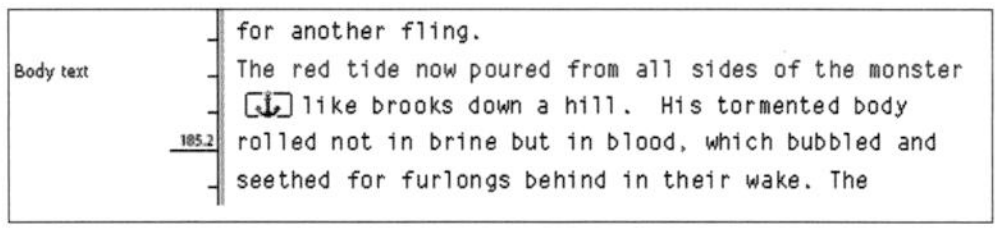

Inline objects, such as shapes or images pasted into the text (see page 70), are indicated with the anchor icon shown above. Deleting the icon deletes the inline object, so be careful. Also, take care not to confuse it with a hyperlink anchor, which has a completely different icon.

Bookmarks and hyperlink anchors

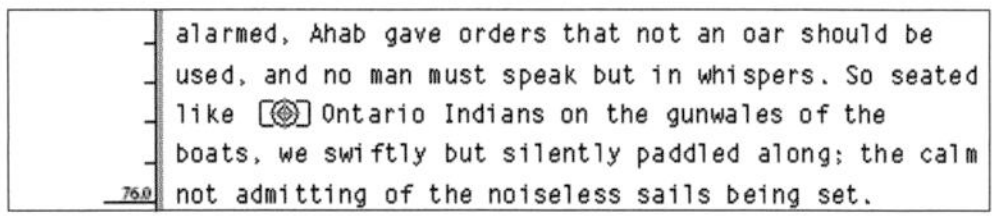

Bookmarks and hyperlink anchors (see page 158) are virtually impossible to see in a layout, even after applying the **Type > Show Hidden Characters** command. Story Editor indicates them clearly with "target" icons.

Hyperlinks

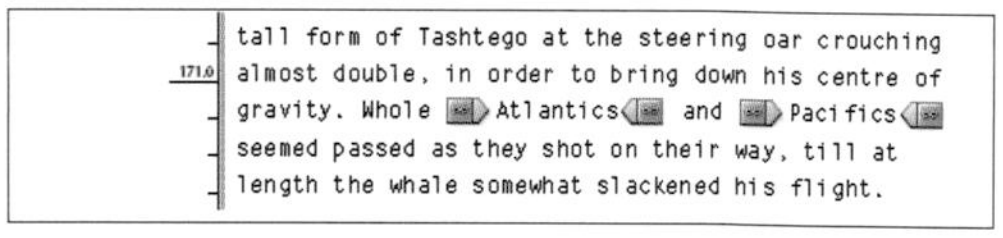

Unless you specify Visible Rectangle in the Appearance section of the Hyperlink Options window, embedded hyperlinks (see page 158) can also be difficult to see. Story Editor, however, indicates their location with colored blocks.

Index markers

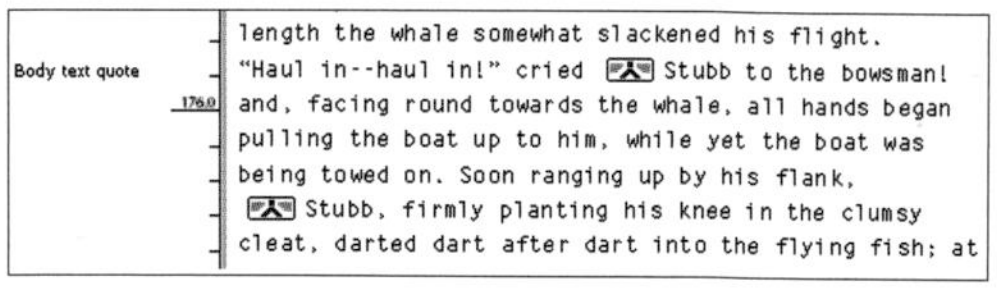

When building an index (see pages 150–153), index markers are fairly clear in your layout when hidden characters are shown, but Story Editor makes them clearer still with the insertion icon shown above.

34

XML tags

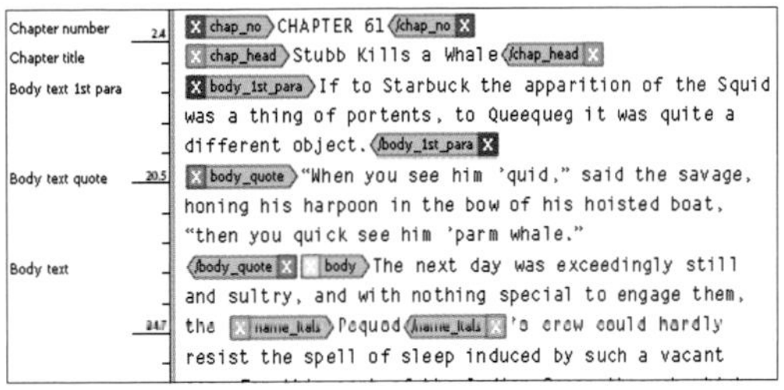

Assigning InDesign styles with XML tags within an XML workflow is not difficult, but only Story Editor gives visual feedback on which tags have been applied where. Each XML tag is indicated complete with color coding and the tag name.

Changing Story Editor's appearance

1 The default appearance of Story Editor may not be to your liking, but it can easily be changed. Go to **InDesign > Preferences** (Mac) or **Edit > Preferences** (Win) and choose Story Editor Display.

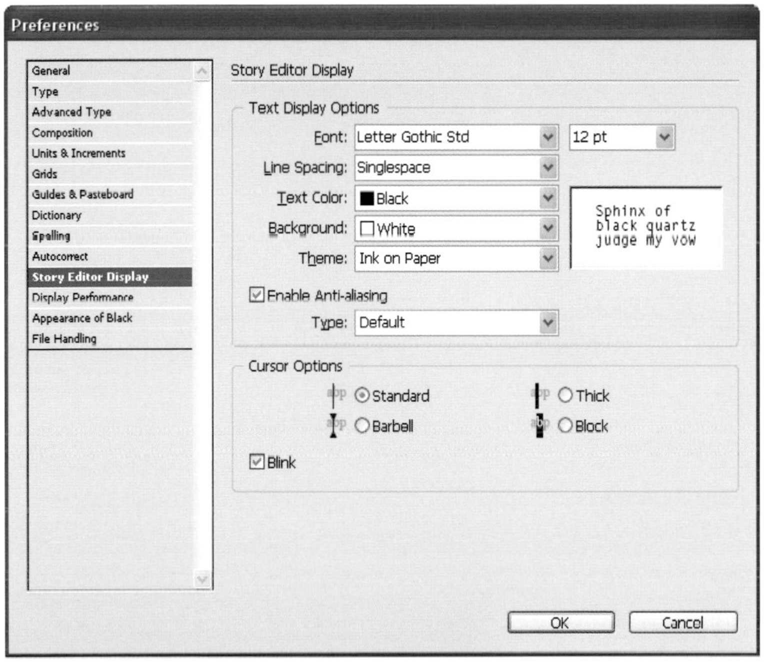

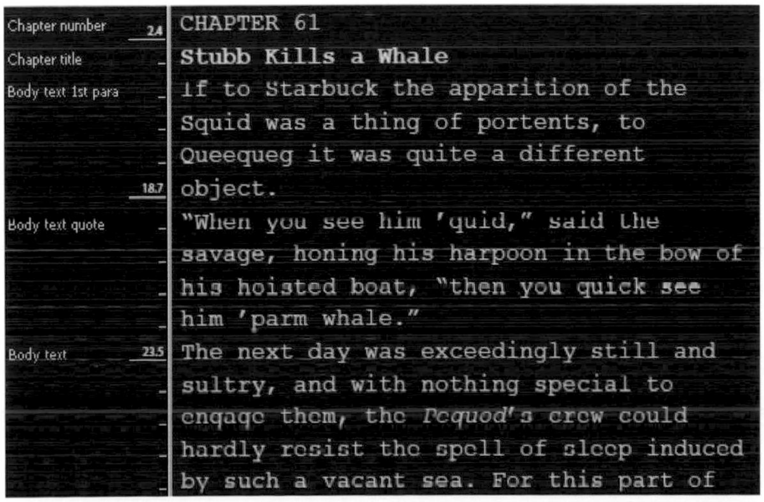

2 If you work on a large, high-resolution screen, increase the type to 16pt or 18pt, and switch to a more expressive serif monospaced font such as Courier. You may find it helpful to customize the text and background colors, to distinguish the Story Editor window from other InDesign windows. If you want basic font formatting, such as bold and italic, to be displayed more clearly, check the Enable Anti-aliasing option and pick Soft or LCD Optimized from the Type pop up.

Tip

THE PROS AND CONS OF STORY EDITOR

InDesign's Story Editor has many points in its favor…

- It is a free-floating window. You do not need to close it before returning to work on your page layout.

- You may keep several Story Editor windows open simultaneously to work on different stories in the document.

- You may open multiple Story Editor windows for the same story: just use the Window > Arrange > New Window command.

- Embedded data such as footnotes, indexed words, and hyperlink anchors are much easier to locate and edit.

- You can use all of InDesign's commands and palettes with it.

- You can enable drag-and-drop text editing for the Story Editor independently of the main layout window.

But on the other hand…

- Character styles are not indicated.

- Only very basic type formatting is represented.

- It cannot edit cell contents within tables.

- It can only open one story per window, not all the text in a document.

Tip

EDITING TEXT BEHIND OBJECTS

On rare occasions, you may find that the text you want to edit is in a frame buried behind a stack of other objects. Hold down the Ctrl/Cmd key and repeatedly click on the stack until the frame you want to edit becomes selected, then call up the Story Editor. This lets you work on that text exclusively without fear of accidentally reselecting other objects in the stack by clicking in the wrong place. If you think you may need to re-edit the text again later, just keep this Story Editor window open, minimizing it to the Dock (Mac) or Task bar (Win).

Optical alignment

nDesign's type engine has the ability to fine-tune typography according to font appearance. Do not confuse this with OpenType features (see page 24) or the standard type controls explained earlier in this chapter. Rather, they are functions that adjust text flow settings automatically, depending upon the shape and size of the fonts you are using. Use them to improve the visual design of your page layouts.

Fine-tuning text with Optical kerning

Tell it to the judge

This is an option accessible from the Character palette (see page 16). To see it in action, type a headline and make it fairly big on the page. Here we have added ruler guides (see page 144) to mark the beginning and end of each word.

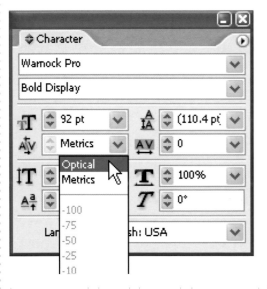

1 Select the text using the Type tool and open the Character palette. Click on the Kern pop-up and choose Optical in place of Metrics.

Tell it to the judge

2 The text is automatically tugged together with tighter kerning.

Note that the specific kern values that InDesign applies differ according to the font and type size. As with manual kerning, optical kerning is only really noticeable at large type sizes, so do not enable optical kerning for ordinary body text.

Adjusting word-spacing with Paragraph Composer

Justified text in narrow columns tends to suffer from large, unsightly word spaces on certain lines. InDesign's Paragraph Composer can help.

> Hither, and thither, on high, glided the snow-white wings of small, unspeckled birds; these were the gentle thoughts of the feminine air; but to and fro in the deeps, far down in the bottomless blue, rushed mighty leviathans, sword-fish, and sharks; and these were the strong, troubled, murderous thinkings of the masculine sea.

1 Open the Paragraph palette, click on the fly-out menu button, and choose Adobe Paragraph Composer.

Show Options

✓ Adobe Paragraph Composer
Adobe Single-line Composer

Only Align First Line to Grid
Balance Ragged Lines

Justification...   Alt+Shift+Ctrl+J
Keep Options...   Alt+Ctrl+K
Hyphenation...
Drop Caps and Nested Styles...   Alt+Ctrl+R
Paragraph Rules...   Alt+Ctrl+J
Bullets and Numbering...
Convert Bullets and Numbering to Text

2 The result is a more regularly spaced paragraph. InDesign has looked for large white spaces, and adjusted the text flow accordingly to minimize them. The system works equally well for non-justified text. It is worth enabling Adobe Paragraph Composer for all your text.

> Hither, and thither, on high, glided the snow-white wings of small, unspeckled birds; these were the gentle thoughts of the feminine air; but to and fro in the deeps, far down in the bottomless blue, rushed mighty leviathans, sword-fish, and sharks; and these were the strong, troubled, murderous thinkings of the masculine sea.

Punctuation at the beginning or end of a justified line can interrupt the clean column edges, as shown here.

1 To correct this, open the Story palette (**Window > Type & Tables > Story**) with the text frame selected, and check the Optical Margin Alignment option.

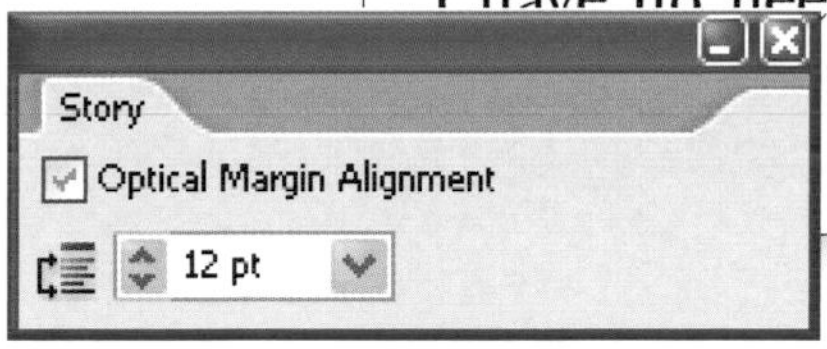

> "For the white fiend! But now for the barbs; thou must make them thyself, man. Here are my razors—the best of steel; here, and make the barbs sharp as the needle-sleet of the Icy Sea. Take them, man, I have no need for them; for I ... shave, sup, nor ... here—to work!"

Story
☑ Optical Margin Alignment
12 pt

2 This allows punctuation—and serifs—to overhang the column edges, so keeping the body of the text neatly aligned. You may need to adjust the point value in the Story palette in order to optimize the result.

> "For the white fiend! But now for the barbs; thou must make them thyself, man. Here are my razors—the best of steel; here, and make the barbs sharp as the needle-sleet of the Icy Sea. Take them, man, I have no need for them; for I now neither shave, sup, nor pray till—but here—to work!"

3 Take a closer look at what it has done to the opening quote marks...

...and to the punctuation at the ends of the lines.

Optical margin alignment is particularly useful for typographically precise publications, such as poetry books.

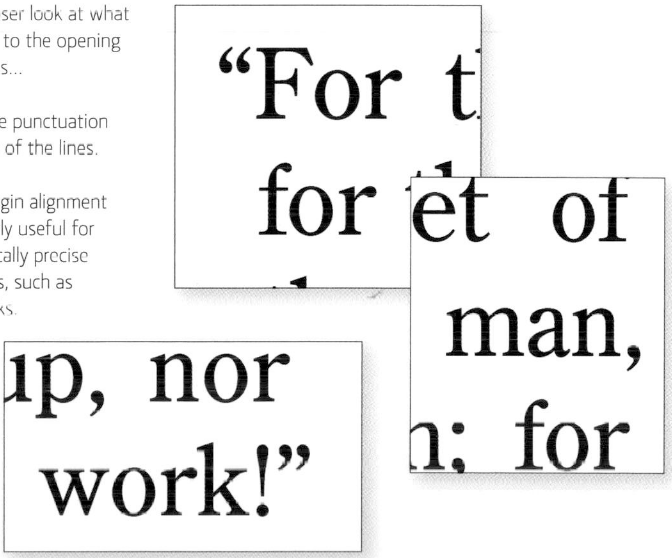

"For t
for et ot
man,
: for
up, nor
work!"

Here's how to balance ragged lines quickly and easily with InDesign.

1 Write a headline or standfirst over two or more decks, allowing the last line to fall short of the full width of the text frame.

2 With the text selected, open the Paragraph palette and choose Balance Ragged Lines from the fly-out menu.
 InDesign analyzes the paragraph, spots that the last line does not balance up with those above, and adjusts the line turns automatically to make the decks as equal as possible in length.

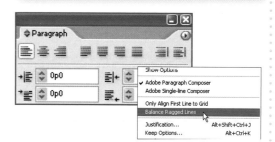

When good cops turn bad on today's mean streets

Paragraph
Show Options
✓ Adobe Paragraph Composer
Adobe Single-line Composer
Only Align First Line to Grid
Balance Ragged Lines
Justification... Alt+Shift+Ctrl+J
Keep Options... Alt+Ctrl+K

When good cops turn bad on today's mean streets

Techno frustration has a traceable history. Urban myths of people throwing their PCs out of office windows were popular in the late 1980s.

3 This feature works well on non-justified body text, too, as a way of eliminating orphans. For example, the paragraph on the left has an ugly orphan.
 When you apply the Balance Ragged Lines command, InDesign adjusts the line turns to produce a more pleasing typographical result.

Techno frustration has a traceable history. Urban myths of people throwing their PCs out of office windows were popular in the late 1980s.

4 Note that InDesign is not actually trying to balance all the ragged lines, only the very last line, so don't expect this feature to solve ragged line problems throughout a paragraph. To do this, enable Adobe Paragraph Composer. By using both features together for headlines and non-justified body text, you can save yourself hours of unnecessary rewriting and editing work

37

Tabs

InDesign tabs allow you to determine and align horizontal spacing in text, and are treated as a paragraph attribute. Tabs generally work best for simple listing alignment tasks, such as price lists, tables of contents (see page 148), and indexes (see page 150–153). For multi-column layouts, use tables instead (see page 40).

The Tabs palette

A **Alignment buttons**
Choose whether a new tab stop or currently selected tab stop will be left-aligned, centered, right-aligned, or aligned to a decimal (or other specific character).

B **Tab position**
This field shows the position of the currently selected tab stop, measured from the left-hand edge of the text frame. When a tab stop is selected, entering a new value here will move it to that new location.

C **Leader character**
Fill wide tab spaces with one or more "leader" characters to aid legibility. Just type the characters you want to use in here.

D **Fly-out menu**
This menu contains only two commands. Clear All simply deletes all the default tab stops you have set up. Repeat Tab fills out the width of the text frame with additional tab stops, spaced out using the same measurement as the currently selected tab stop and the one on its immediate left.

E **Tab stops**
Click in this narrow strip to add new tab positions ("stops"). Click-and-drag on the tab stop indicators to more them. Drag them off the strip and release the mouse button to delete them.

F **Align On character**
Type in a character here to tell an align-to-decimal tab stop what you want it to align to.

G **Ruler**
This is a rough visual indicator of the width across the currently selected text frame.

H **Resize window**
Click-and-drag on this corner to resize the Tabs palette whenever you want.

I **Position palette over text frame**
The Tabs palette is a floating palette that you can keep on screen as you edit your page layout. When switching from one frame to another, click on this magnet button to snap the palette directly over the currently selected text frame.

Choosing the correct alignment option

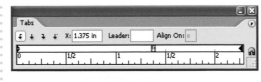

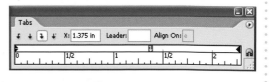

1 Type a simple listing using a tab on each line to separate the text. Select the text using the Type tool, call up the Tabs palette, click on the left-aligned tab button, and click once in the tab stops strip. The tabbed text immediately aligns to this new tab stop.

3 Click on the right-aligned tab button to convert the tab stop once again, this time right-aligning the text.

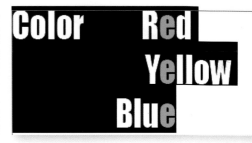

2 With the tab stop still selected, click on the center-aligned tab button. This converts the tab stop without changing its position or creating a new one, centering the text.

4 Now try the align-to-decimal tab button. By default, it will try to align to a full point. Replace whatever is in the Align On field with a character you have used in the text. InDesign duly aligns the text to that character (in this example, the letter "e").

Aligning to decimal

1 The align-to-decimal tab stop is extremely useful for listings that do not conform to conventional layout rules.

Look at this short price list. No matter whether the tab stop is left, right, or center-aligned, it looks untidy.

2 By changing the tab stop to align-to-decimal, you can force a logical alignment. In this instance, we have entered the Euro currency symbol in the Align On field, instantly tidying up the listing.

Using tab leaders

1 Create a simple tabbed listing, aligned however you wish, but make the tab space quite wide.

Remember to keep all the text selected as you edit tabs.

2 Select the tab stop in the Tabs palette and enter a full point in the Leader field.

This adds dotted leader lines across the tab space.

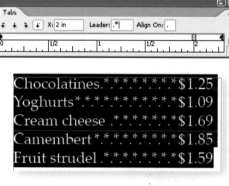

3 There's a problem: the full points are chunky and typographically unattractive. To fix this, double-click on one of the tab spaces in your text frame to select it and reduce its type size using the Character palette or Control palette. This makes the leader dots smaller and finer

4 You're not limited to just full points. Here, we've added an asterisk to the Leader field to create this interesting effect.

Inserting hanging indents

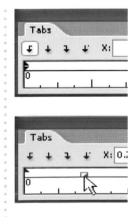

A hanging indent is the opposite of a first-line indent (see page 20). That is, the entire paragraph is indented except for the first line. Here's the easy way to do it.

1 Select the paragraphs you want to indent, open the Tabs palette and click once on the left-aligned tab button to select it.

2 There are two tiny black triangles on the left-hand edge of the tab stop strip. Hold down the Shift key

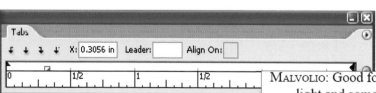

and carefully click on the bottom triangle, dragging it across toward the right. Your indent is now set.

3 In addition to being quick and easy, this method does not require you to insert tabs into your text or juggle with the first line and left indents in the Paragraph palette. It also leaves single-line paragraphs alone. Whenever adjusting the position of this hanging indent stop in the Tabs palette, just remember to hold down the Shift key before clicking and dragging on the triangle.

MALVOLIO: Good fool, help me to some light and some paper. I tell thee, I am as well in my wits as any man in Illyria.
FESTE: Well-a-day, that you were, sir!
MALVOLIO: By this hand, I am! Good fool, some ink, paper, and light; and convey what I will set down to my lady. It shall advantage thee more than ever the bearing of letter did.

Tables

Use tables rather than tabs (see page 38) when you want to lay out a list with several columns. Tables are easier to edit and provide instant options for coloring and styling. Tables are treated by InDesign as inline objects within a text frame. This allows a table to flow in position with the rest of a text story from frame to frame and page to page.

Adding a table

immediately into a table. It exists as an inline object within the text frame.

	Breakfast	Lunch	Dinner
Monday	Cereal	Tuna	Pasta
Tuesday	Grapefruit	Steak	Rice
Wednesday	Porridge	Eggs	Potatoes
Thursday	Muffins	Burger	Meat loaf
Friday	Pancakes	Salad	Fish

Body text can then continue in the same text frame after the table. Both table and body text can be threaded from frame to frame and page to page just like any story.

1 If you already have some tabbed text in a frame, perhaps as part of a text story, just select it with the Type tool and go to **Table > Convert Text To Table**.

Convert Text to Table

- Column Separator: Tab
- Row Separator: Paragraph
- Number of Columns:
- OK
- Cancel

2 Accept the defaults in the dialog box that appears, and the text is reformatted as an InDesign table.

or created on the page can be converted immediately into a table. It exists as an inline object within the text frame.

	Breakfast	Lunch	Dinner
Monday	Cereal	Tuna	Pasta
Tuesday	Grapefruit	Steak	Rice
Wednesday	Porridge	Eggs	Potatoes
Thursday	Muffins	Burger	Meat loaf
Friday	Pancakes	Salad	Fish

Body text can then continue in the same text frame after the table. Both table and body text can be threaded from frame to frame and page

Microsoft Excel Import Options

Options
- Sheet: weekly meals
- View: [Ignore View]
- Cell Range: A1:D6
- ☐ Import Hidden Cells Not Saved in View

Formatting
- Table: Unformatted Table
- Cell Alignment: Current Spreadsheet
- ☑ Include Inline Graphics
- Number of Decimal Places to Include: 3
- ☑ Use Typographer's Quotes
- OK
- Cancel

3 You can also import tables from external files using the **File > Place** command. Simple tabbed text files are placed as they are, letting you convert them to a table on the page. If the external file is a Microsoft Word or Excel document, InDesign prompts you with conversion and formatting options.

Insert Table

Table Dimensions
- Body Rows: 4
- Columns: 4
- Header Rows: 0
- Footer Rows: 0
- OK
- Cancel

4 The text will then be placed as an InDesign table as above. If you prefer to create the table from scratch in your layout, make a new text frame or click somewhere within an existing text frame, then go to **Table > Insert Table**. Enter the number of rows and columns when prompted, and start typing into the empty InDesign table.

immediately into a table. It exists as an inline object within the text frame.

Monday			
Tuesday			

Body text can then continue in the same text frame after the table. Both table and body text

	Breakfast	Lunch	Dinner
Monday	Cereal	Tuna	Pasta
Tuesday	Grapefruit	Steak	Rice
Wednesday	Porridge	Eggs	Potatoes

5 Navigate from cell to cell in a table using the Left, Right, Up, and Down cursor keys, or Tab and Shift+Tab keys.

Insert Row(s)

Insert
- Number: 2
- ○ Above
- ● Below
- OK
- Cancel

6 To add more rows and columns to a table, select a row or column and go to **Table > Insert > Row** or **Column**. Enter the number of rows or columns you want, and where you want them to appear in relation to the currently selected row or column. You can type more text into them immediately.

	Breakfast	Lunch	Dinner
Monday	Cereal	Tuna	Pasta
Tuesday	Grapefruit	Steak	Rice
Wednesday	Porridge	Eggs	Potatoes
Thursday			

The Table palette

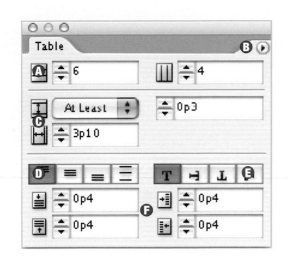

To edit table attributes, the flashing Type cursor can be anywhere within the table. To edit row, column, or cell attributes, you must first select those rows, columns, or cells.

A The number of rows and columns in the current table.

B Fly-out menu
This is just a subset of InDesign's main Table menu.

C Height and width of selected rows and columns.

D Vertical alignment in selected cells
Align text to the top, center or bottom of the cell, or justify multi-line text to fill the cell height.

E Rotate text in selected cells.

F Text inset of selected cells
Insert space or "padding" between text in a cell and the cell border.

Several table functions, including strokes around cell borders, are available in the Control palette when one or more cells are selected.

Removing border strokes

By default, all new InDesign tables are given black border strokes. Here's how to get rid of them.

1 With the type cursor anywhere inside the table, go to Table > Table Options > Table Setup. In the Table Border section, set the Weight value to zero.

	Breakfast	Lunch	Dinner
Monday	Cereal	Tuna	Pasta
Tuesday	Grapefruit	Steak	Rice
Wednesday	Porridge	Eggs	Potatoes
Thursday	Muffins	Burger	Meat loaf
Friday	Pancakes	Salad	Fish

The result is a table with dividers, but no border.

2 To remove the inner strokes instead, go to Table > Table Options > Alternating Row Strokes.

Choose Custom Row from the Alternating Pattern pop-up, and set both Weight values to zero.

	Breakfast	Lunch	Dinner
Monday	Cereal	Tuna	Pasta
Tuesday	Grapefruit	Steak	Rice
Wednesday	Porridge	Eggs	Potatoes
Thursday	Muffins	Burger	Meat loaf
Friday	Pancakes	Salad	Fish

3 Click on the Column Strokes tab at the top of the Table Options window and repeat the Weight zeroing to achieve a rather empty table.

	Breakfast	Lunch	Dinner
Monday	Cereal	Tuna	Pasta
Tuesday	Grapefruit	Steak	Rice
Wednesday	Porridge	Eggs	Potatoes
Thursday	Muffins	Burger	Meat loaf
Friday	Pancakes	Salad	Fish

4 Sometimes you need to remove borders from specific areas of a table. First, select an area of cells.

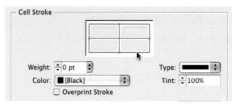

5 Go to Table > Cell Options > Strokes and Fills. In the Cell Stroke "proxy" thumbnail, click on each of the outer borders to toggle them from blue (selected) to grey (deselected). Set the Weight value to zero to achieve the result shown below.

	Breakfast	Lunch	Dinner
Monday	Cereal	Tuna	Pasta
Tuesday	Grapefruit	Steak	Rice
Wednesday	Porridge	Eggs	Potatoes
Thursday	Muffins	Burger	Meat loaf
Friday	Pancakes	Salad	Fish

Tip

EDITING TEXT IN CELLS

• To select an empty cell, double-click in it.

• To select any cell, click in it and drag to one of its edges.

• To select any cell containing the flashing Type cursor, hold down the Shift key and press the Up or Down cursor keys. Press once if the cell is empty, press twice if it is not.

• To select all cells in a table, select at least one cell and use the Edit > Select All command.

• To select multiple cells, click-and-drag across them. Or select one cell using any method above, then hold down the Shift key and press the cursor keys to expand the selection.

• To select one row or column, position the Type cursor near the table edge until the cursor appears as a solid arrow, then click.

• To select multiple rows or columns, select one row or column as above, then drag the mouse or hold down Shift and press the cursor keys to expand the selection.

41

TÇUT

Tables continued

Styling tables

InDesign tables can be styled with automatically applied strokes and background fills to enhance the appearance of rows and columns. We'll begin with this basic table, and add some styles to it.

	Breakfast	Lunch	Dinner
Monday	Cereal	Tuna	Pasta
Tuesday	Grapefruit	Steak	Rice
Wednesday	Porridge	Eggs	Potatoes
Thursday	Muffins	Burger	Meat loaf
Friday	Pancakes	Salad	Fish

1 With the Type cursor flashing somewhere in the table, go to **Table > Table Options > Table Setup**. Remember, you can access this command from the Table palette menu, and also the Control palette when one or more cells are selected. Check the Preview option at the bottom of the Table Options window to see your changes as you work. To begin, set the Weight value under Table Border to zero to remove the outer border from around the table.

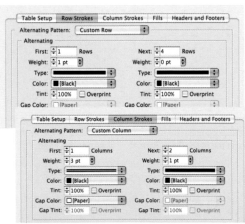

2 Click on the Row Strokes tab at the top of the Table Options window. Choose Custom Row from the Alternating Pattern drop-down. Set First Rows to 1, and give it a Weight of 1pt. Set the Next Rows (however many you have in the table) to a stroke weight of zero.

Click on the Column Strokes tab. Choose Custom Column from the Alternating Pattern drop-down. Set First Columns to 1 with a Weight of 3pt, and pick a stroke style from the Type pop-up. Set the Next Columns (again, however many are in the table) to a Weight of 1pt.

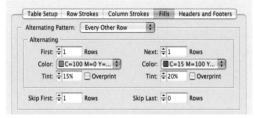

This is the result so far.

3 Click on the Fills tab. Choose Every Other Row from the Alternating Pattern drop-down. Set First Rows and Next Rows to 1, but give them different colors from the Color pop-ups and apply pale tints of around 20%. Increase the Skip First Row value to 1, and click OK.

	Breakfast	Lunch	Dinner
Monday	Cereal	Tuna	Pasta
Tuesday	Grapefruit	Steak	Rice
Wednesday	Porridge	Eggs	Potatoes
Thursday	Muffins	Burger	Meat loaf
Friday	Pancakes	Salad	Fish

The result is a horizontally striped table with vertical column strokes.

4 With the table still selected, return to **Table > Table Options > Alternating Row Strokes**. Set First Rows to 1 with a Weight of 1pt, and choose a color from the Color pop-up. Give the remaining Next Rows a Weight of 1pt as well, but a different color.

5 Click on the Column Strokes tab, and give the First Columns and Next Columns a Weight of zero.

	Breakfast	Lunch	Dinner
Monday	Cereal	Tuna	Pasta
Tuesday	Grapefruit	Steak	Rice
Wednesday	Porridge	Eggs	Potatoes
Thursday	Muffins	Burger	Meat loaf
Friday	Pancakes	Salad	Fish

This is the result so far.

6 Click on the Fills tab. Choose Every Other Column from the Alternating Pattern drop-down. Set First Columns and Next Columns to 1, but give them different colors from the Color pop-ups and apply pale tints of around 20%. Increase the Skip First Columns value to 1, and click OK.

	Breakfast	Lunch	Dinner
Monday	Cereal	Tuna	Pasta
Tuesday	Grapefruit	Steak	Rice
Wednesday	Porridge	Eggs	Potatoes
Thursday	Muffins	Burger	Meat loaf
Friday	Pancakes	Salad	Fish

The result is a vertically striped table with horizontal row strokes.

42

RAFFAELLO SANTI			
Year	Title	Physical Data	Current Location
1500	Angel (fragment of the Baronci Altarpiece)	Oil on wood, 57 x 36 cm	Musée du Louvre, Paris
	Angel (fragment of the Baronci Altarpiece)	Oil on wood, 31 x 27 cm	Pinacoteca Tosio Martinengo, Brescia
	St Sebastian	Oil on wood, 43 x 34 cm	Accademia Carrara, Bergamo
1501	Portrait of a Man	Oil on wood, 45 x 31 cm	Galleria Borghese, Rome
	Crucifixion (Città di Castello Altarpiece)	Oil on wood, 281 x 165 cm	National Gallery, London
1502	The Crowning of the Virgin (Oddi altar)	Oil on canvas, 267 x 163 cm	Pinacoteca, Vatican
	The Annunciation (Oddi altar, predella)	Oil on canvas, 27 x 50 cm	Pinacoteca, Vatican

1 Long tables may need to flow across a number of threaded text frames over several pages. Here's how to deal with them. Begin by placing the table on your page and removing all the borders (see page 40). If the table runs into overmatter, link more frames to the parent text frame in the usual way (see page 10).

RAFFAELLO SANTI			
Year	Title	Physical Data	Current Location

2 If the top-left cell of the table contains the table's title, select the entire row and choose **Table > Merge Cells** or simply click on the Merge Cells button in the Control palette. The top row is now a single cell. Use the Character styling tools (see page 16) to center the text in this cell.

3 The first column of our table contains groups of cells that can be merged in the same way. After merging them, use the Control palette buttons to center these cells both horizontally and vertically, and to rotate the text. These merged, centered, and rotated cells in the first column now look like this:

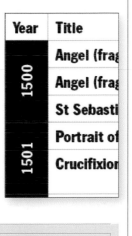

Year	Title
1500	Angel (frag...
	Angel (frag...
	St Sebasti...
1501	Portrait of...
	Crucifixion...

4 The top two rows in our table contain headings. Select them and go to **Table > Cell Options > Strokes and Fills**. Choose a color from the Color pop-up in the Cell Fill section, and set a pale tint such as 20%. Click OK.

Cell Fill
Color: [R=160 G=64 B...] Tint: 20%
☐ Overprint Fill

5 You may want to set a different tint for each of the heading rows. Use the same method to fill other cells with color. Alternatively, drag and drop colors from the Color and Swatches palettes (see Chapter 4) onto specific cells.

RAFFAELLO SANTI			
Year	Title	Physical Data	Current Location
1500	Angel (fragment of the Baronci Altarpiece)	Oil on wood, 57 x 36 cm	Musée du Louvre, Paris
	Angel (fragment of the Baronci Altarpiece)	Oil on wood, 31 x 27 cm	Pinacoteca Tosio Martinengo, Brescia
	St Sebastian	Oil on wood, 43 x 34 cm	Accademia Carrara, Bergamo
1501	Portrait of a Man	Oil on wood, 45 x 31 cm	Galleria Borghese, Rome
	Crucifixion (Città di Castello Altarpiece)	Oil on wood, 281 x 165 cm	National Gallery, London
1502	The Crowning of the Virgin (Oddi altar)	Oil on canvas, 267 x 163 cm	Pinacoteca, Vatican
	The Annunciation (Oddi altar, predella)	Oil on canvas, 27 x 50 cm	Pinacoteca, Vatican
	The Adoration of the Magi (Oddi altar)	Oil on canvas, 27 x 150 cm	Pinacoteca, Vatican
	The Presentation in the Temple (Oddi altar, predella)	Oil on canvas, 27 x 50 cm	Pinacoteca, Vatican

6 Select the heading rows again and choose **Table > Convert to Header Rows**. These rows now appear at the top of every frame that the table runs across.

RAFFAELLO SANTI			
Year	Title	Physical Data	Current Location
1500	Angel (fragment of the Baronci Altarpiece)	Oil on wood, 57 x 36 cm	Musée du Louvre, Paris
	Angel (fragment of the Baronci Altarpiece)	Oil on wood, 31 x 27 cm	Pinacoteca Tosio Martinengo, Brescia
	St Sebastian	Oil on wood, 43 x 34 cm	Accademia Carrara, Bergamo
1501	Portrait of a Man	Oil on wood, 45 x 31 cm	Galleria Borghese, Rome
	Crucifixion (Città di Castello Altarpiece)	Oil on wood, 281 x 165 cm	National Gallery, London
1502	The Crowning of the Virgin (Oddi altar)	Oil on canvas, 267 x 163 cm	Pinacoteca, Vatican
	The Annunciation (Oddi altar, predella)	Oil on canvas, 27 x 50 cm	Pinacoteca, Vatican
	The Adoration of the Magi (Oddi altar)	Oil on canvas, 27 x 150 cm	Pinacoteca, Vatican
	The Presentation in the Temple (Oddi altar, predella)	Oil on canvas, 27 x 50 cm	Pinacoteca, Vatican

RAFFAELLO SANTI			
Year	Title	Physical Data	Current Location
1506	St Michael and the Dragon	Oil on wood, 31 x 27 cm	Musée du Louvre, Paris
	St George Fighting the Dragon	Oil on wood, 32 x 27 cm	Musée du Louvre, Paris
	Young Man with an Apple	Oil on wood, 47 x 35 cm	Galleria degli Uffizi, Florence
	Lady with a Unicorn	Oil on wood, 65 x 51 cm	Galleria Borghese, Rome
	Portrait of a Woman (La Donna Gravida)	Oil on panel, 66 x 52 cm	Galleria Palatina (Palazzo Pitti), Florence
	St George and the Dragon	Oil on wood, 28.5 x 21.5 cm	National Gallery of Art, Washington
1506	The Blessing Christ	Oil on wood, 30 x 25 cm	Pinacoteca Tosio Martinengo, Brescia
	Self-Portrait	Oil on wood, 45 x 33 cm	Galleria degli Uffizi, Florence
	Portrait of Agnolo Doni	Oil on wood, 63 x 45 cm	Galleria Palatina (Palazzo Pitti), Florence
	Portrait of Maddalena Doni	Oil on panel, 63 x 45 cm	Galleria Palatina (Palazzo Pitti), Florence
	Madonna of Belvedere (Madonna del Prato)	Oil on wood, 113 x 88 cm	Kunsthistorisches Museum, Vienna
	Madonna del Cardellino	Oil on wood, 107 x 77 cm	Galleria degli Uffizi, Florence
	The Virgin and Child with Saint John the Baptist (La Belle Jardinière)	Oil on wood, 122 x 80 cm	Musée du Louvre, Paris
1507	The Canigiani Madonna	Oil on wood, 131 x 107 cm	Alte Pinakothek, Munich
	The Canigiani Madonna	Oil on wood, 131 x 107 cm	Alte Pinakothek, Munich
	The Canigiani Madonna (detail)	Oil on wood	Alte Pinakothek, Munich
	The Canigiani Madonna (detail)	Oil on wood	Alte Pinakothek, Munich
	Portrait of a Woman (La Muta)	Oil on wood, 64 x 48 cm	Galleria Nazionale, Urbino
	The Holy Family with a Lamb	Oil on wood, 29 x 21 cm	Museo del Prado, Madrid
	Madonna del Baldacchino	Oil on canvas, 276 x 224 cm	Galleria Palatina (Palazzo Pitti), Florence
1508	Madonna and Child (The Large Cowper Madonna)	Oil on wood, 81 x 57 cm	National Gallery of Art, Washington
	Madonna and Child (The Tempi Madonna)	Oil on wood, 75 x 51 cm	Alte Pinakothek, Munich
	St Catherine of Alexandria	Oil on wood, 71,1 x 54,6 cm	National Gallery, London
	Madonna and Child with the Infant St John	Tempera and oil on wood, 28,5	Museum of Fine Arts, Budapest

7 If your table has a "key" or other such footnote row at the end of the table, merge the cells in this final row into one, then select the row and choose **Table > Convert to Footer Rows**. Go to **Table > Table Options > Headers and Footers**. From the Repeat Footer pop-up, pick Once Per Page.

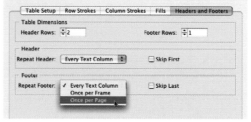

Table Setup | Row Strokes | Column Strokes | Fills | **Headers and Footers**
Table Dimensions
Header Rows: 2   Footer Rows: 1
Header
Repeat Header: [Every Text Column] ☐ Skip First
Footer
Repeat Footer: [Every Text Column] ☐ Skip Last
✓ Every Text Column
Once per Frame
Once per Page

RAFFAELLO SANTI			
Year	Title	Physical Data	Current Location
1503	Madonna and Child	Oil on wood, 55 x 40 cm	Norton Simon Museum of Art, Pasadena
	Portrait of Pietro Bembo	Oil on wood, 54 x 69 cm	Museum of Fine Arts, Budapest
	Portrait of Perugino	Tempera on wood, 57 x 42 cm	Galleria degli Uffizi, Florence
	Spozalizio (The Engagement of Virgin Mary)	Oil on roundheaded panel, 170 x 117 cm	Pinacoteca di Brera, Milan
	Spozalizio (detail)	Oil on roundheaded panel	Pinacoteca di Brera, Milan
	Spozalizio (detail)	Oil on roundheaded panel	Pinacoteca di Brera, Milan
	Allegory (The Knight's Dream)	Oil on wood, 17 x 17 cm	National Gallery, London
1504	Madonna with the Book (Constabile Madonna)	Tempera on canvas transferred from wood, diameter 17,9 cm	The Hermitage, St. Petersburg
	Madonna and Child (The Small Cowper Madonna)	Oil on wood, 58 x 43 cm	National Gallery of Art, Washington
	Madonna and Child Enthroned with Saints	Tempera and gold on wood, 172,4 x 172,4 cm (main panel)	Metropolitan Museum of Art, New York
	The Three Graces	Oil on panel, 17 x 17 cm	Musée Condé, Chantilly

RAFFAELLO SANTI			
Year	Title	Physical Data	Current Location
1505	St Michael and the Dragon	Oil on wood, 31 x 27 cm	Musée du Louvre, Paris
	St George Fighting the Dragon	Oil on wood, 32 x 27 cm	Musée du Louvre, Paris
	Young Man with an Apple	Oil on wood, 47 x 35 cm	Galleria degli Uffizi, Florence
	Lady with a Unicorn	Oil on wood, 65 x 51 cm	Galleria Borghese, Rome
	Portrait of a Woman (La Donna Gravida)	Oil on panel, 66 x 52 cm	Galleria Palatina (Palazzo Pitti), Florence
	St George and the Dragon	Oil on wood, 28.5 x 21.5 cm	National Gallery of Art, Washington
1506	The Blessing Christ	Oil on wood, 30 x 25 cm	Pinacoteca Tosio Martinengo, Brescia
	Self-Portrait	Oil on wood, 45 x 33 cm	Galleria degli Uffizi, Florence
	Portrait of Agnolo Doni	Oil on wood, 63 x 45 cm	Galleria Palatina (Palazzo Pitti), Florence
	Portrait of Maddalena Doni	Oil on wood, 63 x 45 cm	Galleria Palatina (Palazzo Pitti), Florence
	Madonna of Belvedere (Madonna del Prato)	Oil on wood, 113 x 88 cm	Kunsthistorisches Museum, Vienna
	The Virgin and Child with Saint John the Baptist (La Belle Jardinière)	Oil on wood, 122 x 80 cm	Musée du Louvre, Paris
1507	The Canigiani Madonna	Oil on wood, 131 x 107 cm	Alte Pinakothek, Munich
	The Canigiani Madonna	Oil on wood, 131 x 107 cm	Alte Pinakothek, Munich
	The Canigiani Madonna (detail)	Oil on wood	Alte Pinakothek, Munich
	The Canigiani Madonna (detail)	Oil on wood	Alte Pinakothek, Munich
	Portrait of a Woman (La Muta)	Oil on wood, 64 x 48 cm	Galleria Nazionale, Urbino
	The Holy Family with a Lamb	Oil on wood, 29 x 21 cm	Museo del Prado, Madrid
	Madonna del Baldacchino	Oil on canvas, 276 x 224 cm	Galleria Palatina (Palazzo Pitti), Florence
1508	Madonna and Child (The Large Cowper Madonna)	Oil on wood, 81 x 57 cm	National Gallery of Art, Washington
	Madonna and Child (The Tempi Madonna)	Oil on wood, 75 x 51 cm	Alte Pinakothek, Munich
	St Catherine of Alexandria	Oil on wood, 71,1 x 54,6 cm	National Gallery, London
	Madonna and Child with the Infant St John	Tempera and oil on wood, 28,5 x 21,5 cm	Museum of Fine Arts, Budapest
	Madonna and Child with the Infant St John (detail)	Tempera and oil on wood	Museum of Fine Arts, Budapest

8 Looking again at the layout of the table across multiple pages, you can see how the header rows have been set to repeat at the top of every frame, but the footer row only appears once on each page

Pictures in tables

Pictures do not behave as you might expect when they are inside tables. This is because a table is an inline anchored object within its parent text frame. So, if you place a picture in a table, it is in turn treated as an inline anchored object within its parent cell. (See page 70 for more on inline objects, and pages 40–43 for more on tables.) Unlike QuarkXPress tables, there is no such thing as a picture cell in InDesign—all cells are text cells. You can persuade InDesign to work more intuitively for cropping pictures in tables by using this borderless clipping technique.

Tip

RESIZE FIRST

You can place pictures directly into a table cell by using the File > Place command, or by pressing Ctrl/Cmd+D. You cannot drag and drop pictures from your Desktop or Bridge into specific cells in your layout, although this technique does work when replacing one inline picture with another. However, it's best not to do any of these things. If the picture is too big for the table, or its text frame parent, the entire table will be forced into overmatter and become very difficult to retrieve. Instead, place the picture anywhere else on your page, scale it down to a more manageable size, and then cut and paste it into the table cell.

44

Borderless clipping

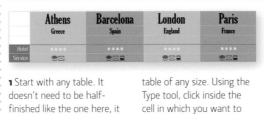

1 Start with any table. It doesn't need to be half-finished like the one here, it can be a brand new, empty table of any size. Using the Type tool, click inside the cell in which you want to place a picture.

2 Place the picture into the cell using whichever method you choose (see the Resize First tip box). You will notice that the picture has spilled out into the adjacent column and is inset slightly from the top left corner of its own cell. What you really want is for the picture edges to be flush with the cell edges.

Cell Options

| Text | Strokes and Fills | Rows and Columns | Diagonal Lines |

Cell Insets
Top: 0 mm   Left: 0 mm
Bottom: 0 mm   Right: 0 mm

Vertical Justification
Align: Top   Paragraph Spacing Limit: 0 mm

First Baseline
Offset: Ascent   Min: 0 mm

Clipping
☑ Clip Contents to Cell

Text Rotation
Rotation: 0°

☑ Preview   (Cancel)   (OK)

3 Select the cell with the Type tool, and open the Cell Options dialog window at the Text section. You can do this by choosing **Cell Options > Text** from the Table menu, or the Table palette menu, or the Control palette menu, or from the Right/Ctrl+click contextual menu. Alternatively, just press Ctrl/Cmd+Alt/Option+B. Change all four Cell Insets to 0 (zero). Further down the dialog window, check the option under Clipping entitled Clip Contents to Cell. Then click OK.

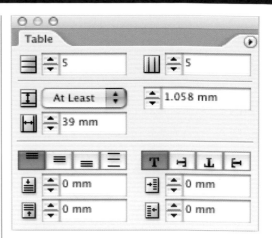

4 Note that you can change the cell inset values directly within the Table palette— they are the four fields at the bottom of the palette. You will still need to open the Cell Options Text dialog window to check the Clip Contents to Cell option.

5 Your picture should now fit cleanly inside the cell. The overlapping area has been cropped from the adjacent column, and the picture runs flush against all the cell edges.

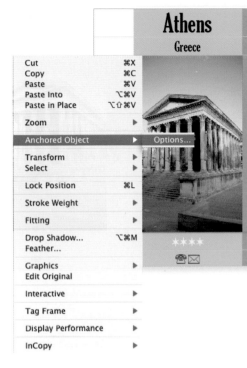

Cut	⌘X
Copy	⌘C
Paste	⌘V
Paste Into	⌥⌘V
Paste in Place	⌥⇧⌘V
Zoom	▶
Anchored Object	▶ Options...
Transform	▶
Select	▶
Lock Position	⌘L
Stroke Weight	▶
Fitting	▶
Drop Shadow...	⌥⌘M
Feather...	
Graphics	▶
Edit Original	
Interactive	▶
Tag Frame	▶
Display Performance	▶
InCopy	▶

6 You will find that you cannot crop the picture from the bottom by dragging the row divider upward—the minimum row height appears to be locked to that of the picture itself. To fix this,

click on the picture with the Selection tool, then choose **Anchored Object** > **Options** from the Object menu, or from the Right/Ctrl+click contextual menu.

7 In the Anchored Object Options dialog window, choose Inline or Above Line from the Position drop-down, click on the Inline radio button just underneath it, then reduce

the Y Offset value into minus figures. If you have the Preview option checked at the bottom, you can watch the table row in which the picture is sitting reduce in height. Click OK.

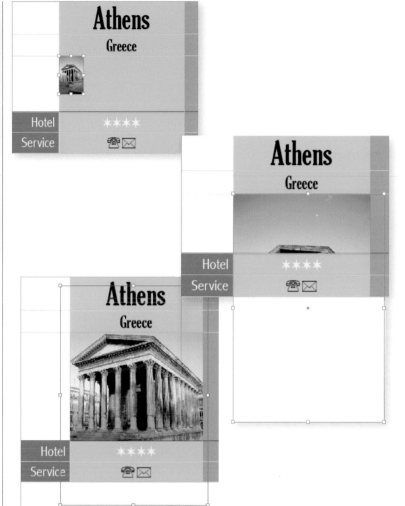

11 You can set up cells for borderless clipping before or after placing the pictures, as you wish.

8 Here's a quick-and-dirty alternative method to calling up the Anchored Object Options dialog window. With the picture selected, resize it inside its cell by dragging on its bottom-right corner while holding down Ctrl/Cmd+Shift, and then let go. The row height reduces with the picture size.

9 Now increase the picture size again using the same method. You have just achieved the same result as before, without having to call up any dialog windows.

10 Switch to either the Direct Selection tool or the Position tool. You can now move, crop, and scale the image in the conventional manner. Of course, you are actually cropping within the inline picture frame, but it looks and feels as if you are cropping within the cell edges.

Text wrap is a property that forces text to wrap around the edge of an overlapping object instead of printing over it or being hidden behind it. QuarkXPress calls this function "Runaround." Text wraps are applied to the object, not the text.

Using Text Wrap

To view or change the text wrap settings for a selected object, open the Text Wrap palette. By default, InDesign does not assign any text wrap to objects you place on the page.

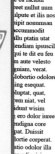

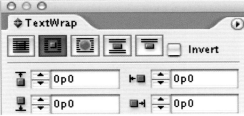

1 An object placed over the text—in this example an Adobe Illustrator graphic inside a stroked frame—will not automatically cause the text to wrap. The text is hidden behind the image.

2 With the object still selected, click on the Wrap Around Bounding Box button in the Text Wrap palette.

This forces the text to wrap around the object frame.

3 Notice that the Text Offset fields below the row of buttons in the palette are no longer grayed out. Use these to push the text away from the object edge on all four sides. The Text Offset is visible as a second thin object frame, and this can be edited manually by dragging on its handles.

For non-rectangular objects, you can only enter a single, uniform Offset value. The reason these fields are called "offset" rather than "outset" is because you can also enter negative values to cause text to overlap the wrapping object slightly. You may want to do this if the object has pale or gradient edges, and only if the text frame is in front of the object.

Tip

WRAPPING TEXT THAT APPEARS BEHIND/BENEATH OBJECTS
Unlike QuarkXPress, InDesign does not care whether the text frame is in front of or behind the text-wrapping object. Text wrap applies to all text on the page no matter where it is in the stacking order of overlapping objects, and across all visible layers. If you want InDesign to work like QuarkXPress, by which only the text frames that are behind text-wrapping objects are affected, click on the InDesign (Mac) or Edit (Win) menu and go to Preferences > Composition. In the Text Wrap section, check the option labelled Text Wrap Only Affects Text Beneath.

The Justify Text Next to an Object option only applies to text to the left of an object that is floating in the middle of a single column.

You can also set individual text frames to ignore text wraps. Select the text frame(s) and go to Object > Text Frame Options, then tick the Ignore Text Wrap option at the bottom left-hand corner of the Text Frame Options window.

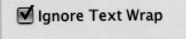

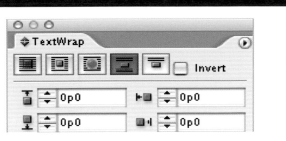

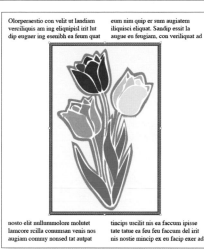

4 The Jump Object button prevents text from wrapping around the sides of the object: it jumps straight from the top to the bottom.

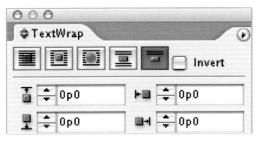

5 The Jump To Next Column button halts the text at the top of the object, then forces the remainder into the next column or threaded frame.

Wrap around object shape

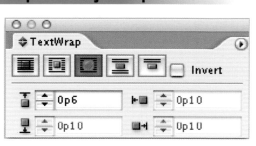

The "Wrap around object shape" button in the Text Wrap palette only applies to irregularly shaped objects. For example, having removed the frame border and fill color from our Illustrator graphic, the text now follows the irregular contour of the graphic itself.

This also works with shapes created with InDesign's drawing tools (see Chapter 3) and images containing alpha channel masks or clipping paths, or that have a pure white background (see page 60)

In this mode, you can only enter a single, uniform Text Offset value. However, if you switch to the Direct Selection tool, the Text Offset path becomes visible and can be edited just like any other Bézier path (see Chapter 3).

47

Tip

WRAPPING AROUND GROUPED OBJECTS

The Wrap Around Object Shape feature does not work on object groups. As soon as you group two or more objects, text will only wrap around the group's overall rectangular bounding box, not the shape of its components. One way around this is to assign the Wrap Around Object Shape property to each individual object before grouping them. Ensure the No Text Wrap button is selected in the Text Wrap palette for the group, and it will then wrap as expected.

Type effects

In addition to putting text inside frames and irregular shapes, InDesign can run text along lines and paths. To do this, you must use the Type on a Path tool, which can be found in the Type tool fly-out in the Tools palette. When this tool is active, the cursor is similar to the normal Type cursor except it has a little dotted line through it to indicate a path. When you bring the tool into proximity with a path, the cursor changes to show a tiny plus (+) symbol, indicating that it is ready to place some text on it.

Type on a
Path toolbar
icon

Type on a Path
cursor over a
blank area

Type on a
Path cursor
over a path

Using the Type on a Path tool

click-and-drag

1 Simply clicking on a path with the tool is enough to start typing, but you will achieve better control by clicking and dragging across the path. As you drag, you will see visual indicators of the start and end points of the text area.

And the women of New

2 When you type, these indicators temporarily vanish. To see them again, select the path using the Selection or Direct Selection tool. If the text you have typed has fallen into overmatter, this will be indicated in the usual manner.

And the women of New

Bedford, they bloom like their own red roses.

3 You can thread a story across a mixture of frames and paths, or even use the **File** > **Place** command to bring text from an external file onto a path in the normal way.

Running text along a path

Cut carefully with scissors

1 Draw a text frame, or indeed any other kind of shape, and style its stroke as required (see Chapter 3). Use the Type on a Path tool to run text along the outside of this frame. In this example, we gave the text frame a thick, dashed stroke because it will contain a cut-out coupon. We used the Type on a Path tool to add the cutting instructions to the outside.

Cut carefully with scissors

2 To lift the text away from the dashed stroke around the frame, select it with the Type on a Path tool and simply increase the baseline shift value in the Character or Control palette (see page 16).

1 pt

3 Often you will want to make the path stroke invisible, leaving just the text. To do this, select the path and change its weight (thickness), which is normally 1pt by default, to zero. You can find the stroke weight control at the top of the Stroke palette (see page 80) and in the middle of the Control palette.

Twinkle twinkle little star, how I wonder what you are up above the clouds so high...

4 This enables you to use the text alone to suggest the path shape, producing interesting results. See page 74 to find out how to draw starbursts with InDesign.

Special effects

The **Type > Type on a Path > Options** command opens a window for applying special type effects. These affect the entire text on a selected path, so you do not need to use the Type on a Path tool to select the text itself before using the command.

The Align drop-down lets you choose how to place the text on the path in relation to the text's baseline, mid-height center point, ascenders, or descenders. The Effect pop-up presents five styling choices:

3D Ribbon

Stair Step

Skew

Gravity

Rainbow (this is the default)

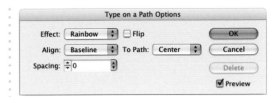

Creating a simple logo with the Skew effect

1 Here's a simple logo you can create with the Skew effect. Using the Ellipse tool (see page 74), draw a shallow oval, then add text to it with the Type on a Path tool. Start the text at the left side of the oval and run it over to the right, then repeat the text again to run around the underside, as shown.

2 Hide the path by setting its stroke to zero. Select the text with the Type on a Path tool, and thicken its font and increase its vertical scale using the Character or Control palette (see page 16).

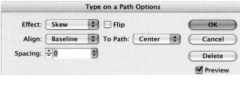

3 Go to **Type > Type on a Path > Options**. From the Effect pop-up, choose Skew and click OK.

4 If necessary, you can adjust the text by selecting the path with the Selection or Direct Selection tool, and dragging on the start and stop bars on the left-hand side of the oval. You can also re-open the Type on a Path Options window and adjust the Spacing value.

5 To complete the logo, select characters using the Type on a Path tool and apply color to them using the Color and Swatches palettes (see Chapter 4). The text remains editable, so it's easy to fix mistakes.

Find/Change

The Find/Change dialog box

Go to **Edit > Find/Change** to open a floating palette for locating and amending text content and type formatting. If you need to use the palette several times as you work on a layout, keep it on-screen: it is not necessary to close it between uses.

(A) Find What
Type in the text you want to search for.

(B) Recent searches
Click here for a list of up to 15 of your most recent previous searches.

(C) Special characters
Click here for a pop-up list of special and hidden characters. Any of these can be entered manually into the Find What and Change To fields if you can remember their symbols, but it's easier to pick them from this list.

Auto Page Number
Section Marker
End of Paragraph
Forced Line Break
Anchored Object Marker
Footnote Reference Marker
Bullet Character
Caret Character
Copyright Symbol
Ellipsis
Paragraph Symbol
Registered Trademark Symbol
Section Symbol
Trademark Symbol
Em Dash
En Dash
Discretionary Hyphen
Nonbreaking Hyphen
Em Space
En Space
Flush Space
Hair Space
Nonbreaking Space
Thin Space
Figure Space
Punctuation Space
Double Left Quotation Mark
Double Right Quotation Mark
Single Left Quotation Mark
Single Right Quotation Mark
Tab Character
Right Indent Tab
Indent To Here
End Nested Style
Any Digit
Any Letter
Any Character
White Space

(D) Change buttons
When you click Find or Find Next, InDesign scrolls to the next instance of the Find What word or phrase, highlights it and waits for your order. Click Change to change the found word or phrase. Click Change/Find to change the found word or phrase and immediately search for the next instance. Click Change All to make all the changes automatically without stopping at each instance.

(E) Change To
Type in the text with which you want to replace the found text.

(F) Search pop-up
Choose whether to search across the entire document or current story, or from the cursor position to the end of the current story, or only the currently selected text. If you have several documents open at the same time, you can run the search across them all at once.

> **All Documents**
> ✓ **Document**
> **Story**
> **To End of Story**
> **Selection**

(G) Text options
Check Whole Word to ensure that a search for the word "reign", for example, does not also highlight "foreign." Check Case Sensitive to ensure that a search for the name "Jack," for example, does not also highlight the word "jack."

(H) More Options
Click here to expand the Find/Change palette to let you search for type formatting as well as text content.

Tip

WILDCARD SEARCHES

Use the symbols ^? to represent "any character" in the Find What field. This helps you to broaden the search to find similar alternative words and phrases in one sweep rather than having to run several searches each with slightly different criteria. For example, entering "a^?roplane" in the Find What field and "airplane" in the Change To field will find all instances of "aeroplane" and the misspelled "airoplane" and let you change them all to "airplane."

Tip

FIND FONT

Go to Type > Find Font for a quicker and more direct way of finding and changing fonts in the current document. Just select a font from the list of those in use and pick a replacement font and style from the Replace With pop-ups at the bottom of the window.

However, if you want to find and change fonts across several open documents at the same time, open the Find/Change palette instead, pick the fonts from the Find Format Settings and Change Format Settings windows, and choose All Documents from the Search pop-up.

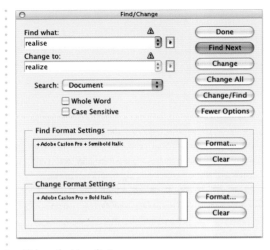

1 Click on the More Options button in the Find/Change palette. The palette expands to offer two new boxes: Find Format Settings and Change Format Settings.

2 When you click on either of the Format buttons, you are presented with a Settings window that looks similar to the Paragraph Style Options window (see page 28).

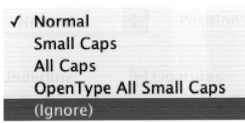

3 By default, all settings are blank to begin with: InDesign only finds and changes formatting attributes that you choose to set. As with Paragraph Styles, you can clear any existing setting by deleting it from its field or by choosing "(Ignore)" from its pop-up. To clear all formatting settings, click OK or Cancel to return to the Find/Change palette and click on the Clear buttons.

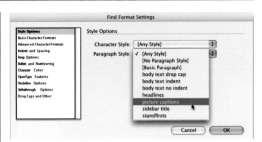

4 The Style Options section of the Find Format Settings and Change Format Settings windows lets you specify the Find/Change action to particular character and paragraph styles.

This is extremely useful for restricting the search to a smaller range of text content within a long document—for example, only searching across picture captions.

5 If you work with multilingual documents, remember that you can find and change according to language. This way, for example, you could find all instances of text assigned as "German: Traditional" and change them to "German: Reformed" to ensure your spellcheck (see page 14) is appropriate for magazine work. Just remember to leave the Find What and Change To fields blank, forcing InDesign to concentrate exclusively on the formatting.

Drag and Drop Text Editing

☑ Enable in Layout View
☑ Enable in Story Editor

1 The easiest way to search for a complex string of characters—one that includes paragraph returns, bullet points, and tabs, for example—is to copy it from your document and paste it into the Find/Change palette. InDesign also supports drag-and-drop copying. To enable this, click on the InDesign menu (Mac) or Edit menu (Win) and go to **Preferences > Type**, then check the Enable in Layout View option under Drag and Drop Text Editing.

2 Click OK. Select a range of text in your layout that you want to use as a search string, then click on it and drag it over to the Find What field in the Find/Change palette.

3 Let go of the mouse button to drop the selection into the field. The search symbols for the special characters in the selection are entered automatically.

Tip

FIND AND DELETE
To delete a word or phrase using the Find/Change palette, simply leave the Change To field blank.

51

Footnotes

Traditionally, footnotes appear in scholarly works and long documents such as textbooks, and it's been difficult to keep them tied to the appropriate page. InDesign, however, makes this much easier. When you insert a footnote reference into a story, InDesign adds a footer area at the bottom of the relevant text frame in which you enter the reference text. This footer is moved from frame to frame and page to page automatically as you edit the layout, keeping the reference indicator and its footnote together at all times.

Tip

REFERENCE SYMBOLS

The Numbering Style pop-up in the Footnote Options window supports various alternative series:

If you pick the symbols style—the asterisk, cross, and so on—check the Restart Numbering Every option and choose Page from the drop-down.

This ensures you adhere to a convention which dictates that reference symbols start afresh on a new page. If you do not restart them in this way, the series of different symbols becomes increasingly bizarre. It's better to keep returning to those symbols with which readers are most familiar.

Adding footnotes

1 To insert a footnote at the cursor position, go to **Type > Insert Footnote**. You may find it more convenient to use the Right/Ctrl-click contextual menus, as they contain more footnote commands. When the flashing type cursor is adjacent to a reference number in your body text, you can call up the contextual menu and choose Go To Footnote Text.

2 Similarly, while editing a footnote, you can jump back to its reference location in the body text by calling up the contextual menu again and this time choosing Go to Footnote Reference.

By default, the reference indicators in the text look like this...

... and the footnotes at the bottom of the text frame look like this:

3 Note how the footnote area is outlined by its own horizontal frame line in addition to the short black rule, and that each footnote is separated by additional horizontal frame lines.

Customizing footnote styling

1 Here's how to reformat InDesign's footnotes if you want a different look. Create a new character style in the Character Styles palette (see page 26) for the footnote reference numbers that appear in the body text. If your body text is in a serif font, choose a sans serif for the numbers, or vice versa, and set the font size to about three-quarters of the size of the body text.

2 In the Advanced Character Formats section, set the Baseline Shift to raise the characters several points off the baseline. Then click OK.

3 Go to **Type > Document Footnote Options**. Under the Numbering and Formatting tab, pick a Numbering Style, and ensure the Start At field is set at 1.

4 Further down the Footnote Options window, tick the Show Prefix/Suffix In option and choose Footnote Reference from the drop-down. Use the drop-down menu next to the Prefix field to enter a "hair space" and an opening square bracket. In the Suffix field, enter a closing square bracket.

5 In the Formatting section, click on the Position pop-up and change it from Apply Superscript to Apply Normal. In the Character Style pop-up, choose the character style you created a moment ago, then click OK.

was, in Venice, part of institutions". [1] This de gates the contemporary n Marco [2] and Rialto B

6 The footnote reference numbers in the body text now look like this. They are larger and more evenly spaced, but do not interfere with the typography.

7 Create another new character style in the Character Styles palette, this time for the footnote text numbers. Choose a bold sans serif from the same family as the font you used for the reference numbers, then click OK.

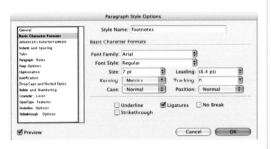

8 Create a paragraph style in the Paragraph Styles palette. This will be for the footnote text itself. Assign a font and set the type size smaller than the body text, but still readable.

9 In the Drop Caps and Nested Styles section, click on New Nested Style. Choose the character style you created for the footnote text numbers, then set it to be applied "through 1 Characters" as shown. Click OK.

10 Go to Type > Document Footnote Options. Under the Numbering and Formatting tab, click on the Paragraph Style drop-down in the Footnote Formatting section and select the paragraph style you just created. Delete the tab symbols in the Separator field and replace them with an "En Space."

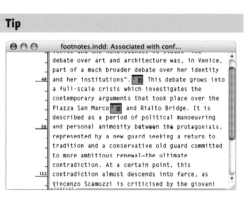

11 Click on the Layout tab at the top. Increase the two Spacing Options at the top by a small amount in order to add a bit of space above and between the footnotes.

12 Further down the window, in the Rule Above section, click on the Weight drop-down and choose 0.5pt. Increase the Offset value at the bottom of the window a little, adding space between the rule and the first footnote. Then click OK.

and a conservative old guard co the ultimate contradiction. At a c descends into farce, as Vincenzo as a "subverter of tradition" at th

1 Manfredo Tafuri and Jessica Levine, *Venice and* (Cambridge (Mass.) & London: The MIT Press, 19

2 Carla Keyvanian, 'Manfredo Tafuri: From the Cr Ideology to Microhistories', *Design Issues*, 16 no.1

13 The footnotes now look smarter and more professional.

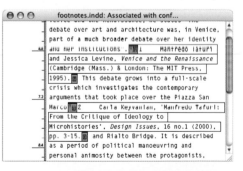

EDITING FOOTNOTES IN THE STORY EDITOR
When working on long documents, the easiest way to edit footnotes is to use the Story Editor (see page 34). The position of each inserted footnote reference is impossible to miss in the Story Editor window.

Click on a reference marker to expand the reference text for editing. Click on one of the markers again to collapse the reference text. You can also Right/Ctrl-click anywhere in the Story Editor window, then choose Expand/Collapse All Footnotes from the contextual menu.

53

PICTURES

Picture frames

Placing, positioning, cropping, resizing, and framing pictures are tasks that can all be accomplished in a few seconds if you're familiar with way InDesign handles frames and their contents. The new Position tool streamlines the process, combining the functions of the Selection and Direct Selection tools.

Adobe Bridge

The Place dialog box doesn't tell you much about the image you're placing—you can't even see a preview thumbnail, unless you've selected Show Import options, by which time it's too late to change your mind without canceling the operation and starting again. Adobe Bridge provides a more visual method for placing pictures. To place an image from Bridge, drag it from the content area and drop it on the page.

To replace any image on the page (it doesn't have to be selected) drag an image from Bridge and drop it on top of the picture you want to replace.

Placing pictures

1 Press Ctrl/Cmd+D to open the Place dialog box and place a picture on an InDesign page. InDesign automatically creates a frame for the new image. Unless you want to replace an existing picture, uncheck the Replace Selected Item box.

2 If you check Replace Selected Item, the new picture adopts the same position and scaling attributes within the frame as the old one.

3 If you mistakenly replace a selected image, press Ctrl/Cmd+Z to undo. The original image is restored and the cursor is loaded with the new image ready to place elsewhere on the page.

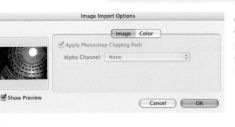

4 Click the Show import options box to see a preview and apply clipping path and color management options.

Drag and drop

You can also drag and drop images from the Finder (Mac) or Explorer (PC) onto an InDesign page. The process works in exactly the same way for multiple images.

Importing vector artwork

1 Vector artwork files imported using the Place command or using drag and drop can be edited in the same way as other graphics files—you can scale and transform them, but you can't edit individual paths, or change fills. If you want to do this, drag and drop, or copy and paste, the graphic directly from the Illustrator document.

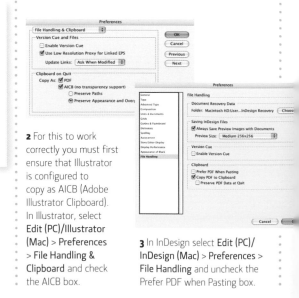

2 For this to work correctly you must first ensure that Illustrator is configured to copy as AICB (Adobe Illustrator Clipboard). In Illustrator, select **Edit (PC)/Illustrator (Mac) > Preferences > File Handling & Clipboard** and check the AICB box.

3 In InDesign select **Edit (PC)/ InDesign (Mac) > Preferences > File Handling** and uncheck the Prefer PDF when Pasting box.

56

Resizing picture frames using the Selection tool

1 InDesign pictures and their frames can be manipulated independently of one another, or together, depending on the desired outcome.

2 Drag any handle to resize the frame, effectively cropping the image. Click and momentarily hold a handle to see a ghosted image of the cropped area of the picture.

3 Hold down the Shift key to crop the image while maintaining the original frame aspect ratio.

4 Hold down Ctrl/Cmd to resize the frame and the image at the same time.

5 Hold down Ctrl/Cmd+Shift to proportionally resize both the frame and its contents.

The Position tool

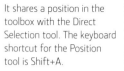

Direct Selection Tool A
Position Tool   Shift+A

The Position tool combines some of the functions of the Selection and Direct Selection tools for working with frames and their contents at the same time.

It shares a position in the toolbox with the Direct Selection tool. The keyboard shortcut for the Position tool is Shift+A.

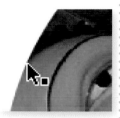

When it's over a picture, the Position tool icon changes to a hand. Click the picture to select it, and the Position tool behaves like the Direct Selection tool, allowing you to move the image within the frame, and resize it independently of the frame.

When positioned over a frame edge, or on a corner point, the Position tool icon changes to a solid black arrow. With the frame selected, the Position tool behaves like the Selection tool. You can resize the frame to crop the picture and use the same keyboard modifiers as for the Selection tool.

Resizing pictures using the Direct Selection tool

1 Drag any handle to resize the image independently of the frame, holding down the Shift key while dragging to maintain the aspect ratio. If the resized image is smaller than the frame, the background color shows through (the default is None). If larger, the image is cropped by its frame.

2 Move an image within its frame when the Direct Selection tool becomes a hand icon. This is useful for adjusting the visible portion of a cropped image within its frame. Click and momentarily hold before dragging to display a ghosted image of the cropped areas.

3 Change the shape of a frame by dragging the corner points to alter the frame's shape.

4 You can delete corner points by selecting them and pressing Backspace, but to add points to the frame you need to use the Pen tool.

5 To revert to a rectangular frame, or to convert the frame to another shape, select one of the options from the **Object > Convert Shape** menu.

Fit to Frame options

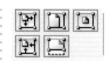

1 You can automatically fit pictures to frames using the content fitting buttons on the Control palette, or the options on the **Object > Fitting** menu.

2 Fit Content to Frame scales the image to fit the frame, disproportionally if necessary.

3 Fit Frame to Content scales the frame to fit the image.

4 Fit Content Proportionally resizes the image to fit the frame while maintaining its proportions. If the proportions of the frame and the image are different, InDesign fits the longest edge of the picture to the frame.

5 Fill Frame Proportionally is a new InDesign CS2 command which works like Fit Content Proportionally, but fits the shortest edge of a picture to the frame and crops the rest, so there's no white space.

6 Center content centers the image horizontally and vertically in the frame.

Working with images

InDesign's display quality can be configured to match your hardware capabilities and the task in hand. Use the Links palette to manage and locate images throughout the document. Two new InDesign CS2 features—Photoshop layer visibility control and Object styles—can save hours of effort producing multiple variations of artwork and applying multiple frame styling attributes.

Display quality options

1 Set display performance options from the **View > Display Performance** menu.

2 Use fast display if you're working on a slow machine with limited RAM. In previous versions of InDesign, Fast Display was called Optimized Display. Gray boxes are displayed in place of images, and all transparency effects are turned off.

3 The Typical Display setting uses low-resolution placeholder images either saved with the file, or generated by InDesign. These look fine at 100 percent view, but pixelate at higher magnifications and when scaled.

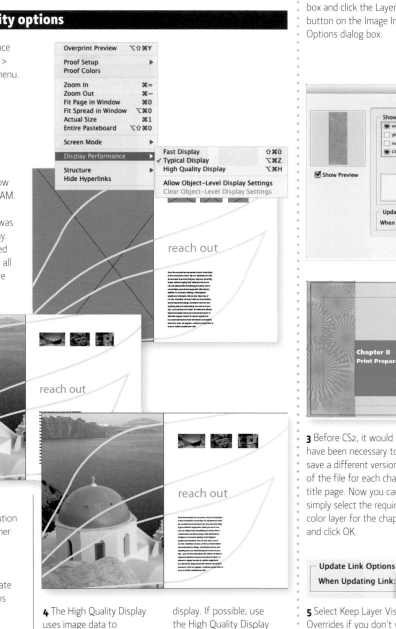

4 The High Quality Display uses image data to produce the screen image. The quality is very good, but slower systems may struggle to update the

display. If possible, use the High Quality Display when carrying out image editing, e.g. creating clipping paths, and to evaluate transparency effects.

Using image layers

1 InDesign CS2 supports the import of native Photoshop files with layers and layer comps intact. To select which layers or layer comps you want to display in a placed PSD file, check the Show Import options box and click the Layers button on the Image Import Options dialog box.

2 In the Show Layers pane, select which layers you want to be visible. The image used here is a graphic for the chapter title page in a book. The file consists of a different-colored fill layer for each chapter in the book and a top layer with the sunburst graphic. The blend mode of the sunburst layer has been set to Luminosity so that it takes on the color of the underlying fill layer.

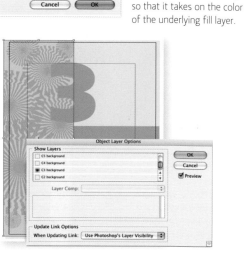

3 Before CS2, it would have been necessary to save a different version of the file for each chapter title page. Now you can simply select the required color layer for the chapter and click OK.

4 You can change the layer visibility for a placed image at any time by Right/ Ctrl+clicking it, and selecting Object Layer Options from the context menu.

5 Select Keep Layer Visibility Overrides if you don't want layer visibility to revert to the Photoshop file defaults if the image is edited and updated. You might, for example, need to add a new color fill layer to the Photoshop file for an additional chapter. If you update the modified image with Use Photoshop's Layer Visibility selected, all of the chapter title pages would revert to the same layer visibility, and you'd have to go through the document to manually reset them.

58

Using the Links palette

The Links palette lists all of the linked images in a document and tells you which page they appear on. Press Ctrl/Cmd+Shift+D to display the palette.

If an image has been deleted, renamed, or moved from its original location, this red icon is displayed.

If an image has been modified, this warning icon is displayed alongside its entry in the Links palette.

To show the location on the page of a file selected in the Links palette, click the Go To Link button. The spread on which the image appears becomes the target spread, and the image is selected and centered in the document window.

Go To Link

Update Link

To update the document with the modified version, click the Update Link button at the bottom of the palette. To update multiple modified images, click the vacant space at the bottom of the palette to ensure no files are selected, and click the Update Link button.

Relink...

To recover a missing image, click the Relink button at the bottom of the palette and locate the missing image.

To edit a linked file using the application in which it was created, click the Edit Original button. (Be aware that this may have unexpected results with EPS graphics, and is also dependent on the operating system file associations.)

Edit Original

All of the commands available as palette icons can be found on the Palette fly out menu, which also contains some useful sort options, plus Reveal in Finder, Reveal in Bridge, and Link Information.

Relink...
Go To Link
Edit Original
Update Link
Copy Link(s) To...

Save Link Version...
Versions...
Alternates...

Purchase This Image...

Reveal in Finder
Reveal in Bridge

Embed File

Link File Info...
Link Information...

Sort by Name
✓ Sort by Page
Sort by Status

Small Palette Rows

Using object-level display settings

The display performance settings apply to all images throughout the document. If your display hardware can't cope with the demands of the High Quality Display, a good compromise is to use the Fast or Typical Display for the document, and set High Quality Display only for those images where it's really necessary.

1 First select **View > Display Performance > Allow Object-Level Display Settings**.

2 Then select the images you need to see at high resolution, Right/Ctrl+click them, and select **Display Performance > High Quality Display** from the context menu.

Fast Display   ⇧⌘0
Typical Display   ⌥⌘Z
✓ High Quality Display ⌥⌘H

✓ Allow Object-Level Display Settings
Clear Object-Level Display Settings

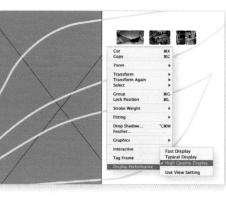

Object styles

1 Use object styles to quickly apply frame formatting to placed images. First, apply styling to the frame, selecting fill and stroke colors, corner effects, and any other attributes.

2 Select the styled frame, and choose New Object Style from the Object Styles palette menu. Name the style and click OK.

3 To apply the object style to other frames, select the frames using the Selection tool, and click the style in the Object Styles palette.

General
☑ Fill
☑ Stroke
☑ Stroke & Corner Effects
☑ Transparency
☑ Drop Shadow & Feather
☐ Paragraph Styles
☑ Text Frame General Options
☑ Text Frame Baseline Options
☑ Story Options
☑ Text Wrap & Other
☑ Anchored Object Options

4 Object styles can be used to apply fills, strokes, corner effects, transparency, drop shadows and feather, text wrap, and anchored object options to any graphic frame. To enable or disable any of these categories, double-click the style in the Object Styles palette to open the Object Style Options dialog box.

Clipping paths

InDesign's support for imported images with alpha channel transparency has marked a move away from the use of clipping paths to produce cut-out images. But clipping paths still have their uses, and InDesign provides a range of options both for utilizing embedded paths in Photoshop files, and for creating clipping paths in situ.

Importing a Photoshop image with a clipping path

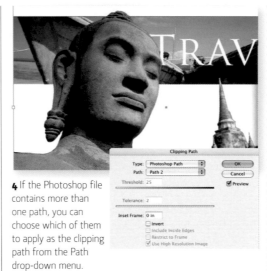

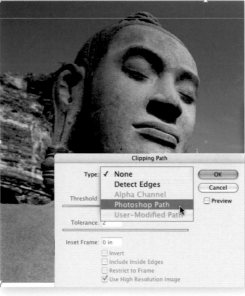

1 When you place an image with a Photoshop clipping path, if you check the Show Import Options box in the Place dialog box, you'll have the opportunity to apply the clipping path to the image on import.

2 The clipping path masks (or, if you prefer, clips) everything outside its boundary. One of the few advantages of clipping paths over alpha channels is that they are PostScript paths, and are therefore resolution independent.

3 Check the Preview box, and you'll immediately see the effect of applying the clipping path.

4 If the Photoshop file contains more than one path, you can choose which of them to apply as the clipping path from the Path drop-down menu.

5 Even if you don't apply the clipping path on import, you can still do it later. Select the image with the Selection tool and choose Object > Clipping Path to display the Clipping Path dialog box. Select Photoshop Path from the Type drop-down menu.

Tip

PLACING MULTIPLE IMAGES
If you're placing lots of images with clipping paths, you don't need to display the Image Import Options dialog box every time. It remembers the previous settings, so once you've applied a clipping path to one image, subsequent images will be treated the same way.

Tip

CREATING A CLIPPING PATH USING AN ALPHA CHANNEL
You can also create an InDesign clipping path from any alpha channels in an image, although you're usually better off simply using the alpha transparency rather than creating a clipping path from it. Nonetheless, the option appears on the Type drop-down menu and the process is the same as for the Detect Edges option.

Creating an InDesign clipping path using Detect Edges

1 You can create a clipping path in InDesign for a placed image that has no embedded path. This is a good quick fix for visuals, but no substitute for an accurate Photoshop clipping path. It relies on good color differentiation between the subject and background, and works best on images with plain light- or dark-colored backgrounds. It won't work on this photo because it can't distinguish the detailed background from the rest of the image.

7 Invert the path to switch the visible and hidden areas.

8 To cut "holes" in the image, e.g. the gap between the man's legs in this image, check the Include Inside Edges box.

2 Select the image and press Ctrl/Cmd+Alt/Option+Shift+K to open the Clipping Path dialog box. Select Detect Edges from the Type drop-down menu and, with the Preview box checked, adjust the Threshold and Tolerance sliders to achieve the best result. Set the object or document display performance settings to High Quality (see pages 58–59) so you can see precisely where the clipping path is.

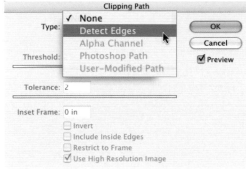

3 Increase the Threshold slider to make more of the Image pixels transparent. At some point, pixels you want to keep will start to disappear. When this happens, reduce the Threshold setting slightly until they reappear

4 If the image background isn't a flat color, but contains detail similar to the cut-out subject, you'll need to set a higher Tolerance value. This will create a smoother path that follows the subject edges less tightly.

5 Inset Frame contracts the path by the specified amount. You'll probably need to use this to remove any background halo, but keep the amounts small.

6 The Inset Frame units are the same as the document units set in the Units and Increments preferences. For a 300ppi image, a value of 1/300th of an inch (you can enter this as 1/300 in) will inset the frame by one pixel.

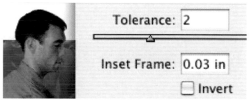

9 Ordinarily, Detect Edges creates a clipping path for the entire image, regardless of any cropping. Selecting Restrict to Frame creates the clipping path only for visible parts of the image and not for cropped areas. This will speed things up, as InDesign doesn't have to create the path for parts of the image you can't see. If you later change the crop to reveal more of the image, however, you'll have to recreate the clipping path.

☑ Use High Resolution Image

10 Always check the Use High Resolution Image box. This ensures the clipping path is calculated using the actual image pixel data, rather than the low resolution proxy, and produces much better results.

61

Text Wrap and clipping paths

Images with clipping paths are almost invariably used in combination with InDesign's Text Wrap feature, which flows a column of type around the shaped edge of any object. InDesign's automatically generated clipping paths may need a bit of cleaning up with the Direct Selection and Pen tools to produce effective text wraps. You can also convert clipping paths to frames, a technique with both creative and practical applications.

Tip

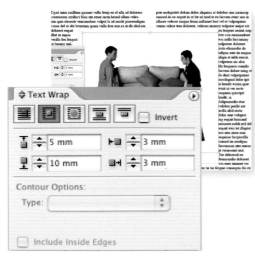

EDITING CLIPPING PATHS
Select an image with the Direct Selection tool to view and edit the clipping path. You can pan the image around within the frame in the same way as for a non-clipped image—the clipping path moves with the image.

Add and delete points from the clipping path using the Pen tool to create a clean path around the object.

Setting independent text offsets

When Wrap Around Bounding Box is selected, you can set the text offset independently for all four sides in the Text Wrap palette.

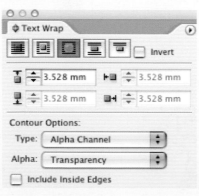

Manually editing the text wrap contour

It's often the case that you don't want a text wrap to rigidly follow the outline of a clipping path. Images with complex edge detail or unusual shapes can make text difficult to read. In these circumstances you'll need to manually edit the boundary.

Manual editing is often also the quickest way to sort out problematic line breaks caused by text wrap—moving a node in or out by a small amount is usually enough to take a word back or over. Use the Direct Selection tool to select and move control points on the boundary and the pen tool to add and delete them.

Once a boundary has been edited you can no longer set the offset in the Text Wrap palette.

Tip

TRANSPARENT IMAGES
You don't need a clipping path in order to create a text wrap. For images with a transparent background (or any alpha channel), click the Wrap around object shape button and select Alpha Channel from the Type drop-down menu in the Text Wrap palette.

Tip

TEXT WRAP RECAP
The Text Wrap palette is covered in more detail on pages 46–47. Here's a quick recap of the five Wrap options:

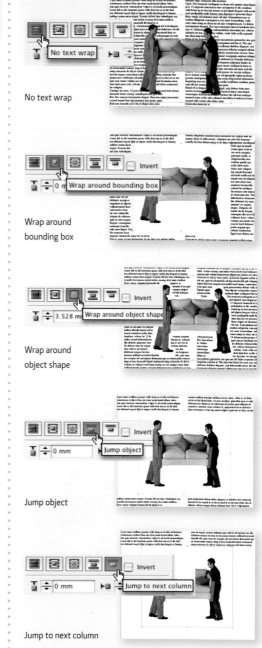

No text wrap

Wrap around bounding box

Wrap around object shape

Jump object

Jump to next column

Using multiple alpha channels

If the image has a transparent background, Transparency is automatically selected in the Alpha drop-down menu. For images with multiple alpha channels, use this menu to select the one you want to use for the text wrap boundary.

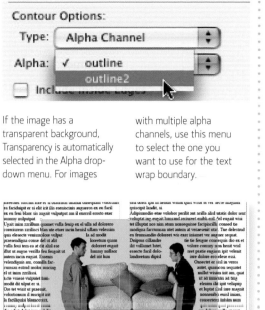

Alpha channel text wraps (and non-clipping path Photoshop path text wraps) can be used to flow text around objects within an image

Choosing contour options

1 For images with clipping paths, you'll usually want to select the Wrap Around Object Shape button. The Contour Options drop-down menu provides a number of choices for determining the text wrap path, but the default "Same as Clipping" is usually the one used. You can use Detect Edges for an image without a clipping path, or Photoshop Path if you've included an additional path in the image specifically for text wrap purposes.

2 With the clipping path selected as the text flow boundary, three of the offset boxes are grayed out. The Top offset box is used to set the text offset all the way around the image

3 If you select the image with the Direct Selection tool, you'll see both the clipping path and the offset contour. The contour appears in the layer color and the clipping path is in the complementary color.

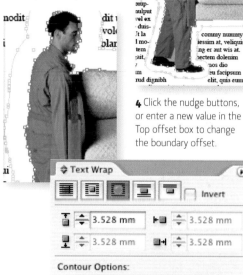

4 Click the nudge buttons, or enter a new value in the Top offset box to change the boundary offset.

Converting clipping paths to frames

1 To convert a clipping path to a frame, first select it with either the Selection or Direct Selection tools, then Right/Ctrl click and select Convert Clipping Path to Frame from the context menu.

2 Converting clipping paths to frames is one way to produce interesting masks for images. Select the converted frame, place a new image, and check the Replace Selected Item box in the Place dialog box.

3 Another common technique is to use a converted clipping path to produce a spot varnish plate for images. Duplicate the clipped image to a new layer, convert its clipping path to a frame, then select the image with the Direct Selection tool and delete it.

4 Apply a solid fill of your varnish spot color to the frame and check the overprint fill box in the Attributes palette. To see the image under the spot varnish frame, you'll either need to temporarily hide the spot varnish layer, or

select Separations View in the Separations palette (or choose Overprint Preview from the View menu, which is the same thing).

63

Transparency cut-outs

Few people are continuing to use clipping paths to produce cut-outs in InDesign. Alpha channel transparency is a much easier, and more versatile, method of displaying cut-out images with no background. Alpha channels make it possible to produce soft-edged and semi-transparent cut-outs—an impossibility with hard-edged PostScript clipping paths.

Automatic transparency

When you place an image with a transparent background on an InDesign page, you can see through the background areas of the frame to objects behind and on lower layers. Transparency is automatically enabled, you don't have to do anything else.

File formats that support transparency

If you're producing files with transparent backgrounds or alpha channel masks for use in InDesign, save them either in PSD or TIFF format, both of which will include the alpha channels—providing you check the Alpha Channels box. You don't need to check the Alpha Channels box to include background layer transparency, it only applies to alpha channels that appear in the channels palette. If there are none, the Alpha Channels box is grayed out.

Colored fills

The background will only be transparent if the frame fill color is set to the default of [None]. If an image that should be transparent isn't, check to make sure that you haven't inadvertently set the frame fill to [Paper], White, or a 0 percent tint of another color.

Used deliberately, this is a useful method of applying a background color to an image.

Flattening files

1 Layered Photoshop and TIFF files can grow very large—file sizes of several hundreds of megabytes are not unusual. Unless you plan on using the Photoshop layer visibility controls (see page 58 for more about this) it's better to reduce the file sizes by merging the layers in the files.

2 The easiest way to do this is to turn off all unrequired Photoshop layers. Select all of the layers in the Layers palette, and choose Merge Layers from the Layers palette fly-out menu.

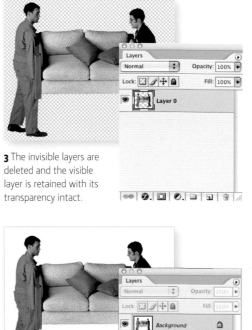

3 The invisible layers are deleted and the visible layer is retained with its transparency intact.

4 If you flatten the image instead of merging it, it will end up on a white background.

Saving TIFF transparency

An alternative to merging the image layers in Photoshop is to use the Save As command to save the image, and then uncheck the Layers box in the Save As dialog. If you do this, Photoshop flattens the image and you end up with a white background, just as if you had flattened it in the usual way. To avoid this, check Save Transparency in the TIFF Options dialog box.

Dragging and dropping

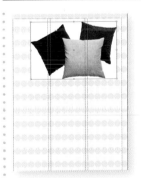

You can't drag and drop transparent images from Photoshop into InDesign, but images dragged and dropped from the Finder or Windows Explorer maintain their transparency, as do pictures dragged and dropped from Bridge. This is the quickest way to import multiple transparent images into an InDesign document.

Making an alpha channel mask

1 One of the biggest advantages of alpha channel transparency over clipping paths is that you can produce soft-edged cut-outs and even translucent effects in InDesign. This pyrotechnic image would be impossible to cut out using a conventional PostScript clipping path.

2 Making an alpha channel mask in Photoshop is literally just a few seconds' work. For this image, the Red channel, which provided the best separation between the flames and the background, was copied to a new alpha channel called "fire mask." The image was saved as a Photoshop file.

3 When the image was placed in InDesign, the fire mask alpha channel was selected in the Image tab of the Image Import Options dialog box. The image was then placed in a layer on top of the layer containing the text box, which has a black fill.

Using layer mask transparency

1 This light bulb image has been cut out using Corel KnockOut, an application for producing cut-out images from photos of "difficult" subjects like hair, glass, water, and smoke. It could equally have been produced in Photoshop (though probably not as easily). It's now been saved as a Photoshop PSD file consisting of a single layer with a layer mask. The mask removes the opaque background while retaining the shadow detail and shading on the glass light bulb.

2 The file can be imported into InDesign and then placed over any background detail—in this case on top of another image—with no further work required.

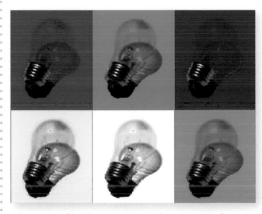

3 Transparent files like this lend themselves to quick manipulation for graphic effects.

65

Transparency cut-outs, continued

Because Photoshop files can contain multiple alpha channels, you can import the same image with several different cut-outs—showing different parts of the image, or producing differently shaped vignettes, for example. InDesign supports partial transparency in Photoshop layers, and you can apply InDesign transparency effects such as drop shadows, feathering, and even blend modes to images.

Applying drop shadows to transparent images

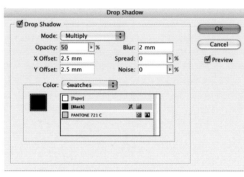

1 Drop shadows applied to images with transparent backgrounds in Photoshop work fine. The only

limitation is that blend modes applied in Photoshop don't work in InDesign, but this isn't really an issue.

3 One advantage of InDesign's drop shadows over Photoshop's is that if you crop a Photoshop

drop shadow—as we have done to the bottom edge of this image—the shadow is cropped as well.

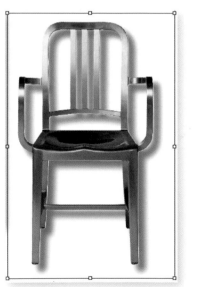

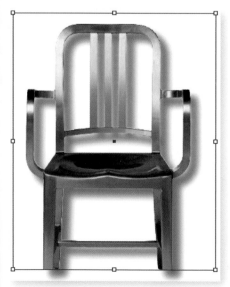

2 In any case, it's far easier to apply drop shadows to images with transparent backgrounds in InDesign. The drop shadow follows the contour of the cut-out image just as it would had

you applied it in Photoshop. InDesign CS2's drop shadow feature now has a noise slider, so you can also introduce texture into drop shadows.

4 However, if you crop an image with an InDesign drop shadow, it's handled more intelligently. InDesign extends the drop shadow beyond the frame.

Images with multiple alpha channels

1 If an image has more than one alpha channel, show the Import Options dialog box when placing it to select the channel that you want to

use. Click the image button and select a channel from the Alpha Channel drop-down menu.

2 The Image options dialog box shows a preview of the alpha channel. If the image in the preview thumbnail doesn't coincide with the selected alpha channel mask, it's probably because

the image has a clipping path in addition to the alpha channels. Uncheck the Apply Photoshop Clipping path button and everything should work as expected.

3 Once the document is placed, you can't change the alpha channel selection. The only way to do this is to select the original image and place it again with the

Replace Selected Item box checked. Choose a different alpha channel and click OK to replace the original image with the new alpha channel transparency.

Feathering transparent images

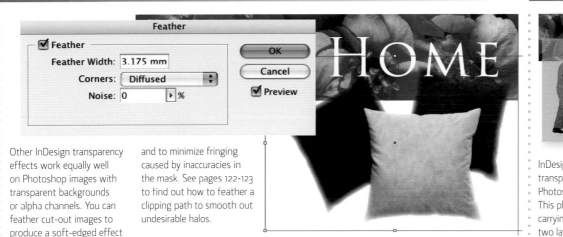

Other InDesign transparency effects work equally well on Photoshop images with transparent backgrounds or alpha channels. You can feather cut-out images to produce a soft-edged effect and to minimize fringing caused by inaccuracies in the mask. See pages 122-123 to find out how to feather a clipping path to smooth out undesirable halos.

Partial transparency

InDesign's support for transparency extends to Photoshop layer opacity. This photo of the two men carrying the couch has two layers. The topmost layer contains the men and couch with a transparent background, and underneath is a pattern fill layer where the fill has been reduced to 75 percent opacity.

PDF layer visibility

In addition to enabling you to control the visibility of layers and layer comps in Photoshop PSD files, InDesign provides similar features for layered PDF files. See page 58 to find out how this works for layered Photoshop files.

✓ **Adobe Illustrator Document**

Illustrator EPS (eps)
Illustrator Template (ait)
Adobe PDF (pdf)
SVG Compressed (svgz)
SVG (svg)

Acrobat 4 (PDF 1.3)
Acrobat 5 (PDF 1.4)
✓ Acrobat 6 (PDF 1.5)
Acrobat 7 (PDF 1.6)

1 Primarily, this feature is used to import and manipulate graphics files from Adobe Illustrator. When saving files from Illustrator, choose Adobe PDF from the format menu and select Acrobat 6 (1.5) or later.

Options
☑ Preserve Illustrator Editing Capabilities
☑ Embed Page Thumbnails
☐ Optimize for Fast Web View
☐ View PDF after Saving
☑ Create Acrobat Layers from Top-Level Layers
☐ Create Multi-page PDF from Page Tiles

2 Check Create Acrobat Layers from Top-Level Layers and save the PDF.

3 When you place the illustration in InDesign, check the Show Import options box, click the Layers button, and select the layers you want to be visible from the list in the Show Layers pane. Alternatively, you can alter layer visibility using the Object Layer Options dialog box.

Being able to selectively turn layers on and off in this way means that you can use one file for a variety of purposes, rather than having to make the layer visibility changes in Illustrator and then saving a different file every time.

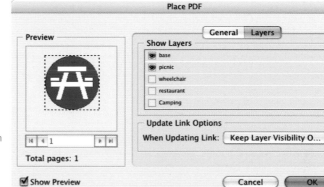

4 For example, a leaflet that uses icons to provide details of facilities at tourist locations would require a different graphic for each symbol. Normally, you'd create the base artwork on one layer and place each symbol on a different layer. Then you'd need to save a multitude of EPS files, each with a different symbol layer made visible and all the others turned off. Now, you need only save one file, which can be placed throughout your template and configured whenever the information becomes available.

5 One thing you need to take care of with layer visibility is the Update Link Options. You'll nearly always want to set this to "Keep Layer Visibility Overrides," then if you update the graphic, for example to add a new symbol layer, the individual layer visibility settings for each instance of the graphic will be maintained. If the link options are set to "Use Photoshop's Layer Visibility," then every instance of the placed graphic will revert to the layer visibility of the updated Photoshop file, which is probably not what you want.

Exporting artwork

You can export an InDesign page, spread, or document in a variety of formats including PDF, EPS, JPEG, SVG, XML, and the InDesign interchange format INX. Inevitably, you'll use some of these options more than others, and, unless you operate an XML-based workflow, PDF, which is used for everything from soft-proofing to handing off pre-press files, is the one you'll need the most.

Here, we'll look at methods for exporting pages to be used as images in their own right. If you want to know about exporting PDFs for pre-press output, see pages 174–175.

Compression options

A Click compression in the menu on the left to view and edit the compression settings for images in the InDesign document. Color images are downsampled to 100ppi and jpeg compressed with low quality.

B There are separate setting for grayscale and monochrome bitmaps, but, as most documents contain few of these, they are less of an issue where file size is concerned.

C Increasing the resolution will do nothing to improve the quality of images on-screen (other than at views greater than 100 percent) and will inflate the file size. If you want to improve the display quality of images, select Medium from the Image Quality drop-down menu in the Color images panel.

D The consequences of this for the size of your PDF file will depend on the number of images. On the Low setting, this 12-page brochure produces a PDF 336Kb in size. A PDF of the same document produced on the Medium setting is 424Kb. A file size overhead almost certainly worth paying for the improved quality.

Exporting a PDF for the Web

Download report by section (PDF format)

	PDF	Text	Size
Chairman's foreword			335KB
Governors' details			145KB

It's increasingly the case that organizations want to put a PDF copy of printed publications—annual reports, brochures, catalogues, etc.—on the web. We're not talking about an interactive document with links, forms, buttons, and other interactive elements here, just something that can be viewed online. Here's how to do it.

1 The first step in exporting any kind of file is the Export dialog box. Select **File > Export**, or press Ctrl/Cmd+E to launch it.

2 The format drop-down menu at the bottom of the dialog box lists the file export types. Select Adobe PDF, and click Save to open the Export Adobe PDF dialog box.

✓ **Adobe PDF**
EPS
InDesign Interchange
JPEG
SVG
SVG Compressed
XML

[High Quality Print]
[PDF/X–1a:2001]
[PDF/X–3:2002]
[Press Quality]
✓ **[Smallest File Size]**

3 Five presets are available. Even though you may not want to use these in their existing configurations, they make a good starting point.

✓ Acrobat 4 (PDF 1.3)
Acrobat 5 (PDF 1.4)
Acrobat 6 (PDF 1.5)

4 Select the [Smallest File Size] preset from the menu at the top of the Export Adobe PDF dialog box. Though there are probably few people still using Acrobat 4 Reader, setting Acrobat 4 (PDF 1.3) in the compatibility menu will widen the potential audience without any discernible difference in quality. PDF 1.3 doesn't support live transparency, but this just means that InDesign does the flattening. You only need to export a PDF with live transparency if you want transparency flattening to be handled by your output bureau. Neither PDF 1.3 nor PDF 1.4 supports layers, but that's not an issue here.

Pages
◉ All
○ Range: 10–11
☑ Spreads

5 Check the All radio button or a page range, and check the Spreads button to display spreads as a single page in the PDF.

Options
☑ Embed Page Thumbnails
☑ Optimise for Fast Web View
☐ Create Tagged PDF

6 Selecting Embed Page Thumbnails is useful for long document navigation, but will add significantly to the file size. Optimize for Fast Web View enables background downloading—the first page, or selected page of the document is displayed as quickly as possible, while the remainder of the PDF downloads in the background.

Saving settings

Save Preset

Save Preset As: Web pdf   OK   Cancel

The PDF export settings are retained and used the next time you open the dialog box. To permanently retain them, click the Save Preset button to add them to the Adobe PDF Preset drop-down menu.

Security settings

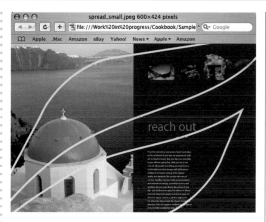

The Security tab of the Export PDF dialog box is used to password protect against unauthorized opening, printing, and copying of the PDF and its contents. If you're putting a PDF on the web, it's unlikely that you'll want to prevent people from opening it, but you might want to prevent them printing it, copying the text and images, or otherwise editing it. To do this, check the "Use a password to restrict printing, editing, and other tasks" box, enter a password in the Permissions Password field, select None from both the Printing Allowed and Changes Allowed drop-down menus and uncheck the "Enable copying of text, images and other content" box.

Advanced settings

The Advanced tab determines image processing and transparency flattener settings. you can leave the Send Data setting on All (unless for some reason you want to use the low-resolution proxy images rather than the high-res linked files), and ignore the OPI panel, unless the page contains OPI image links. For information on transparency flattening see pages 172–173, and to find out how to use the Ink Manager, see pages 106–107.

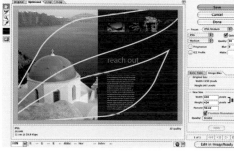

JPEG export

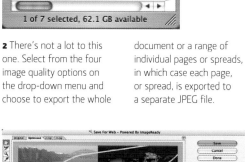

Although Acrobat reader is widespread, it's not universal, and if you want to show someone who doesn't have it a spread, or a cover, then a JPEG is a good option as it can be opened in a web browser. This is also a useful way of creating thumbnails for a web portfolio, or to provide a preview of and link to a PDF.

1 Select JPEG from the Format drop-down menu in the Export dialog box. and click Save to open the Export JPEG dialog box.

2 There's not a lot to this one. Select from the four image quality options on the drop-down menu and choose to export the whole document or a range of individual pages or spreads, in which case each page, or spread, is exported to a separate JPEG file.

3 The JPEG is exported at 72ppi resolution and the original document dimensions, Clearly, an A3 spread exported this way isn't going to be much use for the web, and you'll need to downsample it first in Photoshop.

EPS export

To export an InDesign page as an EPS (Encapsulated PostScript) file, select EPS from the Export dialog box Format drop-down menu. EPS is a single-page format, so if you print a range of pages you'll produce a separate file for each one

Select Level 3 from the PostScript drop-down menu if you know the file will be printed to a Level 3 PostScript printer. If you're not sure, Level 2 provides wider compatibility. If you don't want RGB colors converted to CMYK, change the color drop-down menu setting to Leave Unchanged The CMYK conversion is determined by the Color Setting dialog box (see pages 110–111).

69

Inline and anchored frames

Previous versions of InDesign allowed the insertion of text frames, graphics frames, and grouped objects in a block of text. When the text moved, the inline frames moved with it, and this feature was used for graphic elements like pull-quotes, sidebars, and crossheads.

InDesign CS2 still has inline frames, but now they are a subset of a more flexible feature called anchored objects. In addition to inline anchored objects there are two new types—Above Line and Custom. Custom anchored objects maintain a looser relationship to the text in which they are anchored and can also be configured to maintain a link to page margins so that, for example, a pull-quote in an outside column stays in the outside column even if it moves from a left to a right hand page.

Using inline anchored objects

1 To place an inline frame, first cut or copy it. Next, click with the Type tool where you'd like the object to go, and then paste it. You can insert a graphic frame, text frame, or group in this manner.

2 You can now select the inline frame with either of the selection tools, or the Type tool, as if it were a character in the text and move it up and down. The bottom of the frame sits on the text baseline. If the frame is taller than the leading, the lines above are shifted upwards in auto-leaded text. If leading is fixed, the inline frame will overlap the preceding lines of text. If the inline frame is on the first line of a text frame, its initial vertical position is determined by the baseline options in the Text Frame options dialog box. The top of the inline frame can't extend beyond the baseline, nor the bottom beyond the leading height.

3 You can control the vertical position of an inline frame beyond the baseline and leading height by using baseline shift.

Creating inline graphics crossheads

Crosshead

1 First create your crosshead. This one consists of a single line text frame and an Illustrator graphic. The text frame is the same width as the page columns. Select both objects and press Ctrl/Cmd+G to group them, then Ctrl/Cmd+C to copy the group to the clipboard.

entering on these personal details, as I give them to show that I have not been hasty in coming to a decision.

Crosshead

My work is now nearly finished; but as it will take me two or three more years to complete

2 Using the Type tool, place an insertion point at the end of the paragraph preceding the crosshead and press Return, then paste the inline group. Because this text is set with 12pt leading, the graphic overlaps the preceding lines.

3 Select the crosshead with the Direct Selection tool, and choose **Object > Anchored Object > Options**. Check the Above Line radio button and enter Space Before and after values as necessary.

4 If you use the Type tool to select and copy the crosshead, you can paste it elsewhere in the copy with the Space Before formatting intact.

same object. I hope that I may be excused for entering on these personal details, as I give them to show that I have not been hasty in coming to a decision.

Crosshead

My work is now nearly finished; but as it will take me two or three more years to complete

5 If you want to align the crosshead type to the baseline grid, select the Align to Baseline Grid option from the Control palette with the insertion point in the crosshead text. If you do it with the insertion point on the inline group within the body text, it will align the base of the grouped item. The simplest option is to create the entire crosshead on the page and set all character and paragraph style options prior to grouping and inserting the object into the text.

Creating an inline drop cap

1 To create an inline drop cap, paste the frame in the text, replacing the first character in the paragraph.

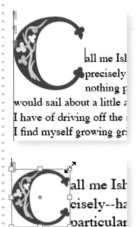

2 Click the paragraph button on the Control palette, and use the nudge buttons or enter the required number in the Drop Cap Number of Lines box.

3 If you need to resize the drop cap frame, do so by using the Selection tool and holding down Ctrl/Cmd+Shift to proportionally resize the frame and its contents.

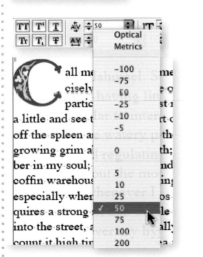

4 Control the gap between the drop cap and adjacent characters using kerning. Position the insertion point on the top line immediately after the drop cap (it you have difficulty doing this, place it farther along the line and use the left arrow key to move it back). Select an initial value from the kerning pull-down menu on the control palette then use the nudge buttons to adjust it.

Creating anchored pull-quotes

Custom Anchored objects are better suited to page elements such as pull-quotes—though associated with a particular text passage, pull-quotes are outside of the text and also have a positional relationship with the page itself. Here's how to set up an pull-quote that stays opposite a paragraph of text, but also stays in the outside margin, even if the text moves from a right- to a left-hand page.

1 Create your pull-quote in the usual way—by copying it from the body copy, pasting to a new text frame, and applying a paragraph or object style. Select it with the Selection tool, cut it, place an insertion point in the text with the Type tool, and then paste it inline.

2 Select the inline object with the Selection tool, and choose **Object > Anchored Object > Options**. Select Custom from the Position drop-down menu, and check the Relative to Spine box to position the pull-quote horizontally with reference to the spine.

3 Click to activate the outside top square on the Anchored Object Reference Point proxy. This means pull-quote will be positioned with reference to its outside top corner.

4 Next, click to activate the outside middle square on the Anchored Position Reference Point proxy. This means the pull-quote will be positioned relative to the outside edge of the page.

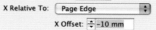

5 Select Page Edge from the X Relative To pull down menu. This tells InDesign to position the outside top corner of the pull-quote on the page edge. Enter -10 in the X Offset field to move it in 10mm.

6 Select Line (Baseline) from the Y Relative To drop-down menu. This tells InDesign to position the outside top corner of the pull-quote on the baseline of the text where you originally pasted it.

7 Enter 35mm in the Y Offset field—you don't want the pull-quote directly opposite its matching text in the body copy. Check the Keep within Top/Bottom Column Boundaries box to prevent the pull-quote from breaking the bottom page margin, and click OK.

8 Now if the text is edited, the pull-quote will move up and down the page, maintaining its 35mm offset from the baseline of the original text.

9 If the page layout is changed and the right-hand page becomes a left, the pull-quote maintains its position in the outside margin 10mm in from the page edge.

71

DRAWING

Shapes

nDesign provides tools for creating three types of basic shapes: rectangles, ellipses, and symmetrical polygons. For your convenience, the Tools palette contains two sets of these three tools. One set creates the shapes as picture frames, the other set creates them as plain shapes.

Tip

THE SHAPE TOOLS

The shape tools can be found in the Toolbar in fly-out menus from the Rectangle and Rectangle Frame tool buttons. Click and hold one of the buttons to reveal the menu.

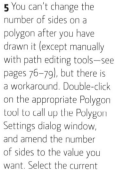

- ☒ Rectangle Frame Tool   F
- ⊗ Ellipse Frame Tool
- ⊗ Polygon Frame Tool

- ☐ Rectangle Tool   M
- ◯ Ellipse Tool   L
- ⬡ Polygon Tool

74

Creating and converting shapes

1 To draw a shape, select a shape tool and click-and-drag across your page. Alternatively, select the tool and click once on the page to call up a dialog window prompting you to enter a Width and Height for the shape at that location.

2 When using the Polygon or Polygon Frame tools, this dialog window also prompts you to enter the number of sides that the polygon should have.

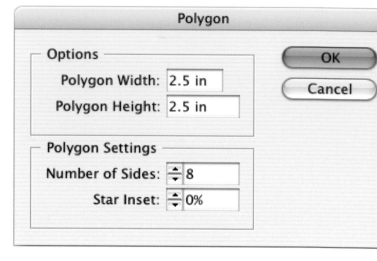

3 To change the default settings for the Polygon tools, double-click on the tool itself in the Tools palette and enter your preferred Number of Sides. InDesign also applies this setting when you use the **Object > Convert Shape > Polygon** command.

4 The **Object > Convert Shape** menu lets you quickly convert your rectangles, ellipses, and polygons into each other, or into triangles, lines, or rectangles with special corner effects. The Rounded Rectangle, Beveled Rectangle, and Inverse Rounded Rectangle commands pick up their default settings from the Corner Effects dialog window. For these settings, or if you are a QuarkXPress user looking for a rounded box tool, turn to page 80.

5 You can't change the number of sides on a polygon after you have drawn it (except manually with path editing tools—see pages 76–79), but there is a workaround. Double-click on the appropriate Polygon tool to call up the Polygon Settings dialog window, and amend the number of sides to the value you want. Select the current polygon shape on your page and choose the **Object > Convert Shape > Rectangle** command to turn it into a rectangle. Then choose **Object > Convert Shape > Polygon** to convert it back to a polygon. This updates the shape with the new polygon settings while maintaining its current size, position, stroke, and fill.

Creating simple starbursts

Polygon Settings

Options
Number of Sides: 12
Star Inset: 30%

[OK] [Cancel]

1 Double-click on the Polygon tool or the Polygon Frame tool to call up the Polygon Settings dialog window. Enter the number of points you want for your star in the Number of Sides field, increase the Star Inset value above 0%, and click OK. Here's how a 12-point starburst will look with a Star Inset value of 30%.

Polygon Settings

Options
Number of Sides: 12
Star Inset: 60%

[OK] [Cancel]

2 Here's the same 12-point starburst with a Star Inset value of 60%.

Stroke

Weight: 6 pt   Cap:
Miter Limit: 7   x   Join:

3 If the tips of the star appear to be flat rather than pointed after having applied a stroke, open the Stroke palette and increase the Miter Limit value until the tips appear.

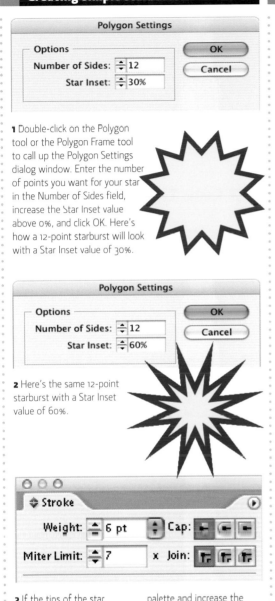

Tip

CREATING TWIRLS
Another pleasing starburst effect can be created by selecting all of the tips in a starburst using the Direct Selection tool, and then using the Rotate tool to twist them around.

Creating random starbursts

Polygon Settings

Options
Number of Sides: 20
Star Inset: 50%

[OK] [Cancel]

1 For a randomized starburst effect, create a new polygon with the Number of Sides set to 20 and a Star Inset of 50%. You will find it helpful to work on an uncolored shape to start with.

2 Using the Direct Selection tool, click on the tip of one of the star points. Hold down the Shift key and click on five more tips randomly around the star. Then switch to the Scale tool, move its anchor point to the center of the starburst, and click-and-drag outward to cause the selected tips to stretch.

3 Now select six other tips at random and use the Scale tool to shrink them, pushing the tool inward this time.

4 Here's the resulting starburst with a stroke, fill, drop shadow (see page 120) and type applied.

Using the PathEffects script

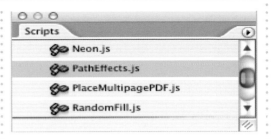

Scripts
Neon.js
PathEffects.js
PlaceMultipagePDF.js
RandomFill.js

1 It's possible to create more diverse polygon effects by using the PathEffects script that is supplied with InDesign. Select a polygon on your page, open the Scripts palette, and double-click on Path Effects.

PathEffects

Effect: Punk
 Bloat
 PunkBloat
 BloatPunk
 Twirl
 AntiTwirl
 RetractAll
 MakeRectangle
 MakeOval

[OK] [Cancel]

Options: Offset from Center Point: 50%
 Copy Path

Refer to the script text for a description of the path effects.

2 Select an effect from the PathEffects dialog window.

3 If you start with this polygon...   ... the Bloat effect creates this...

... and the Twirl effect creates this.

The Pen tool

nDesign's Pen tool works in a way similar to "Bézier"-style vector pen tools. Click once to set the starting point, then click elsewhere to set a second point, and a path will be drawn between them. Subsequent clicks add points to the path until you click back on the Pen tool in the Tools palette to stop.

Using the Pen tool

1 To create straight lines, just click with the Pen tool. Every time you click, a line will be drawn between that point and the previous one.

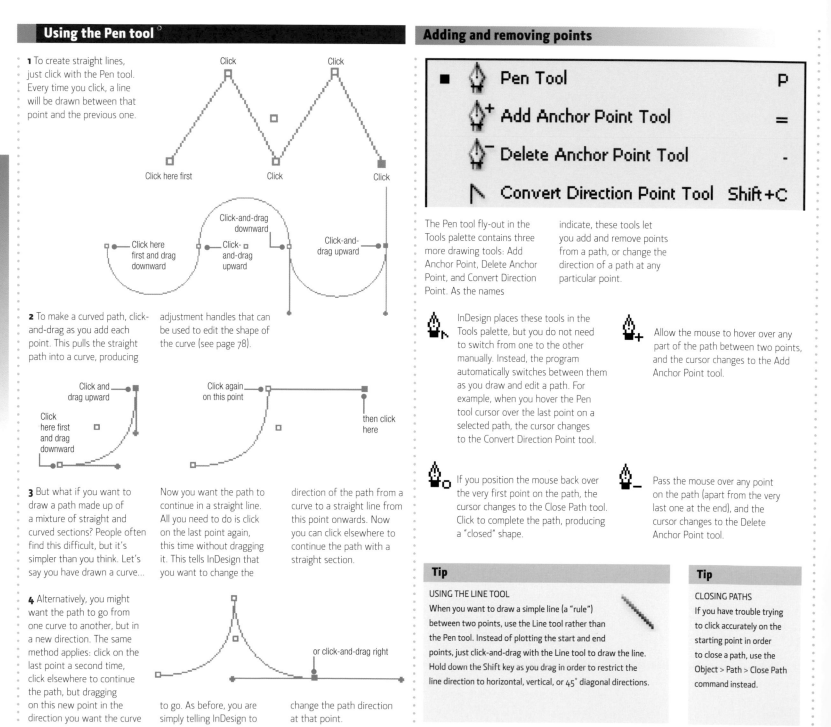

Click

Click here first

Click

Click

Click

Click-and-drag downward

Click here first and drag downward

Click-and-drag upward

Click-and-drag upward

Click-and-drag upward

2 To make a curved path, click-and-drag as you add each point. This pulls the straight path into a curve, producing

adjustment handles that can be used to edit the shape of the curve (see page 78).

Click and drag upward

Click here first and drag downward

Click again on this point

then click here

3 But what if you want to draw a path made up of a mixture of straight and curved sections? People often find this difficult, but it's simpler than you think. Let's say you have drawn a curve…

Now you want the path to continue in a straight line. All you need to do is click on the last point again, this time without dragging it. This tells InDesign that you want to change the

direction of the path from a curve to a straight line from this point onwards. Now you can click elsewhere to continue the path with a straight section.

4 Alternatively, you might want the path to go from one curve to another, but in a new direction. The same method applies: click on the last point a second time, click elsewhere to continue the path, but dragging on this new point in the direction you want the curve

to go. As before, you are simply telling InDesign to

or click-and-drag right

change the path direction at that point.

Adding and removing points

Pen Tool — P
Add Anchor Point Tool — =
Delete Anchor Point Tool — -
Convert Direction Point Tool — Shift+C

The Pen tool fly-out in the Tools palette contains three more drawing tools: Add Anchor Point, Delete Anchor Point, and Convert Direction Point. As the names

indicate, these tools let you add and remove points from a path, or change the direction of a path at any particular point.

InDesign places these tools in the Tools palette, but you do not need to switch from one to the other manually. Instead, the program automatically switches between them as you draw and edit a path. For example, when you hover the Pen tool cursor over the last point on a selected path, the cursor changes to the Convert Direction Point tool.

Allow the mouse to hover over any part of the path between two points, and the cursor changes to the Add Anchor Point tool.

If you position the mouse back over the very first point on the path, the cursor changes to the Close Path tool. Click to complete the path, producing a "closed" shape.

Pass the mouse over any point on the path (apart from the very last one at the end), and the cursor changes to the Delete Anchor Point tool.

Tip

USING THE LINE TOOL

When you want to draw a simple line (a "rule") between two points, use the Line tool rather than the Pen tool. Instead of plotting the start and end points, just click-and-drag with the Line tool to draw the line. Hold down the Shift key as you drag in order to restrict the line direction to horizontal, vertical, or 45° diagonal directions.

Tip

CLOSING PATHS

If you have trouble trying to click accurately on the starting point in order to close a path, use the Object > Path > Close Path command instead.

In addition to drawing irregular lines and geometrical shapes, the Pen tool can be very useful for tracing outlines on the fly. Let's take the example of a magazine feature that interviews a movie star.

1 Place the main photo of the interviewee on the first page, and use the Pen tool to trace a path around his silhouette. If you find the Pen tool a bit finicky, you can draw around him using the Pencil tool instead, although you may need to edit the path afterwards to clean it up (see page 78).

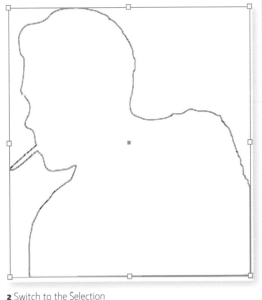

2 Switch to the Selection tool, and move the traced path away from the placed image. It helps to work with a closed path, but this is not essential.

3 You can now treat the path as a standard shape. Resize it by dragging on a corner point while holding down the Ctrl/Cmd+Shift keys, and customize the stroke and fill (see page 80). Here, we have placed the shape behind the interview text to liven up an otherwise dull follow-on page.

4 Alternatively, bring the shape in front of the text, open the Transparency palette and apply the Screen blending mode to produce this white-out text effect.

5 The shape can be scaled down and placed behind pull-quotes to break up plain text pages. This device also adds personality and relevance to the pull-quote.

6 Increase the size of the shape, switch to the Type tool, and double-click inside the shape. This converts the path shape into a text box. Choose **Object > Text Frame Options** (see Chapter 1) and change the number of columns to 2. You can now place the interview text into it, just like any other text box, but the type itself flows in the shape of the interviewee's silhouette.

Editing paths

After drawing a path, you can edit the points, curve direction handles, and the actual sections between them using the Direct Selection tool. Remember that the Pencil tool fly-out in the Tools palette includes a couple of extra path-editing tools.

Using the Direct Selection tool

There are several ways of editing paths with the Direct Selection tool.

 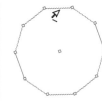 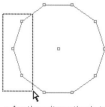

1 Draw a polygon (see page 74) and click on one of the corner points with the Direct Selection tool to select it, leaving all the other points unselected.

3 Alternatively, click on a path section between two points. Notice that the appearance of the cursor changes to indicate that you have selected a path section rather than a point.

5 Another alternative is to select several points on the path at once. You can do this by Shift+clicking on each point that you want to select, or by dragging a marquee area over them. You can then click-and-drag on any of the selected points, or path sections between them, to move them the whole group.

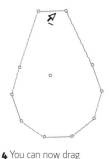

2 Now just click-and-drag on the point to move it.

4 You can now drag the path section to move it and the points connected to it.

Tip

THE SMOOTH AND ERASE TOOLS

Clicking and holding the mouse on the Pencil tool in the Tools palette reveals a fly-out menu containing two more useful path tools. Drag the Smooth tool along a jagged path to make it smoother. Drag the Erase tool along a path to erase the precise sections you are dragging over. You can adjust the sensitivity of the Pencil and Smooth tools in their Preference dialog windows, which are opened by double-clicking on the tools themselves in the Tools palette.

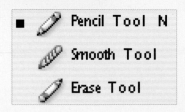

Using the Pencil tool

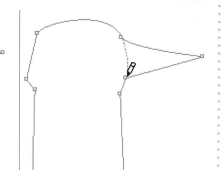

1 In addition to drawing freehand paths, the Pencil tool can redraw sections within existing paths. For example, this bottle-top shape has a big glitch in the path.

2 Select the path with the Direct Selection tool, switch to the Pencil tool, then drag it between any two existing points to indicate how you would like the correct path to appear.

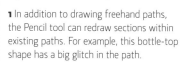

3 As soon as you let go of the mouse button, that section of the path is redrawn as you wanted it.

Using the Scissors tool

Clicking on a path with the Scissors tool splits it in two at the location where you clicked. This can be useful for splitting a complex shape into several parts, but it also has some interesting design potential. Place an image on a page (see Chapter 2), then click once on either side of the image's bounding box.

Switch to the Selection tool and drag the two sliced objects apart. Note that each sliced object contains a full copy of the image. Also, the bounding boxes are now open paths, so you may wish to close them using Object > Paths > Close Path.

1 The Convert Direction Point tool in the Pen tool fly-out in the Tools palette allows you to turn corner points on an existing path into curves, and vice versa. Here's a practical use for it when working with the Button tool (see page 160). First, draw a rectangle with the Button tool. You can customize the fill and stroke now or do it later (see page 80).

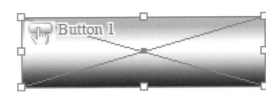

2 Switch to the Convert Direction Point tool, click on the bottom right-hand corner of the rectangle, and drag toward the right while holding down the Shift key to constrain the action horizontally. The corner point turns into a curve.

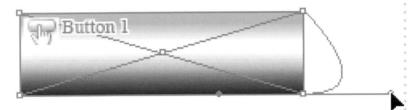

1 Use the Add Anchor Point tool in the Pen tool fly-out in the Tools palette to increase the number of points on a path. It can turn rectangles into custom polygons with just one click. For example, place an image on the page and click with the Add Anchor Point tool on its bounding box. The rectangle now has five points instead of four.

3 Click on the top-right corner of the rectangle and drag toward the left, again holding down the Shift key. The right-hand side of the rectangle is now fully rounded.

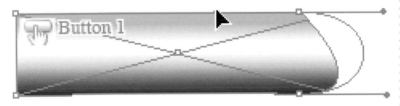

4 Repeat these steps on the left-hand side of the rectangle, reversing the drag directions accordingly, to make this side rounded too. To adjust their depth, switch to the Direct Selection tool and drag on the curve sections, while holding down the Shift key to keep the action horizontal.

2 Switch to the Direct Selection tool and drag on the points individually to customize its shape. This is a very easy way to avoid the rectangular monotony of placed images.

79

Tip

ILLUSTRATOR PATHS

If you have drawn a vector graphic in Illustrator CS2, drag and drop it from its Illustrator window into an InDesign window. You can then immediately edit the paths within InDesign, directly on the page.

5 Select both "corner" points, and drag on the curve sections to stretch out the shape as required. You can now further customize the button's appearance. The result is a classic interactive on-screen button.

Strokes and fills

All objects on an InDesign page are defined as paths, and every path can have a "stroke" and a "fill" attribute. This applies to text in addition to boxes, lines, and shapes. A fill is simply a color applied to the interior area of a path: see Chapter 4 to learn how to apply color fills. A stroke is a visual line effect that follows the path, whose attributes can include weight, color, line style, corner style, and end caps.

The parts of an object

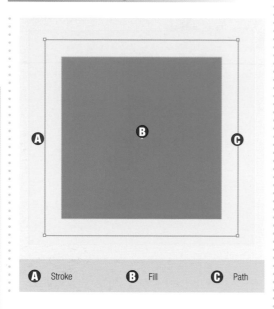

- Ⓐ Stroke
- Ⓑ Fill
- Ⓒ Path

Setting fill and stroke colors

The Tools palette, Swatches palette, and Color palette each provide a fill and stroke selector to help you choose whether your color changes will affect the fill or stroke of a currently selected object. Simply click on either the fill or the stroke symbol to activate it. This selector also appears in the Character Style Options, Paragraph Style Options, and Object Style Options dialog windows.

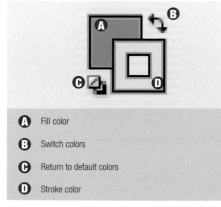

- Ⓐ Fill color
- Ⓑ Switch colors
- Ⓒ Return to default colors
- Ⓓ Stroke color

The Stroke palette

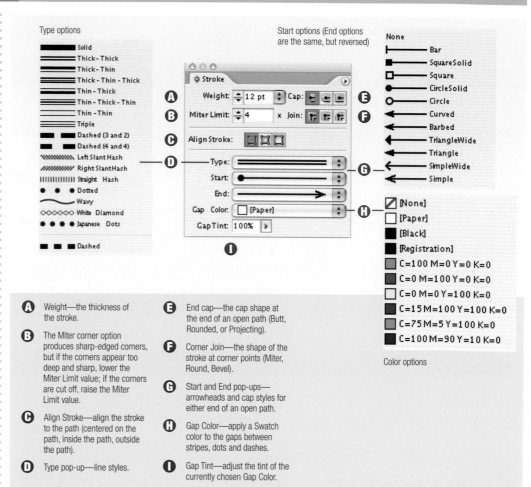

- Ⓐ Weight—the thickness of the stroke.
- Ⓑ The Miter corner option produces sharp-edged corners, but if the corners appear too deep and sharp, lower the Miter Limit value; if the corners are cut off, raise the Miter Limit value.
- Ⓒ Align Stroke—align the stroke to the path (centered on the path, inside the path, outside the path).
- Ⓓ Type pop-up—line styles.
- Ⓔ End cap—the cap shape at the end of an open path (Butt, Rounded, or Projecting).
- Ⓕ Corner Join—the shape of the stroke at corner points (Miter, Round, Bevel).
- Ⓖ Start and End pop-ups— arrowheads and cap styles for either end of an open path.
- Ⓗ Gap Color—apply a Swatch color to the gaps between stripes, dots and dashes.
- Ⓘ Gap Tint—adjust the tint of the currently chosen Gap Color.

Tip

REVERSING PATHS

InDesign paths have a direction—literally a beginning and an end—but often you won't know which is which. For example, you could apply one of the Stroke palette arrowheads to a path, only to find that InDesign has put the arrowhead on the wrong end.

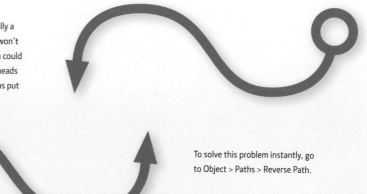

To solve this problem instantly, go to Object > Paths > Reverse Path.

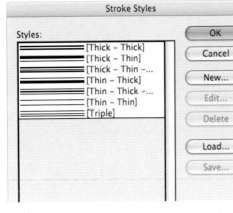

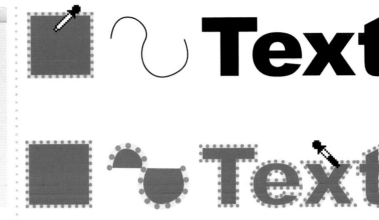

The Eyedropper tool is very handy for copying the fill and stroke attributes of one object and applying them to another.

1 Click with the Eyedropper tool on any object—it does not have to be selected first.

2 The cursor swaps direction and the eyedropper symbol appears full. Now click on any other object, or several objects in turn. The text here, by the way, has been converted to outlines (see page 92). To reset the Eyedropper tool to copy something else, click back on its icon in the Tools palette.

1 Choose Stroke Styles from the Stroke palette menu.

This opens the Stroke Styles dialog window. Click on New.

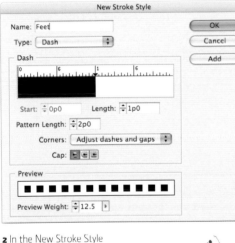

2 In the New Stroke Style window, you can create custom line styles of your own. Pick Stripe, Dotted, or Dash from the Type drop-down, then click-and-drag underneath the ruler pane to add, remove, and adjust line elements.

3 The line styles you can create are somewhat limited, but InDesign has a few secret styles you can access. Choose Dash from the Type pop-up and enter the word "Feet" in the Name field.

4 Click OK, then OK again to close the Stroke Styles window. You now have a stroke style composed of footprints, which you can apply from the Stroke palette like any other.

Object Styles are like Character Styles and Paragraph Styles, but they apply to object attributes. These attributes can include fills and strokes.

1 To see how they work, draw a rectangle and customize its fill and stroke with different colors, and so on. With the object still selected, open the Object Styles palette and Alt/Option+click on the Create New Style button to open the New Object Style dialog window.

2 Click on the Fill and Stroke sections in the list on the left of the window to see how the attributes have been picked up from the selected object. Give the style a name, and click OK. The new style now appears in the Object Styles palette.

3 Select another object in your layout and click on the new style name in the Object Styles palette to apply that style to it. Remember, you can edit that style by ensuring no objects are selected, then double-clicking on its name in the Object Styles palette; any changes you make will immediately update the appearance of all objects in your layout using that style. If you edit the fill and stroke of an object which has an Object Style applied to it, the style name in the palette will appear with a "+" symbol after it. To reapply the unedited Object Style attributes to that object, Alt/Option+click on the style name.

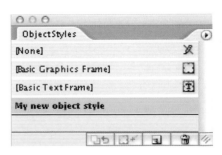

81

Corner effects

Corner effects can be applied to any path in InDesign to give some variety to layouts. This can be anything from rounding the corners of a simple line to creating rosettes from polygons.

Selecting a corner effect

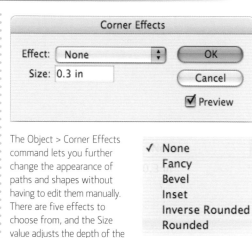

The Object > Corner Effects command lets you further change the appearance of paths and shapes without having to edit them manually. There are five effects to choose from, and the Size value adjusts the depth of the effect on each corner point.

- ✓ None
- Fancy
- Bevel
- Inset
- Inverse Rounded
- Rounded

Starting with a plain rectangle...

Inset

Fancy

Inverse Rounded

Bevel

Rounded

Applying Corner Effects to polygons

Use Corner Effects with a large Size value to transform polygons into highly stylized shapes. For all of the following before-and-after examples, use the Polygon tool to create the initial shape (see page 74).

1 The Inverse Rounded effect with a high Size value produces curved starbursts.

2 The Inset effect with a high Size value produces symmetrical star symbols.

3 Create a polygon with 10 sides and a Star Inset of 10% to produce this gentle starburst. By smoothing off the corners with the Rounded corner effect, you produce a rosette-like shape.

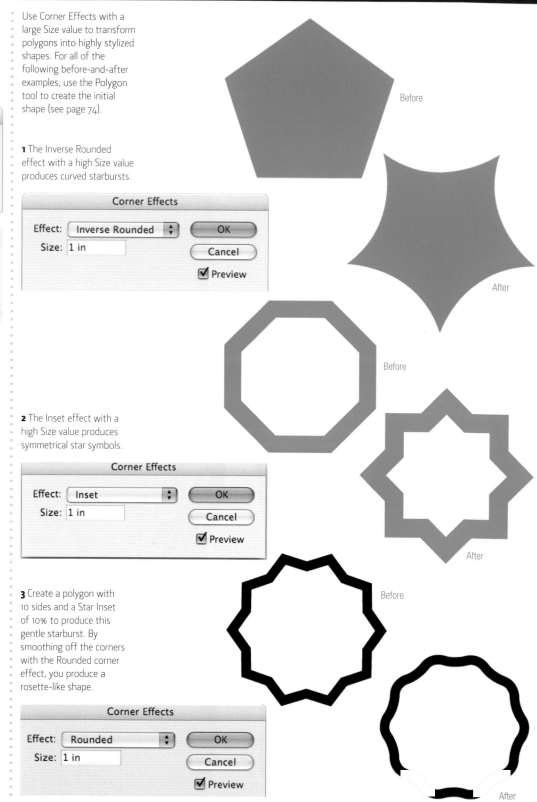

Before

After

Before

After

Before

After

4 As a practical example, here is the rosette shape, duplicated, rescaled, and aligned at the center (see page 84) with differing color fill tints (see page 96–99).

The glow around the text is produced with the Drop Shadow command (see page 120).

(see page 84)

Tip

SMOOTHING PATHS

Don't waste time trying to adjust Bézier handles on complex paths to create neatly curved corners—Corner Effects can do it for you. Plot the path with the Pen tool as a series of straight-line sections...

...then apply the Rounded Corner Effect.

Corner effects script

> Modo lestrud dolor em ametuer in henit erciliq uatuer ipit non ute feugai tam, quat, commodolese doloreet lummy nis adignisse min veliquat at acil incilit adion ullandrem iuscincipis do od eugait landre exer ad magnim quat aliquat, si tet, consed er iliquisit at. Guerostio do od exero dolore diamcoreros atio dolore ero od dit ulput vel etue doloreet, vel eugait nostio cor sequat, quip erat, si. Ud tat ad dolore volor at in ver suscipisl trud exer sequisit ate ming erit ulpute

1 The main limitations of Corner Effects are that you cannot manually adjust the corners, nor can you apply the effects to each corner individually. However, there is an InDesign script, also called CornerEffects, that can do this for you. It works with any path, shape, or text frame.

CornerEffects

Corner Type: ● Rounded
○ Inverse Rounded
○ Bevel
○ Inset
○ Fancy

OK
Cancel

Options: Offset: 48 pt
Pattern: first and last

✓ all points
first point
last point
second point
third point
fourth point
first two
second and third
last two
first and last
odd points
even points

---

2 Open the Scripts palette and double-click on CornerEffects. The dialog window that appears gives you the familiar range of effects, but a Pattern drop-down at the bottom allows you to choose which corners in the selected object will be affected, numbered counterclockwise from the top-left.

> Modo lestrud dolor em ametuer in henit erciliq uatuer ipit non ute feugait am, quat, commodolese doloreet lummy nis adignisse min veliquat at acil incilit adion ullandrem iuscincipis do od eugait landre exer ad magnim quat aliquat, si tet, consed er iliquisit at. Guerostio do od exero dolore diamcoreros atio dolore ero od dit ulput vel etue doloreet, vel eugait nostio cor sequat, quip erat, si. Ud tat ad dolore volor at in ver

3 Rather than applying a special effect, the resulting shape is fully editable with the Direct Selection and Pen tools.

Transform and Align

InDesign has a wealth of tools for transforming and aligning objects. The Rotate, Scale, and Shear tools can be used separately from the Tools palette, or try the Free Transform tool, which combines the effects of the individual tools.

Using the Transform tools

There are three task-specific transformation tools in the Tools palette: Rotate, Scale, and Shear. Although these functions are also available in the Transform palette, the advantage of working with the tools is that you can move the transformation anchor point manually. This anchor point is the center point around which the rotation, scaling, or shearing takes place. It is only visible when using these three tools, and its default starting position is set by the current "proxy" point in the Transform palette. Drag on the anchor point itself to change its position. Click-and-drag elsewhere with the tool to conduct the transformation, or double-click on the tool in the Tools palette in order to enter a precise value using a dialog window.

The Free Transform tool lets you rotate, scale, and shear without switching tools. To rotate, bring the cursor near a selected object's border and drag in the direction you want to turn it. To scale, click-and-drag on any handle around an object, or hold down the Shift key and drag on a corner handle to rescale the object proportionally. To shear, click on any side handle of an object, then hold down the Ctrl/Cmd key before dragging.

Tip

REAPPLYING TRANSFORMATIONS

When you edit an object with the transformation tools, or indeed the Selection and Direct Selection tools, InDesign memorizes your actions. You can then select another object and apply exactly the same transformation to it using Object > Transform Again > Transform Again. For example, if you moved an image across the page, you can select one or more other objects and use this command to move them exactly the same distance in exactly the same direction relative to their original position. If you want to apply the transformation to multiple selected objects individually rather than treating them as a unified group, use the Transform Again Individually command instead.

InDesign also memorizes transformation sequences, such as a scale, move, rotation, and shear, all on the same object. You can then replay the entire sequence on other selections using Object > Transform Again > Transform Sequence Again or Transform Sequence Again Individually.

TOOLS

Rotate tool

Scale tool

Shear tool

Free Transform tool

Anchor point

Direct Selection tool

Selection tool

The Transform palette

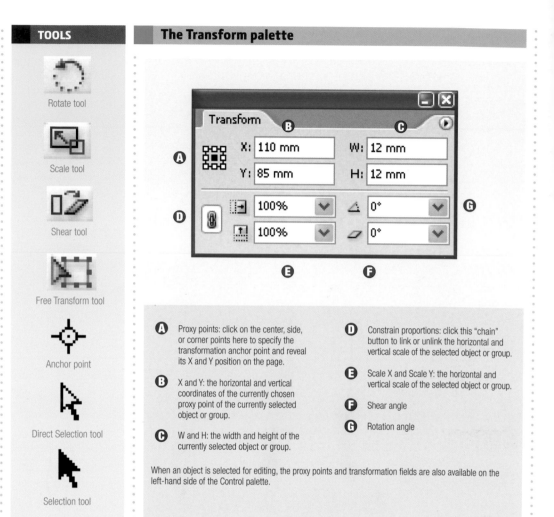

A Proxy points: click on the center, side, or corner points here to specify the transformation anchor point and reveal its X and Y position on the page.

B X and Y: the horizontal and vertical coordinates of the currently chosen proxy point of the currently selected object or group.

C W and H: the width and height of the currently selected object or group.

D Constrain proportions: click this "chain" button to link or unlink the horizontal and vertical scale of the selected object or group.

E Scale X and Scale Y: the horizontal and vertical scale of the selected object or group.

F Shear angle

G Rotation angle

When an object is selected for editing, the proxy points and transformation fields are also available on the left-hand side of the Control palette.

Tip

TRANSFORMING STROKES

When using the transformation tools, you can choose whether or not an object's stroke and its content (text or image) should be scaled accordingly or left alone. These options are enabled or disabled with a check in the Transform palette fly-out menu.

Confusingly, InDesign treats scaling as an independent attribute from an object's core properties. So if you scale up a box by 300% with Scale Strokes checked, the stroke will appear thicker but the Strokes palette still shows the original stroke weight. To update the Strokes palette with the actual weight, choose Reset Scaling to 100% under the same fly-out menu.

Scale Text Attributes
Transform Group Content
Reset Scaling to 100%

Rotate 180°
Rotate 90° CW
Rotate 90° CCW

Flip Horizontal
Flip Vertical
Flip Both

✔ Transform Content
Dimensions Include Stroke Weight
✔ Transformations are Totals
✔ Show Content Offset
✔ Scale Strokes

The Align palette

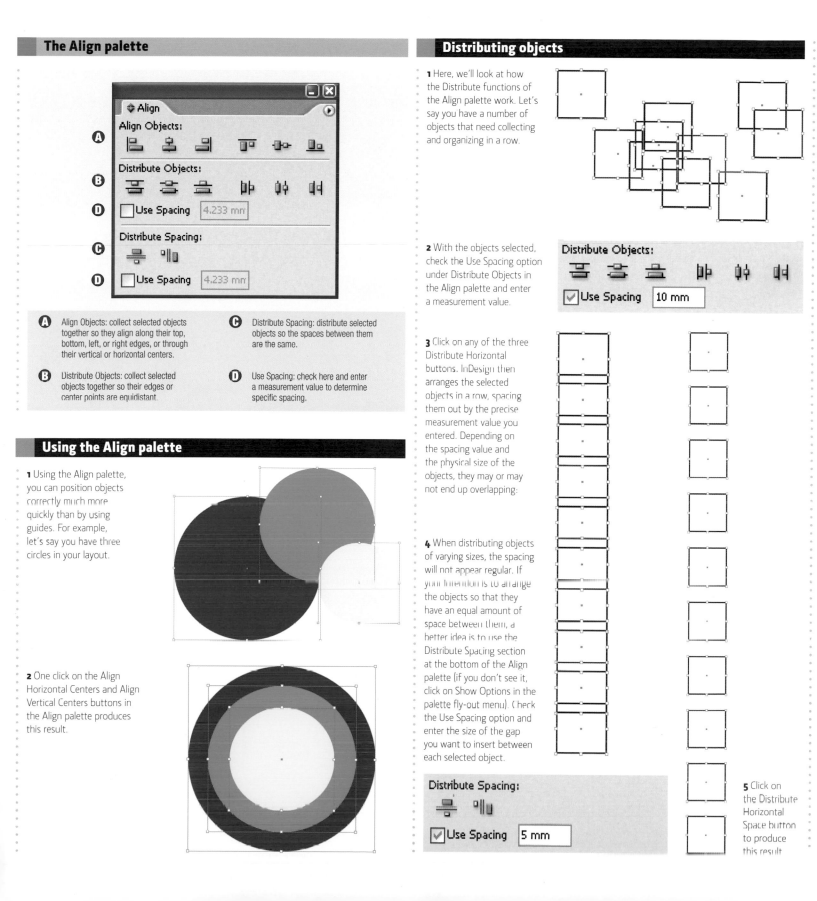

A Align Objects: collect selected objects together so they align along their top, bottom, left, or right edges, or through their vertical or horizontal centers.

B Distribute Objects: collect selected objects together so their edges or center points are equidistant.

C Distribute Spacing: distribute selected objects so the spaces between them are the same.

D Use Spacing: check here and enter a measurement value to determine specific spacing.

Using the Align palette

1 Using the Align palette, you can position objects correctly much more quickly than by using guides. For example, let's say you have three circles in your layout.

2 One click on the Align Horizontal Centers and Align Vertical Centers buttons in the Align palette produces this result.

Distributing objects

1 Here, we'll look at how the Distribute functions of the Align palette work. Let's say you have a number of objects that need collecting and organizing in a row.

2 With the objects selected, check the Use Spacing option under Distribute Objects in the Align palette and enter a measurement value.

3 Click on any of the three Distribute Horizontal buttons. InDesign then arranges the selected objects in a row, spacing them out by the precise measurement value you entered. Depending on the spacing value and the physical size of the objects, they may or may not end up overlapping:

4 When distributing objects of varying sizes, the spacing will not appear regular. If your intention is to arrange the objects so that they have an equal amount of space between them, a better idea is to use the Distribute Spacing section at the bottom of the Align palette (if you don't see it, click on Show Options in the palette fly-out menu). Check the Use Spacing option and enter the size of the gap you want to insert between each selected object.

5 Click on the Distribute Horizontal Space button to produce this result.

Nested frames

In addition to putting text and pictures inside frames, you can put frames inside other frames—that is, you can "nest" them. This lets you use the parent frame to crop the object within, in much the same way as you would crop a picture. However, with nested frames, you can put several objects inside, including live text, and still edit them individually afterwards.

Selecting nested objects

1 Whether nested or just overlapping, all shapes have a center point that acts as a handle for selecting and moving the shape. It is especially useful when working with the Direct Selection tool, because one click on the center point selects the entire shape for moving.

2 Let's say you have a yellow square hidden underneath this pale blue circle.

3 With the Selection or Direct Selection tool active, hold down the Ctrl/Cmd key and click on the circle to select the shape behind it.

4 Now, by clicking and dragging on the center point of the hidden selected shape, you can drag it out into the open.

5 If the hidden shape is empty, the Ctrl/Cmd+click method will not work. Instead, you can drag a selection marquee over the whole area to select all the objects, then Shift+click the center points of the unwanted objects to deselect them before dragging out the one you want.

6 You can also drill through nested or grouped objects using the selection buttons in the Control palette.

Using nested frames

1 Take these three objects, for instance: a text frame and two colored shapes

drawn using the Pen tool (see page 76).

2 Select all three with the Selection tool and choose **Object > Group** to group them. Remember, the objects you want to nest inside another frame must be grouped first. Choose **Edit > Copy** to copy the group to the clipboard.

3 Draw a new frame, such as this ellipse, and choose **Edit > Paste Into**. The grouped objects now appear inside the new frame.

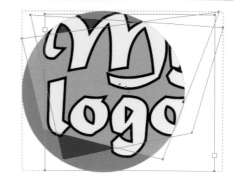

4 Switch to the Direct Selection tool and click inside the new frame. Select and edit any of the objects individually,

or Alt/Option+click on the center point of one of them to select all of the objects together.

5 Click on an object and drag it to a new position. You may find it easier to

click on an object to select it, then click-and-drag on its center point to move it.

6 You can see here how the parent frame (the ellipse) crops the objects inside.

Usefully, the text can still be edited using the Type tool.

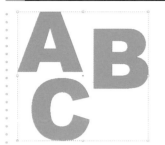

1 Here, we'll combine nested frames with negative Text Wrap values to produce an unusual typographic design. In three text frames, type an A, a B, and a C, give them a solid face (Arial Black here), and use the **Type > Create Outlines** command to convert them to shapes (see page 92). Select all three text shape objects and choose **Object > Group**. Copy them to the clipboard with **Edit > Copy**.

2 Draw a new frame, and choose **Edit > Paste Into** to nest the text shape objects inside it. Use the Direct Selection tool to select each shape and move it beyond the edge of the frame.

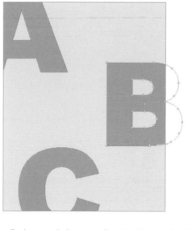

3 Each nested object can be given its own text wrap attributes using the Text Wrap palette (see page 46). In this instance, however, we've set each object to Wrap Around Bounding Box with negative outset values. This makes the wrap outlines smaller than the objects themselves, allowing text to overlap them.

4 Place some text on your page, then move the text frame over the top of the nested frame. Adjust the negative text wrap for the nested objects until you achieve a result that you're happy with.

Nit vel haret irit niametuero corer accum vel iriure tem nissim quismodigna alit alit et wismodo lortisim iustie vulluptat ver suscidunt ad tat ad mod min hendit, vel elit wis nonummodip et augue magna facinciduis nibh et adip ea con er ing el iriliquat, con veraestio odigniatet acip exeraestrud tat. Atet praessit, consequip exeraestie dolor in ullut am nos nonse velisci ncipit eu faccum qui el elestrud tat alit et adipissi. Giamcortis ad minim iustie min henim ilisl etum ipit ullum iure magna feu feu facipsum ipsum del ipit ipit ulpute tatum

1 Nested frames can be used to create photo composites that can be adjusted without having to keep returning to Photoshop. Start by placing some images on your page. Here, we're using a flat landscape photo for a backdrop, and a couple of images with clipping paths.

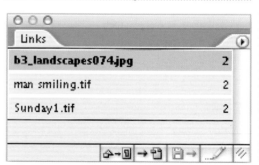

2 Arrange the images on top of each other to create a fake scene, then select them all and group them using **Object > Group**. Copy the group to the clipboard, draw a new frame, and choose **Edit > Paste Into**. You can now use the parent frame to crop the grouped image objects inside, and can also adjust those objects individually.

3 Using the Direct Selection tool, click on the backdrop image inside the nested frame. Open the Links palette and you will see the name of this image file highlighted. Click on the Relink button or choose Relink from the palette menu, then select a replacement image.

4 The selected image is swapped for a new one, while still inside the nested frame. Just try doing that in Photoshop!

87

Compound paths

Paths can be combined, or "compounded" into groups or single complex shapes to produce some interesting layout effects. While it is possible to apply all of the following techniques to open paths, including straight rules and squiggly lines, you would normally only use the compound path commands on closed shapes.

88

Compounding paths

1 Create a pair of overlapping objects like this, and select them both.

2 Open the Pathfinder palette. The compounding effects make up the top row of buttons.

3 If you click on the Add button in the palette, the result is a single merged shape, taking the fill and stroke attributes of the front object.

4 If you click on the Subtract button instead, the front object is used as a "cookie cutter" to punch a hole in the back object where they overlap.

5 If you click on the Intersect button, only the overlapping area between the two objects remains, taking the fill and stroke attributes of the front object.

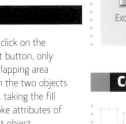

6 If you click on the Exclude Overlap button, InDesign compounds the two objects as a grouped pair and knocks a hole through the overlapping area. The objects can be edited independently using the Direct Selection tool. This is the same as using the menu command **Object > Compound Paths > Make**. The fill and stroke attributes are taken from whichever object was created first, regardless of whether it is in front of or behind the other.

Use the Add command in the Pathfinder palette rather than Exclude Overlap if you want the overlapping sections of certain objects to be combined into solid areas, not punched through.

7 If you click on the Minus Back button, the rear object is used as a "cookie cutter" to punch a hole in the front object where they overlap. This is the opposite of Subtract.

Compound photo fill

1 Draw a series of closed-path objects using the Pen or shape tools. Allow some to overlap, and leave big gaps between others.

2 Select all the objects. In the Pathfinder palette, click on the Exclude Overlap button or choose Object > Compound Paths > Make. The objects act as if they have been grouped.

3 With the compounded objects still selected, choose File > Place and locate an image you want to bring onto your page.

4 Click Open to place the image, whereupon it loads inside the compound objects as if they were a single frame. Use the Direct Selection tool to adjust the position of the image and to change the shape and position of the individual objects.

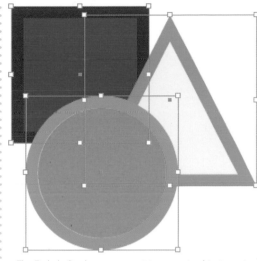

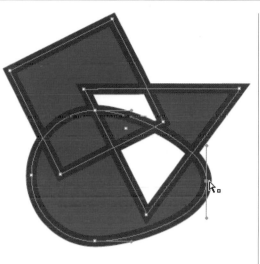

1 The Exclude Overlap command in the Pathfinder palette (being the same as the **Object > Compound Paths > Make** command in the menus) is unlike the other Pathfinder effects. It is the only compound effect that can be broken apart into separate objects again. However, the results can be a little unexpected.

For example, draw three shape objects, and color their fills and strokes differently (see page 80). Overlap them and select them all.

3 Switch to the Direct Selection tool. You can now reshape any of the points on any of the paths. Hold down the Alt/Option key and click on a path to select that object independently of the others in the compounded group, so that you can apply other transformations such as Rotate and Shear on them alone.

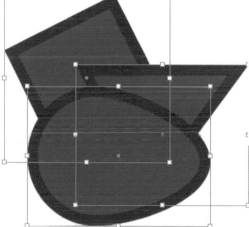

2 Click on the Exclude Overlap button in the Pathfinder palette, or go to **Object > Compound Paths > Make**. Note how the compound path has taken on the fill and stroke attributes of the first shape we drew. Although this first shape (the square) is sitting behind the others here, the front-to-back stacking order of the objects is actually irrelevant.

4 Now choose **Object > Compound Paths > Release**. This "releases" the compound group back to individual shapes, complete with any editing changes you have made. The objects do not, however, retrieve their original fills and strokes.

5 If you had earlier placed an image inside the compound path, releasing it will leave the image inside only the first shape you drew—the other objects will be empty but will still have taken on the fill and stroke attributes of that first object.

Advanced compound paths

Although creating complex shapes is the obvious purpose for compound paths, you can use them in combination with special effects to produce original and effective results. Here we'll create an inset title panel effect that could be used for a product label or brochure cover. Similar results could be produced using Photoshop or Illustrator, but the entire effect is achieved entirely within InDesign using compound paths.

BUTTONS AND TOOLS

Eyedropper tool

Rectangle tool

Subtract button

Eyedropper tool loaded

Type tool

Selection tool

Eyedropper tool loaded with type

Creating a panel using compound paths

1 Special graphics are often best created in an empty document and then copied over to your live layout when they are finished. So, open a new document and add three more layers to the default layer using the Layers palette. Name the four layers, from top to bottom, "text," "hole," "front image," and "back image."

2 Click on "front image" in the Layers palette to select it, then go to File > Place and choose an image to add to the page. Resize and fit the image as required. Copy this image from the "front image" layer to the "back image" layer by holding down the Alt/Option key and dragging the square dot next to the layer name in the Layers palette down, and dropping it onto the "back image" layer below. This makes an identical copy of the image in precisely the same position, but on the lower layer.

3 Hide the "front image" layer by clicking on the eye button next to its name in the palette. Using the Selection tool, click on the image on your page—this selects the copied image sitting in the "back image" layer. Open the Transparency palette (see page 114), and drag on the Opacity slider to reduce its opacity value from 100% to 30%.

Reveal the "front image" layer by clicking on the eye button in the Layers palette, then select the "hole" layer. Draw a shape on this layer using the Pen, Pencil, or shape tools. Here we have used the Rectangle tool and used **Object > Corner Effects** (see page 82) to apply the Fancy effect to its corners. Give the shape a solid black fill and no stroke (see page 80).

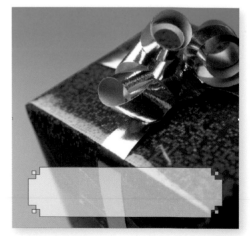

4 With the shape still selected, hold down the Shift key and click on the image behind it. With both objects selected, go to **Object > Compound Paths > Make**. Alternatively, open the Pathfinder palette and click on the Subtract button. This takes the shape from the "hole" layer and uses it to knock a hole through the image in the "front image" layer, revealing the pale image that is sitting on the "back image" layer.

5 With the compound object still selected, choose **Object > Drop Shadow** (see page 120). In the Drop Shadow dialog window, check the Drop Shadow option at the top to activate the effect and also check Preview so you can see the effect in real time.

6 Adjust the settings as required (or just accept the defaults) and click OK. The drop shadow applies to the compound object, overlapping the "back image" layer and producing an inset effect.

7 Select the "text" layer in the Layers palette, switch to the Type tool, click-and-drag to create a new text frame, and type in some text to use as a heading. Position it over the hole in the compound path and, if you like, give it a drop shadow of its own, although you will need to reduce the shadow's X and Y offsets.

Select everything by choosing **Edit > Select All**, and then group the objects by choosing **Object > Group**. This graphic can now be moved to a live page layout.

Tip

CLEAN EDGES

The drop shadow that was applied to the hole in the compound object also appears around the outer edge of the large rectangle. To shave off this outer drop shadow while preserving the effect inside the hole, nest the group inside another frame and crop the edges.

To do this, draw an empty frame using the Rectangle tool. With the Selection tool active, click on the grouped graphic you created and choose Edit > Copy or Edit > Cut. Next, click in the empty frame and choose Edit > Paste Into.

You can then use the Selection tool to alter the size and shape of the parent frame, cropping off the drop shadow edges as required. For more on nested frames, see page 86.

Here, we have also applied a rounded corner effect to the parent frame, creating a label-like result. For more on corner effects, see page 82.

91

Tip

MATCHING TYPE COLORS

Keep the colors in your design coordinated by picking them out of your placed image and applying them to other objects such as text and paths. To do this, switch to the Eyedropper tool and click anywhere on the image.

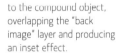

This loads the tool with the color of the pixel you clicked on, and the tool cursor will appear "loaded." Bring the Eyedropper over the text in your compound graphic and you will notice that the loaded cursor now has a tiny text-insertion I-beam in it. This indicates that the Eyedropper tool is ready to apply the loaded color to the text rather than to any other object.

If nothing appears to happen, make sure you have the Fill attribute (not the Stroke attribute) active in the Tools, Swatches, or Color palettes (see page 80). If the Eyedropper tool copies over unwanted attributes in addition to the Fill color, double-click on its icon in the Tools palette to call up the Eyedropper options and uncheck the attributes you want ignored.

To pick up new colors with the Eyedropper tool, hold down the Alt/Option key, click again elsewhere on the image and release the key before applying it to text or other objects.

Create Outlines

The Type > Create Outlines command converts text to vector shapes. This allows you to apply a greater variety of visual effects than are possible with type alone. Here's a guide to the kinds of effects you can achieve with outline text, along with instructions on how to create them.

Convert type to vectors

OUTLINES

Type a word in a text frame, enlarge it, and give it a thick-set font. Then just use **Type > Create Outlines** to convert it to a compound group of vector shapes.

OUTLINES

If you click on the group with the Direct Selection tool, you can see (and edit) the individual shapes using conventional Bézier handles.

Tip

OUTLINES

SELECTED TEXT
You don't have to use the Create Outlines command on entire text frames. Use the Type tool to select part of the text in a frame, then choose Type > Create Outlines. Only the selected letters are converted, and they can be edited as above while sitting alongside the true text characters as anchored inline objects.

Creating special effects

1 To give the outlined text a color fill and a thick, colored stroke, select the group with the Selection tool and use the Swatches palette. Make sure you click on the Fill or Stroke symbol as appropriate at the top of the palette first (for more on this palette, see page 96). To add a thick stroke, pick a value from the Weight drop-down at the top of the Stroke palette (for more on this palette, see page 80). You can also apply this effect to ordinary text that has not been converted to outlines.

OUTLINES

	Solid
	Thick – Thick
	Thick – Thin
	Thick – Thin – Thick
	Thin – Thick
	Thin – Thick – Thin
	Thin – Thin
	Triple
	Dashed (3 and 2)
	Dashed (4 and 4)
	Left Slant Hash
	Right Slant Hash
	Straight Hash
	Dotted
	Wavy
	White Diamond
	Japanese Dots
	Dashed

2 To produce unusual outline effects, choose from the different styles available in the Type drop-down in the Stroke palette. Again, make sure you have clicked on the Stroke symbol in either the Swatches palette or the main Tools palette. This effect cannot be applied to ordinary text, only outline text.

OUTLINES
OUTLINES
OUTLINES
OUTLINES

3 For this rainbow effect, create a multicolored gradient swatch (see page 100) and apply it either as a fill or as a stroke. Here, the same gradient is used for both, running in opposite directions. To do this, drag across the text outlines with the Gradient fill—once for the fill, then back in the opposite direction for the stroke. As before, you must specify whether the fill or the stroke is active by click on the appropriate symbol in the Swatches palette or main Tools palette.

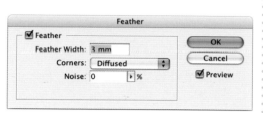

6 To send the text outlines into soft focus, select them with the Selection tool and choose **Object** > **Feather**. Check the Feather option, and adjust the Feather Width value as required. Ensure Diffused is selected from the Corners drop-down.

7 This mottled variant of the soft focus effect is produced by opening the Feather dialog window again, and increasing the value in the Noise slider.

4 Filling text outlines with an image is easy. Just select the outlines with the Selection tool and use the **File** > **Place** command as usual. Alternatively, drag and drop an image onto the text outlines from your Desktop or from Bridge. If you then switch to the Direct Selection tool, you can scale and crop the image across the whole outline group.

5 To add a drop shadow, just select the text outlines and choose **Object** > **Drop Shadow**. Check the Drop Shadow option and you're done. For more on drop shadows, see page 120.

Tip

RECOMBINING LETTERS

With the text outlines selected with the Selection tool, choose Object > Compound Paths > Release. You can now move and apply effects to the letters individually. Note that a peculiarity in InDesign causes holes in certain characters (such as O and A) to be filled in. To fix this, select the filled-in character on its own, choose Object > Compound Paths > Make and then immediately repeat Object > Compound Paths > Release.

Jumble the letters together and make them appear playful by rotating them slightly one by one using the Rotate tool. You could apply transparency effects at this point if you like, using the Transparency palette. For more on transparency, see page 114.

Select all of the letter shapes with the Selection tool (Shift+click them all in turn, or click-and-drag a marquee area over them), then combine them by choosing Object > Pathfinder > Add. Alternatively, just click on the Add button at the top left in the Pathfinder palette. You can now apply more effects, such as this image fill and drop shadow.

COLOR

Color palette

Although most designers, for good reasons, tend to make more use of the Swatches palette, the Color palette is nonetheless worth getting to know. You can use the Color palette to quickly create any color you need; these colors can then be easily converted to swatches, with all their attendant advantages.

Color palette

To show the color palette select **Window > Color** or press F6. The Color palette operates in one of three color modes: CMYK, RGB, and Lab. These

modes are based on color models that provide a method for specifying and manipulating colors by means of their digital components.

The Color palette lets you do this by entering numbers, dragging sliders, or clicking on a color bar to select the color you want.

Show Options

Select CMYK from the Color palette menu and, if you can't see the sliders, select Show Options, or click the triangle to the right of the word Color on the palette tab. For commercial four-color press work you'll use the CMYK mode almost exclusively.

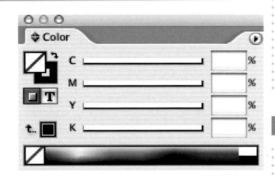

Fill and Stroke selectors

The Fill and Stroke selectors at the top left of the Color palette work in the same way, and are linked to their equivalents on the Toolbar. Click either one to activate it, or press X to toggle between them. The default fill and stroke colors are [None] and [Black], which you can assign by pressing D. To swap the fill and stroke colors, click the swap arrow to the top left of the selectors, or press Shift+X.

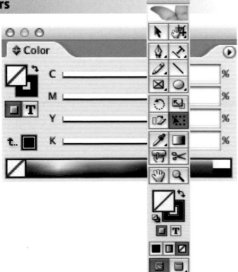

Selecting colors

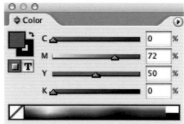

To specify a new fill or stroke color, click the required selector and drag the C, M, Y, and K sliders to the required component levels, or enter a numeric value in the percentage field. You can tab between the fields to do

this quickly, and if you hold down the Ctrl/Cmd key as you press Return, the same percentage change is applied to the other fields.

Alternatively, to make a color selection visually, click anywhere within the

color bar at the bottom of the palette. Use this as a starting point and make adjustments with the sliders.

You can also apply [None], [Paper], or [Black] using the three swatches at either end of the color bar (see below).

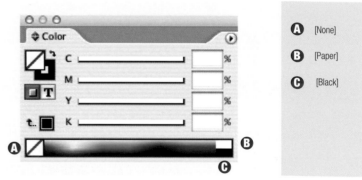

A [None]

B [Paper]

C [Black]

Switching modes

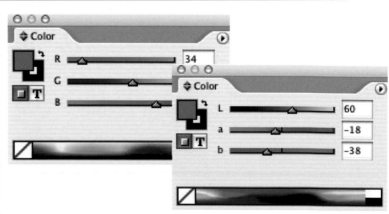

To switch to RGB mode, select RGB from the palette menu. The specified color is unchanged, but is represented by its red, green, and blue components.

Select Lab from the palette menu to display the Lab color components. Shift+click the color bar to quickly switch between color modes.

Out-of-gamut colors

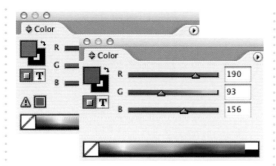

If you're working with a CMYK document and use either the RGB or Lab modes to select colors, it's possible to produce out-of-gamut colors that cannot be reproduced on a CMYK press. A yellow warning triangle appears in the color palette to alert you to this.

Click either the triangle or the color swatch next to it to substitute the closest available in-gamut CMYK color.

Drag and drop colors

 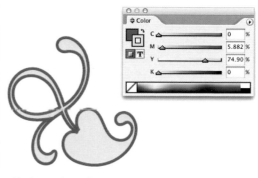

You can drag and drop the Fill or Stroke selector onto an object to apply color. You can even drag the Fill selector onto a stroke to change it, and vice versa.

1 To change a fill, drag either the Fill or Stroke selector over the center of the object until the cursor changes to an arrow with a black dot next to it. Then drop it to apply the fill color.

2 To change the stroke color, drag either the Fill or Stroke selector over the stroke of the object until the cursor changes to an arrow with a short black line next to it. Then drop it to apply the stroke color.

Coloring selected objects

When you create a new object, its fill and stroke colors are determined by those currently set in the Color palette. To change the fill or stroke color of a selected object, first activate the Fill or Stroke selector, then change the color by dragging the sliders, or using one of the other methods already described.

Tip

CMYK, RGB, OR LAB?

The choice of color mode for the Color palette will be determined by the nature of your project and the color settings. If you are producing a four-color process publication for commercial printing, it makes sense to use only CMYK mode. If you're producing material for screen display—an online manual that will be output to PDF, for example—you should use RGB. For single- and spot-color print jobs, it makes little difference. Few people use Lab, a wide-gamut color space that closely resembles human perception (but not printing presses or computer monitors). Lab is primarily used for converting from one color space to another.

Add to Swatches

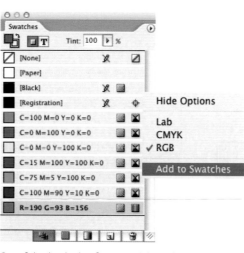

One of the drawbacks of using the Color palette is that it applies unnamed colors to objects. Unnamed colors can't be changed throughout a document, so if there is a change to the overall design, you'll have to select and change the color of each element individually. You can avoid this chore by adding colors you've created in the Color palette to the Swatches palette (see pages 98–99) before applying them.

1 Select Add to Swatches from the Color palette menu. The swatch is added to the Swatches palette and (as long as the Name with Color Value box in the Swatch options dialog box is active) it is automatically named using the color values.

2 The swatch mode and name are defined in the Color palette's current mode, so if you want a CMYK swatch, make sure the Color palette is in CMYK mode.

Coloring text

1 To apply color to text, first select the text with the Selection tool and click the Formatting Affects Text box in the color palette. By default, text has no stroke and a black fill.

2 To change the fill, click the Fill selector in the Color palette (the T icon), select the color mode from the palette menu and specify the color mix.

3 To color the text frame, click the Formatting Affects Container box.

4 To color selected words or letters within the text block, select the required text with the text tool. In this case the Formatting Affects Text box is automatically selected and grayed out.

97

COLOR
Swatches

Use the Swatches palette to create process and spot colors, tints, gradients, and mixed ink colors. Applying "named" colors from the Swatches palette makes the identification of applied colors easy, and enables global editing—you can change the color of items throughout a document by editing the swatch.

The Swatches palette

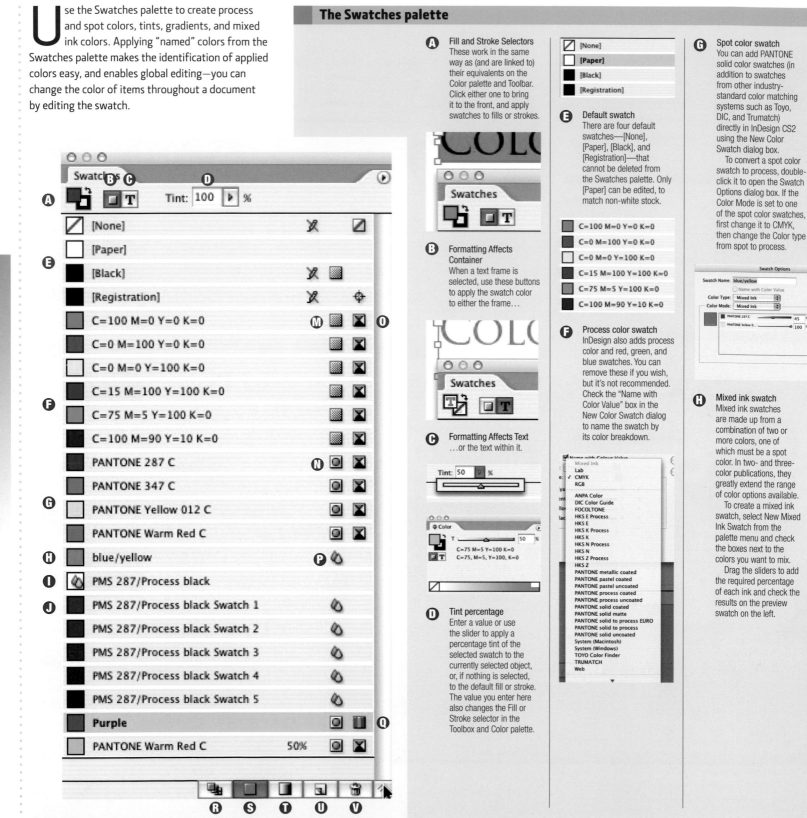

A **Fill and Stroke Selectors**
These work in the same way as (and are linked to) their equivalents on the Color palette and Toolbar. Click either one to bring it to the front, and apply swatches to fills or strokes.

B **Formatting Affects Container**
When a text frame is selected, use these buttons to apply the swatch color to either the frame…

C **Formatting Affects Text**
…or the text within it.

D **Tint percentage**
Enter a value or use the slider to apply a percentage tint of the selected swatch to the currently selected object, or, if nothing is selected, to the default fill or stroke. The value you enter here also changes the Fill or Stroke selector in the Toolbox and Color palette.

E **Default swatch**
There are four default swatches—[None], [Paper], [Black], and [Registration]—that cannot be deleted from the Swatches palette. Only [Paper] can be edited, to match non-white stock.

F **Process color swatch**
InDesign also adds process color and red, green, and blue swatches. You can remove these if you wish, but it's not recommended. Check the "Name with Color Value" box in the New Color Swatch dialog to name the swatch by its color breakdown.

G **Spot color swatch**
You can add PANTONE solid color swatches (in addition to swatches from other industry-standard color matching systems such as Toyo, DIC, and Trumatch) directly in InDesign CS2 using the New Color Swatch dialog box.
To convert a spot color swatch to process, double-click it to open the Swatch Options dialog box. If the Color Mode is set to one of the spot color swatches, first change it to CMYK, then change the Color type from spot to process.

H **Mixed ink swatch**
Mixed ink swatches are made up from a combination of two or more colors, one of which must be a spot color. In two- and three-color publications, they greatly extend the range of color options available.
To create a mixed ink swatch, select New Mixed Ink Swatch from the palette menu and check the boxes next to the colors you want to mix.
Drag the sliders to add the required percentage of each ink and check the results on the preview swatch on the left.

98

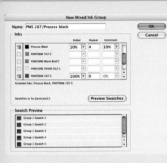

I **Mixed ink group**
A mixed ink group is a set of automatically generated mixed ink swatches based on percentage increments of one or more of the component inks. Typically, they consist of a base spot color with increments of black added to produce progressively darker shades. You can't apply the group swatch—it appears in the palette purely so you can edit the component inks.

To create a mixed ink group select New Mixed Ink Group from the palette menu and check the boxes of the existing swatch colors you want to include in the mixed ink group. Note that at least one of them must be a spot color.

To create additional group swatches, select one of the mixed ink swatches and click the New Swatch icon while holding down the Alt/Option key. The swatch is automatically given the group name plus the next number in the sequence. Adjust the component color sliders as required and click OK to add the new swatch to the group.

J **Mixed ink group member**
The mixed color group generates a swatch for each incremental percentage change. Double-click these swatches to edit them individually.

K **Gradient swatch**
A gradient swatch applies a mix of colors to an object, gradually blending from one to the next. Once a gradient swatch is applied, it can be fine-tuned in the Gradient palette. Find out how to create Gradient Swatches on pages 100–101.

L **Tint swatch**
To create a tint swatch, select a swatch and enter a percentage value in the tint field, then click the New Swatch icon. Double-click the swatch to change the tint value.

M **Process color type icon**
This tells you that the color will separate onto the four process color plates.

N **Spot color type icon**
This is a spot color and will print on its own spot color plate.

O **CMYK color mode icon**
Don't confuse color modes with color types. This PANTONE spot color is defined in CMYK mode, but it prints on a spot color plate. Spot and process color types can be defined in any color mode—CMYK, RGB, or Lab.

P **Mixed color icon**
This icon tells you that this is a mixed ink swatch. Double-click to edit it.

Q **RGB color mode icon**
The mode of this spot color has been changed to RGB, illustrating the point that you can define spot colors using any color mode.

R **Show All Swatches**
Displays all the swatches in the palette.

S **Show Color Swatches**
Displays only the color swatches.

T **Show Gradient Swatches**
Displays only the gradient swatches.

U **New Swatch**
If you click this button with a swatch selected in the palette, the swatch will be duplicated. You can then double-click the duplicate to edit it. Ctrl/Cmd+Alt/Option+click the New Swatch icon to directly open the New Swatch dialog box with the selected swatch settings. It's usually more reliable to use the palette menu to select a specific new swatch type.

V **Delete Swatch**
You need to take care when deleting swatches, as other swatches may be based on them.

99

Tip

SAFE SELECTION
When working with the Swatches palette (or, for that matter, the Color, Gradient, or Tint palettes), always make sure nothing is selected by first pressing Shift Cmd/Ctrl+A (unless it's your intention to make changes to selected objects). Be aware that changes you make in the Swatches palette will affect the default color settings.

Tip

SOLID TO PROCESS
InDesign CS2 includes the PANTONE Solid to Process library, designed to show how PANTONE spot colors will appear when printed in four-color-process inks. By cross-referencing these swatches with a printed PANTONE Swatch book, you can be sure of what will print regardless of color management and on screen appearance.

Gradients

nDesign's gradient swatches provide the opportunity to create subtle color blends for backgrounds and graphics without resorting to Photoshop or Illustrator. Creating and applying blends is a two-step process. First create a blend swatch, then apply it and make adjustments using the Gradient palette.

Using the Gradient Tool

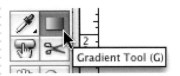

The Gradient tool provides a much more flexible way of applying gradients to selected objects.

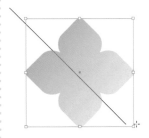

1 Pick the Gradient Tool, and drag at any angle across a selected object to apply a gradient fill. The beginning and end points of the gradient (the first and last color stops on the Gradient Ramp) correspond with where you begin and end dragging. You can start and end the gradient outside of the selected object...

2 ...or inside it.

3 You can also use the Gradient tool to produce off-center radial gradients.

Creating gradient swatches

1 Select New Gradient Swatch from the Swatches palette fly-out menu. There are two types of gradients, Linear and Radial.

Linear gradients change color along a single axis. Radial gradients radiate out in all directions from a central point. We'll create a linear gradient here, but the process is the same for radial gradients.

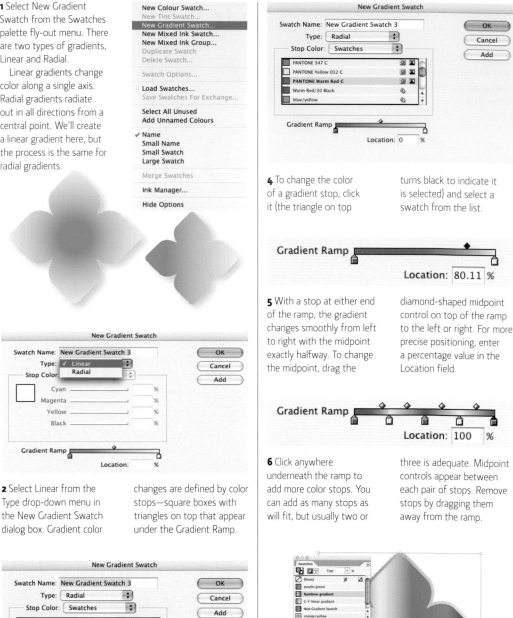

2 Select Linear from the Type drop-down menu in the New Gradient Swatch dialog box. Gradient color changes are defined by color stops—square boxes with triangles on top that appear under the Gradient Ramp.

3 You can define stop colors using CMYK, RGB, or Lab color sliders, or by using existing swatches from the Swatches palette. Click the beginning or end stop, and select Swatches from the Stop Color drop-down menu to display a list of swatches in the dialog box.

4 To change the color of a gradient stop, click it (the triangle on top turns black to indicate it is selected) and select a swatch from the list.

5 With a stop at either end of the ramp, the gradient changes smoothly from left to right with the midpoint exactly halfway. To change the midpoint, drag the diamond-shaped midpoint control on top of the ramp to the left or right. For more precise positioning, enter a percentage value in the Location field.

6 Click anywhere underneath the ramp to add more color stops. You can add as many stops as will fit, but usually two or three is adequate. Midpoint controls appear between each pair of stops. Remove stops by dragging them away from the ramp.

7 Once the gradient is created, it can be applied in the same way as any other swatch. Select an object, choose the Fill or Stroke selector, and then select the gradient swatch from the Swatches palette. Alternatively, you can drag and drop the swatch from the palette.

1 Display the Gradient palette by selecting **Window > Gradient**. The Gradient palette allows you to adjust the gradient for selected objects without altering the properties of the gradient swatch.

2 The Type drop-down menu allows you to set either a linear or radial gradient, regardless of how the swatch was defined.

3 You can change the angle of a linear tint from the default setting of zero degrees, which is horizontal. To make the gradient run vertically with the right end of the ramp at the top, enter 90.

4 To run it vertically the other way, enter -90 (if you enter 270 it is automatically converted to -90).

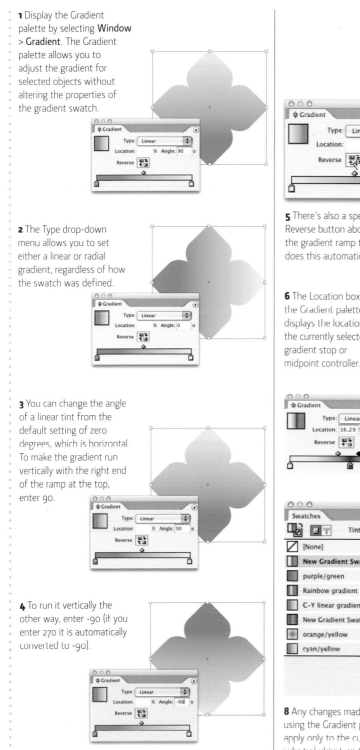

5 There's also a special Reverse button above the gradient ramp that does this automatically.

Click the button a second time to reset the original orientation.

6 The Location box in the Gradient palette displays the location of the currently selected gradient stop or midpoint controller.

7 You can drag and drop swatches from the Swatches palette to the Gradient palette to define new colors for existing stops, and to add new stops.

8 Any changes made using the Gradient palette apply only to the currently selected object, or the default swatch if nothing is selected. To add a gradient created or edited in the Gradient palette to the Swatches palette, drag the preview swatch from the Gradient palette and drop it on the Swatches palette. Double-click the new swatch to rename it.

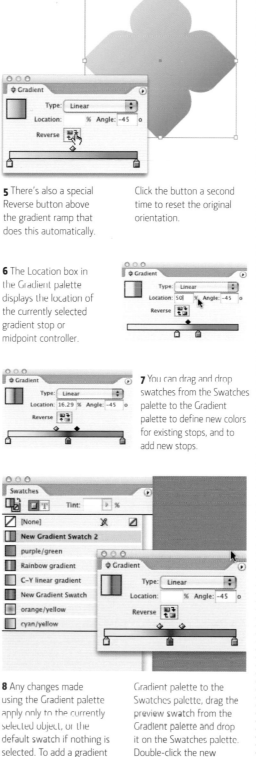

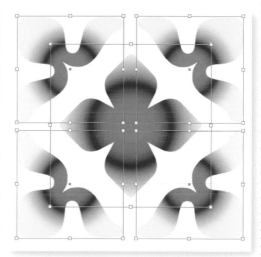

1 If you use the Swatches or Gradient palette to apply a gradient to a multiple selection or a grouped object, the gradient is individually applied to each component.

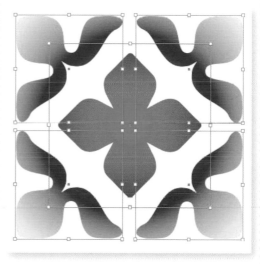

2 To apply a gradient across all the objects as a group, use the Gradient tool or turn the selection into a Compound Path using **Object > Compound Paths > Make**.

Tip

GRADIENT CONVERSION

You can create gradients from spot, process, and mixed ink colors, and mix all color types in one gradient. On output, all gradients are converted to CMYK, so you may experience color shifts with anything other than CMYK gradients.

Applying color to objects

There are several ways to apply color to objects, and, particularly where text is concerned, some are better than others. Sometimes, all you're interested in is speed and convenience; at other times, you need to consider how the method of application will affect your ability to make edits.

Copying attributes with the Eyedropper

The Eyedropper Tool provides a quick and convenient way of copying color and other attributes between page elements.

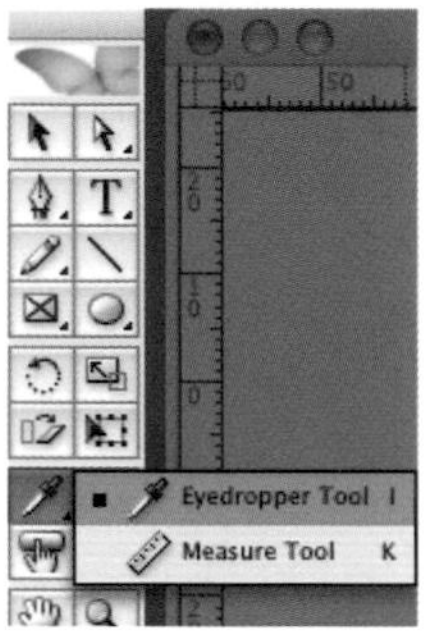

1 Select the Eyedropper tool from the Toolbar. It shares a position with the Measure tool; if it isn't visible press I.

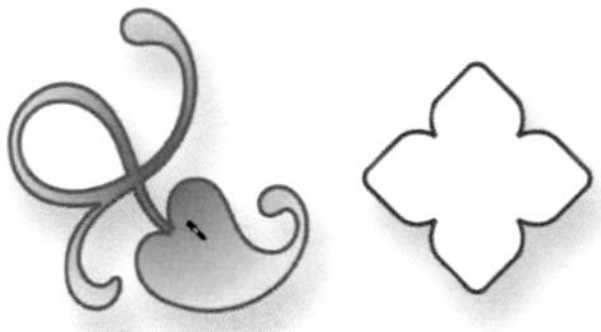

2 Click on a stroked and filled object. The appearance of the tool changes from empty to full, and the icon flips to indicate the Eyedropper is "loaded."

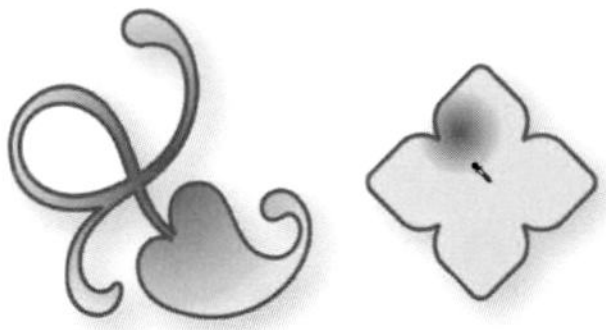

3 Click on any other object to apply the copied fill and stroke attributes.

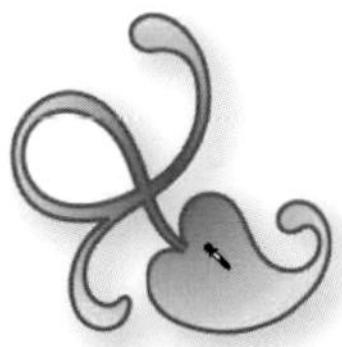

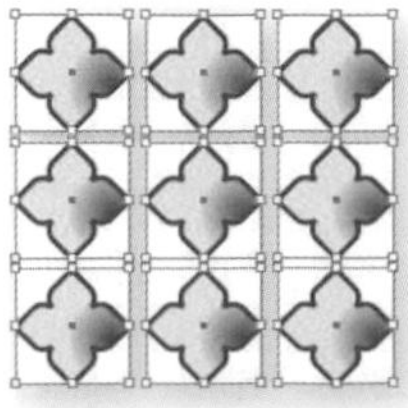

4 Alternatively, first select the object or objects to which you want to apply new attributes, and then click on the object you want to copy with the Eyedropper. The new stroke and fill attributes are automatically applied to all the selected objects.

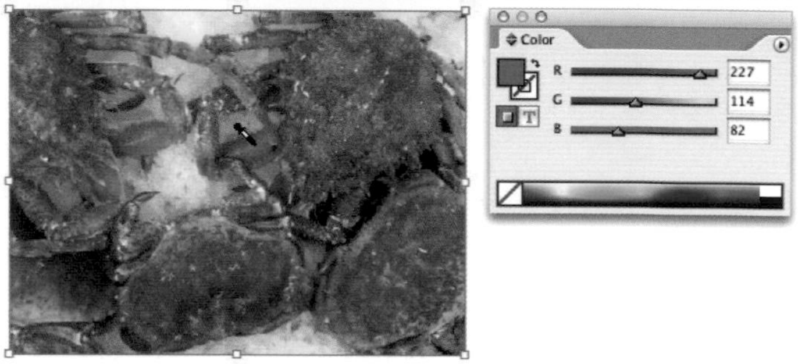

5 You can copy attributes from imported graphics and images in addition to InDesign objects. If you click on an imported bitmap, the color of the pixels under the Eyedropper becomes the fill color. If you haven't applied a stroke to the frame, then the stroke color is [None].

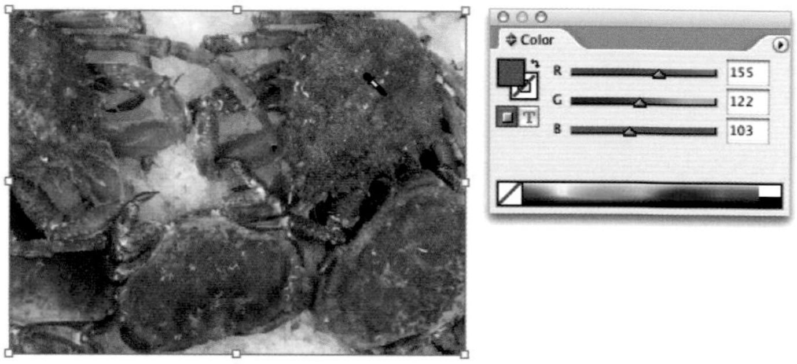

6 To reload the Eyedropper, hold down the Alt/Option key and click elsewhere in the image to sample a new color.

Formatting type with the Eyedropper

In addition to stroke and fill attributes, the Eyedropper tool can transfer type and transparency settings.

1 Select the text you want to format with the Type tool, then select the Eyedropper tool from the Toolbar (this is one situation in which you can't use the keyboard shortcut, I).

2 Click anywhere in the frame of the formatted text you want to copy. All of its character and paragraph settings in addition to its fill and stroke attributes are applied to the previously selected text. If no text is selected, then the Eyedropper icon will change to include an "I-Beam." Now just drag across the text that you would like to select to have the style immediately applied.

Here's how to copy all of the formatting from one piece of text to another:

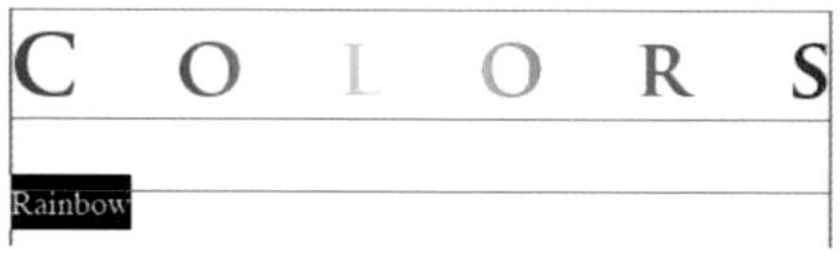

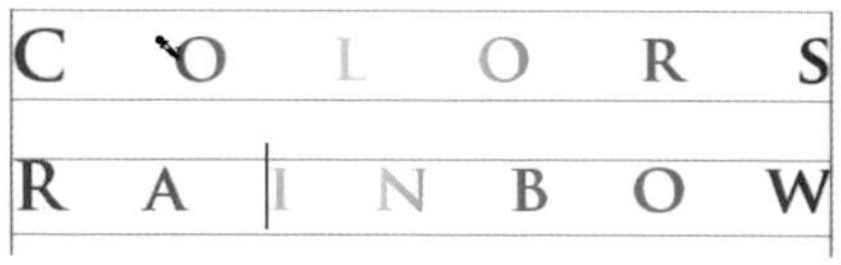

3 You can use the Eyedropper to apply only the fill and stroke attributes of sampled text. Use the Selection tool to select the frame containing the text to be formatted, select the Eyedropper tool, and click the Formatting Affects Text button on the Toolbar, Color, or Swatches palette. Now click with the Eyedropper in the text frame to be sampled.

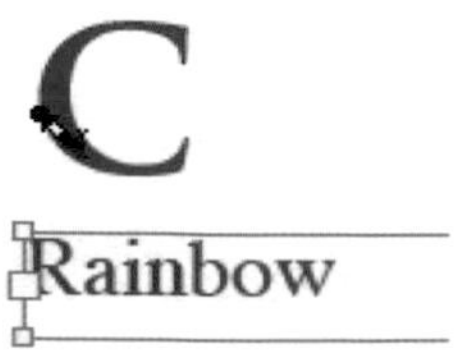

spectrum

1 There's another way to format multiple elements using the Eyedropper tool. Press Shift+Cmd/Ctrl+A to deselect all. Select the Eyedropper tool. Click the text which contains the attributes you want to copy. A small I-Beam text cursor appears when you position the loaded Eyedropper over the text to which you want to apply the attributes.

It used to be the case that to apply fill and stroke attributes to text, you first had to convert it to Postscript paths. With InDesign, you can apply stroke or fill attributes to live text that remains editable.

2 Click-and-drag in the text to select the characters you want to format. The Eyedropper remains loaded, and you can continue to use it to format text and other page elements. Only appropriate formatting is applied, so if you click on a graphic, the text formatting is ignored but other attributes are applied.

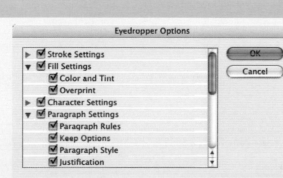

1 To apply a fill color to text, first select it with the Type tool. Next, click the Fill selector. The Formatting Affects Text icon is automatically selected when you make a text selection with the Type tool. Click on a swatch in the Swatches palette to color the selected text. You can apply a color to any amount of text in this way, from a single character to an entire story.

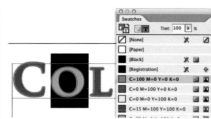

2 Type has a default stroke color of [None]. To stroke selected type, click the Stroke selector in the Swatches palette or Toolbar and select a swatch. The default stroke weight is 1pt.

3 You can't drag and drop swatches onto type to color the fill and stroke—only the text frame can be colored in this way. When text is selected with the Type tool, the Formatting Affects Text icon is automatically checked and you can't select the Formatting affects container icon. But if you try to drag a swatch onto the text, the frame will be filled with the swatch color.

C O L O R S

4 You can add a gradient fill or stroke to type by clicking on a gradient swatch to color the selected text. You can also use the Gradient tool, which gives you more control by enabling you to define the start and end points, and the angle of the gradient.

COLORS

5 When you fill or stroke live type with a gradient, it extends invisibly to fill the bounding box. The type acts like a clipping path on the bounding box gradient. If you edit the type, different parts of the gradient will be exposed.

COLORS

6 There are two ways around this. You can either reapply the gradient with the Gradient tool to achieve the desired effect, or you can convert the type to outlines, in which case it becomes an inline graphic. This "fixes" its relationship with the gradient, but the type is no longer editable.

Tip

EYEDROPPER OPTIONS

Double-click the Eyedropper tool in the Toolbar to open the Eyedropper Options dialog box. Here you can determine what formatting is applied when you click on text and graphics with the loaded Eyedropper Tool.

Eyedropper Options

- ▶ ☑ Stroke Settings
- ▼ ☑ Fill Settings
  - ☑ Color and Tint
  - ☑ Overprint
- ▶ ☑ Character Settings
- ▼ ☑ Paragraph Settings
  - ☑ Paragraph Rules
  - ☑ Keep Options
  - ☑ Paragraph Style
  - ☑ Justification

[OK]
[Cancel]

COLOR
Duotones

The best way to produce a duotone image is to use Photoshop, but if you're in a hurry, or can live without the kind of tonal control Photoshop offers, try using InDesign instead. You can make duotones from grayscale or color photographs, but slightly different techniques are required.

Real duotones

Duotones, tritones, and quadtones use additional inks to enhance the tonal quality of a monochrome image. Photoshop's Duotone mode allows you to assign additional spot or process colors to a black-and-white image and adjust the curves for each color, including black. In this way, you can create a range of effects that substitute the additional colors to a greater or lesser degree in specific parts of the tonal range.

Photoshop uses a transfer function to produce the spot color plate. When you import a Photoshop PSD or EPS duotone into InDesign, the spot color appears in the Swatches palette.

Monotone tint

A simple way of cheating duotones is to use a monotone instead. To create this effect, first import a grayscale file into InDesign. It can be a PSD, TIFF, or JPEG—the file format isn't important. Select the image with the Direct Selection tool and click on a swatch in the Swatches palette. This simply tints the grayscale image, replacing black with an alternative color. It works best with darker colors—the lighter the replacement color, the flatter (less contrasty) images will look.

Creating a duotone effect with mixed ink swatches

You can overcome the contrast problem of monotones, and achieve a result closer to a duotone, by using a mixed ink swatch instead of a straight spot color.

1 This example uses the same PANTONE 287 tint, applied as a mixed ink swatch with 50 percent black. (See pages 98-99 to find out how to create mixed ink swatches.)

2 By varying the combinations of the two inks in the mixed Ink swatch, you can achieve a wide range of duotone effects. Make sure your swatch editing doesn't affect other objects by duplicating and renaming the mixed ink swatch and using it purely for duotone tinting.

3 This more conventional looking duotone was produced by reversing the tint amounts in the original mixed ink swatch to 100 percent black and 50 percent PMS 287.

4 You can assess the ink balance in duotones produced using the mixed ink and other methods using the Separations Preview palette.

104

Creating duotones with Overprint Fill

Another method for producing duotones from grayscale images is to fill the frame with the second color and set the image to overprint.

1 Select the image frame using the Selection tool and choose a swatch from the Swatches palette. Initially, you'll see the highlights in the image change to the color you selected. It's an effect, but probably not the one you were looking for.

2 Click on the image with the Direct Selection tool. If it's not visible, press Shift+F6 to display the Separations Preview palette, select Separations from the View menu and turn on the separations for the black plate and your second image color.

3 Next, display the Attributes palette and check the Overprint Fill box. The tint should now appear throughout the tonal range.

Creating tritones with gradients

The overprint method can also be used to good effect with gradients.

1 Instead of a flat color, fill the frame with a linear gradient. This tritone image has been produced using the overprint method with a linear gradient fill using two PANTONE spot colors.

2 Solid spot colors can be overly heavy, but you can't produce a tint from a gradient. To produce a more subtle tritone effect, define a gradient using spot color tints. This one uses the same PANTONE colors as before but the solid colors have been substituted with 50 percent tints.

Tinting color images

A different approach is required with color images because you can't apply a tint color to them or set them to overprint.

1 If you click on a color image with the Direct Selection tool, the Swatches and Color palettes are grayed out. Applying a color to the frame has no effect.

2 One way around this is to use blend modes. First, select the image frame using the Selection tool and apply a color swatch to fill it. This will have no immediate visible effect.

To see the difference, select the image with the Direct Selection tool and choose the Luminosity blend mode from the drop-down menu on the Transparency palette.

3 This method works well with most colors and tints, adding the secondary color to shadow detail as well as to the midtones. As with grayscale images, you can use gradients, but any spot colors used are converted to CMYK. Because of this, you should only use duotone techniques on color images intended for CMYK output.

105

Ink Manager

The Ink Manager controls what happens to the document colors on output. You can use it to alias spot colors to another plate, convert spot colors to process, and to define ink behavior for trapping.

Opening the Ink Manager

You can display the Ink Manager by selecting Ink Manager from the Swatches palette menu, by clicking the Ink Manager button on the Output pane of the Print dialog box, or on the same pane of the Export Adobe PDF dialog box.

New Color Swatch...
New Tint Swatch...
New Gradient Swatch...
New Mixed Ink Swatch...
New Mixed Ink Group...
Duplicate Swatch
Delete Swatch...

Swatch Options...

Load Swatches...
Save Swatches For Exchange...

Select All Unused
Add Unnamed Colors

✓ Name
Small Name
Small Swatch
Large Swatch

Merge Swatches

Ink Manager...

Hide Options

Color types

The Ink Manager lists the four process colors plus all spot colors defined in the document, whether they've been used or not.

Process colors are indicated by the process color icon.

And spot colors by the spot color icon.

Aliasing spot colors

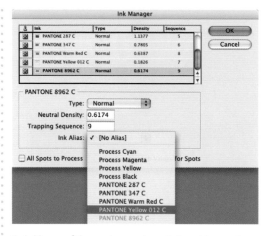

Probably one of the most common uses for the Ink Manager, among designers at least, is to alias one spot color to another. There are a variety of reasons why you might want to do this. A job with two spot colors may have been reduced to one for economic reasons, or imported graphics may have different spot color names, resulting in the creation of multiple plates for the same ink. Select the ink you want to alias from the ink list and choose the ink you want to alias it to (i.e. the plate you want it to print on) from the Ink Alias drop-down menu.

🔒	Ink	Type	Density	Sequence
◉	PANTONE 287 C	Normal	1.1377	5
◉	PANTONE 347 C	Normal	0.7805	6
◉	PANTONE Warm Red C	Normal	0.6387	8
◉	PANTONE Yellow 012 C	Normal	0.1826	7
⚒	PANTONE 8962 C	<PANTONE Yellow 012 C>		

In this instance PANTONE 8962 C will print on the same plate as PANTONE Yellow 012 C. In the Type column of the ink list PANTONE 8962 C is listed as PANTONE Yellow 012 C indicating it is aliased to that ink.

Separations Preview

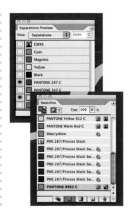

You can check the alias is working by clicking OK to close the Ink Manager, and then opening the Separations Preview palette to view the separate plates. Though the same result could have been achieved by deleting the PANTONE 8962 C swatch and replacing it with PANTONE Yellow 012 C, using the Ink Manager retains the colors in the document.

Convert spot to process

🔒	Ink	Type	Density	Sequence
☒	Process Yellow	Normal	0.16	3
☒	Process Black	Normal	1.7	4
☒	PANTONE 287 C	Normal	1.1377	5
☒	PANTONE 347 C			
◉	PANTONE Warm Red C	Normal	0.6387	7
◉	PANTONE Yellow 012 C	Normal	0.1826	6

To convert a spot color ink to CMYK process, click its spot color icon. The icon type changes to CMYK and all of the usual ink controls are grayed out. You can change the ink back to a spot color at any time by clicking the ink type icon again.

All Spots to Process

🔒	Ink	Type	Density	Sequence
☒	Process Black	Normal	1.7	4
☒	PANTONE 287 C			
☒	PANTONE 347 C			
☒	PANTONE Warm Red C			
☒	PANTONE Yellow 012 C			
☒	PANTONE 8962 C			

PANTONE 347 C
Type:
Neutral Density:
Trapping Sequence:
Ink Alias: [No Alias]

☑ All Spots to Process   ☐ Use Standard Lab Values for Spots

To change all spot colors in the document to process, check the All Spots to Process box. Unchecking this box reverts all converted inks back to spot colors, including those that were individually converted.

Trapping Inks

PANTONE 287 C
Type: Normal
Neutral Density: 1.1377
Trapping Sequence: 5
Ink Alias: [No Alias]

The Type drop-down menu, Neutral Density field, and Trapping Sequence field are used by InDesign to determine how to trap the specified ink. If you're unsure about trapping and are using only process and conventional spot color inks, then leave these set to the defaults. In the majority of cases InDesign's built-in trapping will do an excellent job.

Trapping spot varnish

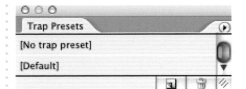

One situation in which changing these settings would be advisable is when using spot varnish or metallic inks. InDesign's trapping engine works by comparing the neutral density values of abutting inks and spreading or choking the lighter of the two into the darker ink.

This approach maintains the shape of objects while avoiding any gaps due to press misregistration. In the case of spot varnish, choose Transparent from the Type drop-down menu to ensure that underlying inks do not choke the spot varnish elements.

Trapping metallic inks

| | PANTONE 8962 C | Opaque | 0.6173 | 9 |

Metallic inks are particularly opaque and even if you've selected a metallic ink from a color library, its neutral density value may not reflect its true printed

characteristics. Choose Opaque to prevent metallic inks from spreading into neighboring colors, but to allow neighboring colors to spread into the metallic ink.

Changing Ink Neutral Density

PANTONE 8962 C

Type:	Normal
Neutral Density:	1.7
Trapping Sequence:	9
Ink Alias:	[No Alias]

An alternative method of altering trapping behavior for individual inks is to edit the Neutral Density values. Process Black has a neutral

density of 1.7, so setting the Neutral Density of metallic inks to 1.7 or higher will cause all other inks to spread into them.

Using Trap Presets

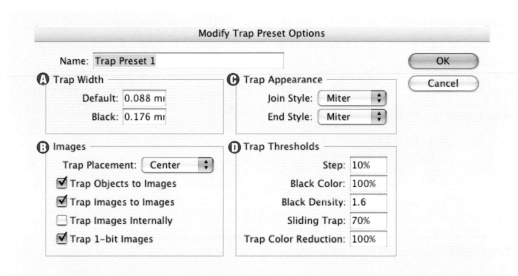

Set the trapping options for the entire document, individual pages, or page ranges (but not individual objects) using the Trap Presets palette. The simplest

way to modify trap settings for the document is to edit the Default preset by double-clicking it to open the Modify Trap Preset Options dialog box.

Most of these settings will produce perfectly good results in their default settings and, unless you have a good understanding of trapping, or are working on the advice of your prepress bureau, are probably best left that way. Here's a brief explanation of what some of them are for.

(A) Trap width
The default box sets the trap width for all inks except black. The black field also defines the "holdback area" which prevents the process color elements in rich blacks from spreading into adjacent inks.

(B) Images panel
These settings control trapping of InDesign objects that interact with imported graphics. To change these settings you need to be aware of the limitations of InDesign's built-in trapping compared with In-RIP trapping carried out by a prepress bureau. Built-in trapping cannot trap placed EPS vector graphics or internally trap placed bitmap images.

(C) Trap Appearance
Use these options to define the join and end style of trap lines around objects. Again, unless you have very specialized trapping requirements this is best left on the default setting of Mitre.

(D) Trap Thresholds
These settings control when and how trapping is applied. Step defines the required difference in process colors for trapping to occur. Sliding Trap handles the complex problem of trapping abutting gradients.

107

Tip

OVERPRINTING

Trapping is only an issue where overlapping objects "knock out" and an object that prints in one color knocks a hole in the other to avoid show-through of the underlying ink.

Very opaque inks can be overprinted because show-through is not a problem. InDesign's default trapping preset overprints black.

You can set any object's fill or stroke to overprint by checking the Overprint fill or Overprint Stroke box in the

Attributes palette. A common manual trapping technique (pictured) involves adding a thin overprinting stroke, which matches the fill color, to an object to create the trap.

Color management settings

Thanks to Adobe Bridge, it's now much easier to achieve consistent color across all of the Creative Suite applications. But successful color management still requires a basic understanding of how color profiling works, and what the Color Settings dialog box in InDesign (and the other CS applications) can do.

Using Creative Suite Color Settings

Unlike previous versions of InDesign, color management in InDesign CS2 is on by default. Your starting point for setting up color management should be Adobe Bridge. Select **Edit > Creative Suite Color Settings** to open the Suite Color Settings dialog box.

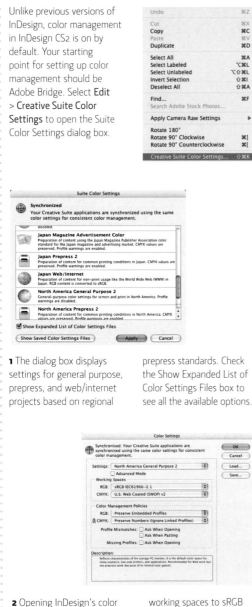

1 The dialog box displays settings for general purpose, prepress, and web/internet projects based on regional prepress standards. Check the Show Expanded List of Color Settings Files box to see all the available options.

2 Opening InDesign's color settings (**Edit > Color Settings**) shows that the North America General Purpose 2 setting adjusts InDesign's RGB and CMYK working spaces to sRGB and U.S. Web Coated (SWOP) v2 respectively. Use this for projects intended for press output and PDF output for the Web.

3 The North America Prepress 2 setting (or the other regional prepress options) uses the same CMYK working space, but sets the RGB working space to Adobe RGB (1998).

4 Adobe RGB has a wider gamut than sRGB, and is better suited for images and graphics that will be converted to CMYK at output time. This is also a better option for RGB output intended for on-screen viewing in a color-managed environment, such as a production department intranet.

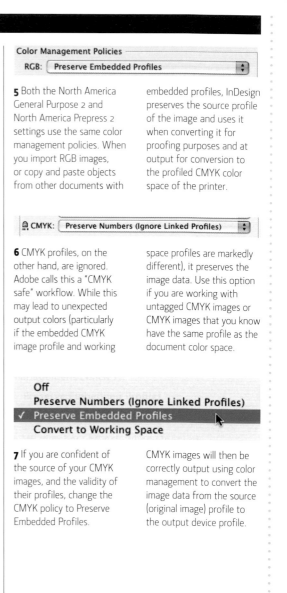

5 Both the North America General Purpose 2 and North America Prepress 2 settings use the same color management policies. When you import RGB images, or copy and paste objects from other documents with embedded profiles, InDesign preserves the source profile of the image and uses it when converting it for proofing purposes and at output for conversion to the profiled CMYK color space of the printer.

6 CMYK profiles, on the other hand, are ignored. Adobe calls this a "CMYK safe" workflow. While this may lead to unexpected output colors (particularly if the embedded CMYK image profile and working space profiles are markedly different), it preserves the image data. Use this option if you are working with untagged CMYK images or CMYK images that you know have the same profile as the document color space.

7 If you are confident of the source of your CMYK images, and the validity of their profiles, change the CMYK policy to Preserve Embedded Profiles.

CMYK images will then be correctly output using color management to convert the image data from the source (original image) profile to the output device profile.

Tip

SYNCHRONIZATION ISSUES

When you change color settings in a Creative Suite application, a message appears at the top of the Color Settings dialog box warning that color settings across Creative Suite applications are no longer synchronized. To re-synchronize the suite, go into the Suite Color Settings box in Bridge, select the correct settings from the list, and then click Apply to apply the settings to all applications in the suite.

Color Settings

⊕ Unsynchronised: Your Creative Suite applications are not synchronised for consistent color. To synchronise, select Suite Color Settings in Bridge.

Save custom settings

You may want to save custom settings so that they can be applied in Bridge and synchronization maintained. This is a good idea if you need to change settings for other reasons, for example if you use a specific press profile as the CMYK working color space. Saved custom settings are added to the Suite Color Settings dialog box.

RGB workflow

Working Spaces	
RGB:	sRGB IEC61966-2.1
CMYK:	U.S. Web Coated (SWOP) v2

Because InDesign allows you to set both CMYK and RGB working color spaces, you can successfully implement a color-managed workflow for documents with multiple outputs—print and PDF, for example. In this case, North America Prepress 2, or the appropriate regional version of it, modified as described provides the best solution.

If an imported RGB or CMYK image has a profile, it is used. Graphics created in the document are profiled with either the RGB or CMYK document color space, depending on the color model used to create them.

Profile Mismatches

Color Management Policies	
RGB:	Preserve Embedded Profiles
CMYK:	Preserve Embedded Profiles
Profile Mismatches:	☑ Ask When Opening
	☑ Ask When Pasting
Missing Profiles:	☑ Ask When Opening

Always ensure that the Profile Mismatches boxes are checked if you want to be told about profile problems when opening InDesign documents. The only circumstances in which you might not want this to happen is if you're opening and converting a lot of documents with profiles that differ from the default application working color space.

It's commonly thought that the Profile mismatch warnings apply to placed graphics, but this is not the case. Placed images with embedded profiles are treated according to the Color Management Policies, but you won't be warned if, for example, you place an RGB image with an embedded sRGB profile in an InDesign document with an Adobe RGB working color space.

Color management for the web

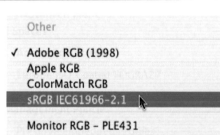

If you are producing a document for on-screen use only, a PDF for web viewing for example, the sRGB working space is probably a better option. Achieving consistent color for web documents is a virtual impossibility. It's likely that the PDF will be viewed on a wide variety of monitors, few, if any, using properly calibrated and configured color management systems. In these circumstances the sRGB color space, which is the default Windows monitor profile, is likely to produce more consistent results.

Conversion Options

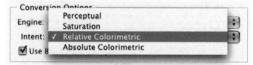

Check the Advanced mode box to display the conversion options. If you don't generally feel confident with color management, leave these settings on their default. The Engine drop-down determines the software that carries out the color space conversion for proofing and output purposes. Different options are available on Macs and Windows platforms, but the choice, which is likely to make very little visible difference, is between the Adobe Color Engine and that of the operating system's CMS.

Rendering intent

Conversion Options	
Engine:	Perceptual
	Saturation
Intent: ✓	Relative Colorimetric
☑ Use B	Absolute Colorimetric

The rendering intent determines how out-of-gamut colors are mapped to the destination color space. Ordinarily, it's not something you need to change because the default Relative Colorimetric setting does a good job in most circumstances. If you're experiencing problems with conversion of out-of-gamut colors, changing to Perceptual is worth trying. And Saturation is useful if you want to maintain saturated colors in imported charts.

Use Black Point Compensation

☑ Use Black Point Compensation

This is turned on by default and maps the black of the source profile to the black of the destination profile, ensuring that the full dynamic range is used.

Handling profiles

A typical production environment (if there is such a thing) is not a closed system. InDesign documents, digital images, and other graphics pour in from a variety of sources, and are unlikely to fit your profile requirements unless you have a good working relationship with the supplier, or are very lucky. Knowing what to do in these situations can help avoid surprises at the hard proofing stage.

Tip

PROFILE HANDLING FOR PLACED IMAGES

In an ideal world, selecting a common color settings file (CSF) for all Creative Suite applications in Bridge would mean virtually transparent color management. The only decision that needs to be made is which RGB and CMYK working color spaces to adopt.

If you've applied a synchronized color setting using Adobe Bridge, then Photoshop and Illustrator files placed in InDesign will have the same RGB and CMYK profiles as the InDesign document profile and working color space.

The reality is that documents and images come from a variety of sources, not all of which operate a color-managed workflow and, even when they do, probably use different profiles.

This raises the question of what to do when placing images with no embedded profile or profiles that differ from the Document working space. Images with no profile are the most problematic because without a profile the color data is meaningless. If possible, try to find out how the image was created and assign a suitable profile. Failing that, assign the document default.

For RGB images with embedded profiles you have two options, both of which will produce accurate color. The Preserve Embedded Profiles policy is the simplest option. The other is to convert images to the document color space in Photoshop prior to importing them.

Reassigning color profiles

It might be necessary to change the document profile if the print specifications have changed—for example, if it has been decided to print on coated, rather than uncoated stock, or to print the job in another part of the world. A job originally intended for printing in the U.S. might be switched to the Far East; or simply switching from one local printer to another might necessitate a profile change.

1 Underneath the Color Settings option on the Edit menu you'll find two further color management options—Assign Profiles and Convert to Profile. These two processes change the document color profile in different ways that produce very different results, so it's important to choose the right one.

2 The Assign Profiles dialog box provides three options each for the RGB and CMYK document profile. You would only use the first of these, Discard (use current working space), if you had altered the current working space, or if you'd opened a document with a mismatched profile and elected to keep it.

3 The second option, Assign current working space, would only be used if the existing document profile and working space were different, or the document had no profile.

4 Assign Profile lets you choose from a drop-down list of all the currently installed RGB or CMYK profiles.

5 The Assign Profiles window changes the document profile without changing the color data. What this means is that the appearance of colors will change because the same color data has been assigned a different profile, and is interpreted differently by the color management system. Consequently, you should only use Assign Profiles when you want to add a profile to a document that previously had no profile (or, for some reason had the wrong profile), for example, one that was created in a workflow that was not color-managed. Check the Preview box to see the resulting color shift.

6 The settings at the bottom of the Assign Profiles dialog box allow you to apply different rendering intents to different kinds of images. You could, for example, use the default Use Color Settings Intent for solid colors, and Perceptual for the Default Image Intent.

Convert to Profile

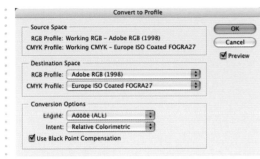

1 Convert to Profile changes the color data in order to maintain consistent colors. The different data will be interpreted by the color management system to produce the same results as the old data did with the old profile. Use this option when you want to convert a color managed document with an existing profile to a new profile.

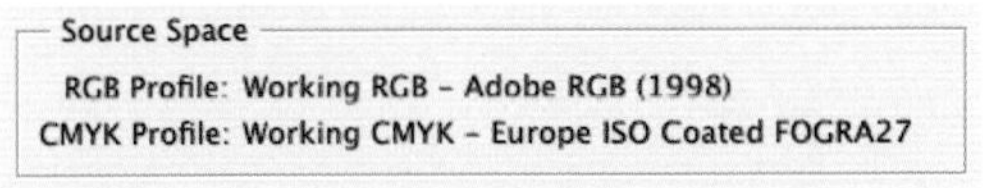

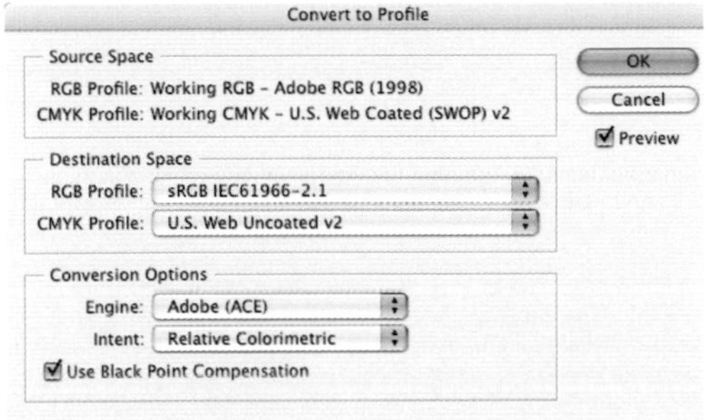

2 One of the useful things about the Convert to Profile dialog box is that it tells you the existing RGB and CMYK source space profiles for the document.

Typically, you would use Convert to Profile to convert a document with an Adobe RGB profile to sRGB, or with a coated profile to an uncoated one. Check the preview box to see color changes that may occur as a result of this remapping of out-of-gamut colors.

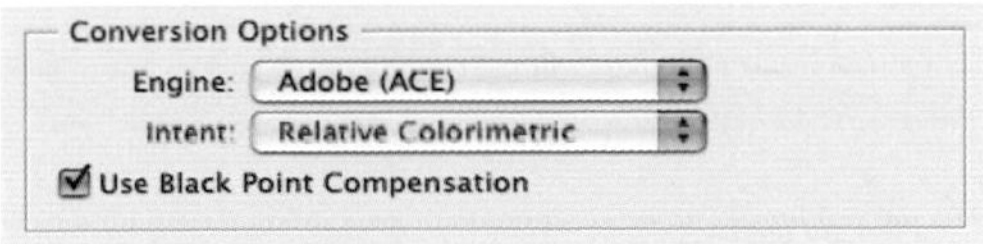

3 The Convert to Profile dialog box also provides the opportunity to change the Conversion options. You can use this in conjunction with the preview to see the effect of using different rendering intents.

Show Import Options

1 When placing images, check the Show Import Options box to display the Image Import Options dialog box. Click the Color tab to display the Profile and Rendering Intent menus.

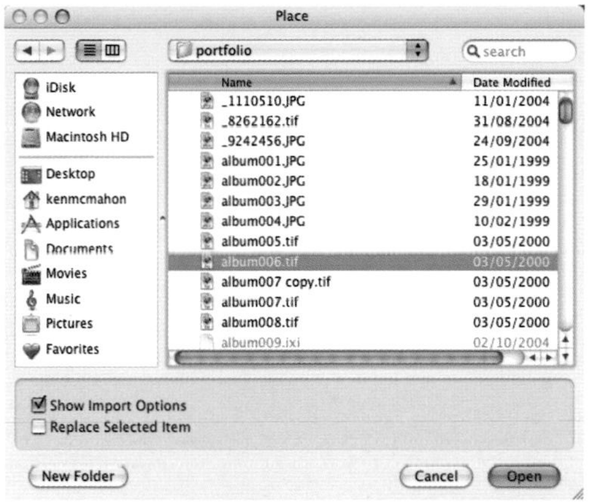

2 What appears in the Profile menu depends on the Color Management Policies in the Color Settings dialog box. If the image has an embedded profile and the chosen policy is to preserve embedded profiles, the image profile will appear here.

If the image has no profile, then the default document profile is used.

Change color settings

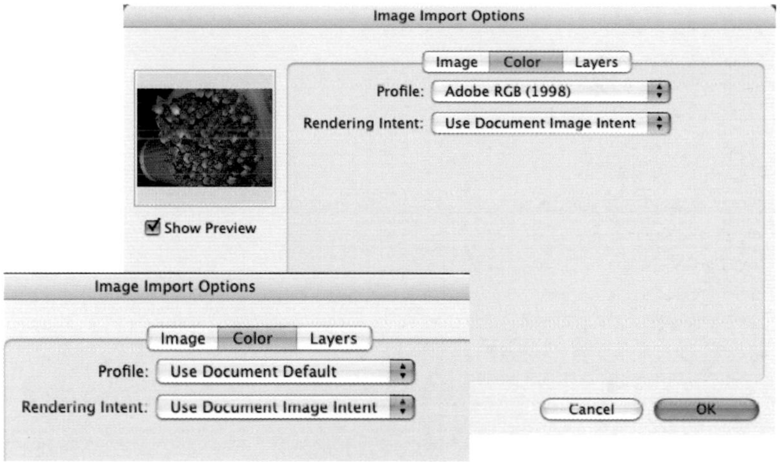

To change the color settings for a placed image, Right/Ctrl+click the image and choose Graphics > Image Color Settings from the context menu.

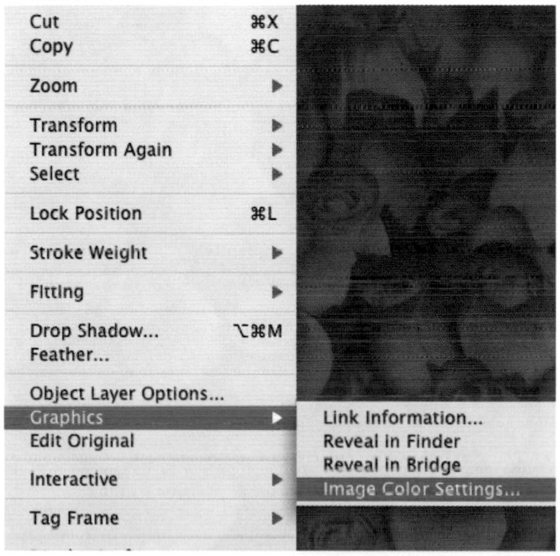

TRANSPARENCY

Transparent objects

Blend modes

Drop shadows

Feather

Transparent objects

One of the most useful and innovative features of Adobe InDesign is its support for transparency. Usually, topmost objects on a page completely obscure those behind it. InDesign gives you the option of selecting that topmost item and reducing its opacity so that the elements behind it (including the white background of the page) "show through." It's simple: go to Window > Transparency, select the Opacity field, and change a selected item's opacity from the default 100 percent to a lower value.

InDesign's transparency handling

The Opacity setting is just one of four ways in which InDesign can apply transparency to a page element. Other ways include changing an object's blend mode (see page 116), applying a drop shadow (see page 120), and applying a feather to its edges (see page 122). Additionally, InDesign supports placed images with native transparency—that is, it honors transparent areas and effects created in a graphics program and saved with the image.

You can modify the opacity of (and/or apply any of InDesign's transparency effects to) any object on the page, whether you created it in InDesign or imported it from another program. This includes text, vectors, shapes and lines, solid color and gradient fills and strokes, and imported graphics and PDFs.

Tip

VIEWING TRANSPARENCY ACCURATELY

To conserve computer processing power, InDesign does not generate accurate previews of transparency and transparency effects by default. This is especially true for the low-resolution previews of imported vector images (AI, EPS, and PDF). They look like they have a white background when they actually have a transparent one. You can change the preview level for vectors and transparency to High Quality in the Preferences > Display Performance palette, which will update all placed graphics' previews, or you can select an individual image and choose View > Display Performance > High Quality Display to redraw the screen preview for just that one image.

Using transparent text

1 Select a text frame with the Selection tool and reduce the opacity in the Transparency palette to make the text transparent. Now you can see artwork behind the filled characters, but the transparent text is still fully editable.

2 You can't apply transparency to just some of the words in a story, because Transparency in InDesign only works on objects— i.e., items you can select with the Selection tool. If you select a range of text with the Type tool, the Transparency commands are grayed out. To apply transparency to a text selection, you'll have cut and paste it into its own text frame, then click on the new text frame with the Selection tool. Alternatively, you could convert the selected text to outlines that are inline frames in the text flow. For further details, see "Adding drop shadows to text" on page 120.

3 If the text frame has a background fill, the background assumes the same opacity setting as the text.

4 To create solid, 100% opaque text on a semi-transparent background, you'll have to use two separate frames: one for the text and one for the text's background. To make the text easier to read, but allow the image to show through behind the text, insert a semi-transparent paper- or color-filled filled frame between the two.

This is 100% Black, no transparency

This is a 20% tint of Black, no transparency

This is 100% Black, 20% Opacity

City Life
Join the Party!

InDesign supports any transparent areas saved in Photoshop and Illustrator files when you place them into the layout. In Photoshop, save the file as a PSD, PDF, or TIFF (with Save Transparency turned on in the TIFF Options dialog); in Illustrator, save the file in AI format. When these images are placed on the page, objects behind the images show through their transparent areas.

1 Unlike the hard edges of images with embedded PostScript clipping paths (as here), true transparency masks often contain edges with a gradual, soft transition from opaque to transparent pixels, allowing natural compositing of this type of image with other images placed into the layout, or with other objects created within InDesign itself.

2 The transparent areas in this Photoshop image (PSD) allow the green color of the background frame to show through the edges of the hair and between the front legs of the dog.

You can modify the opacity of any placed image, regardless of whether the image itself contains transparency. Select the image with the Selection tool, and reduce the opacity in the Transparency palette. If the image frame had a stroke applied, the same opacity setting is applied to the stroke. To make the image transparent but not the stroke, select the image with the Direct Selection tool before modifying the opacity.

Besides allowing you to seamlessly composite InDesign elements with image transparency, another benefit of InDesign's support of transparent areas in placed graphics is the ability to wrap text to the contours of non-transparent pixels in the image.

1 Start by overlapping or underlapping a text frame with the placed image.

2 Then, select the image, click the Wrap Around Object Shape icon in the Text Wrap palette, (**Window > Text Wrap**) and choose Alpha Channel from the Contour Options drop-down menu in the palette.

115

WHERE IS TRANSPARENCY BEING USED?
InDesign alerts you to pages that contain transparency effects or images with native transparency by adding a checkerboard pattern to their page icons in the Pages palette.

Even if only one tiny object on a page has transparency, and nothing else on the spread does, the entire spread gets the checkerboard pattern applied by default. To help you pinpoint which elements on a spread contain transparency, target the spread and set the Flattener Preview palette to highlight Transparent Objects. All objects on the spread are grayed out, but the transparent elements have a red overlay.

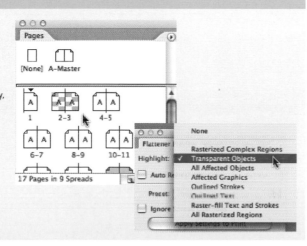

Flattening Transparency

PostScript RIPs (in other words, most printers and imagesetters) and older PDF formats (Acrobat 4 and earlier) do not support transparency. When spreads containing transparent elements are sent to a PostScript device (or exported or distilled into an Acrobat 4-compatible PDF, such as PDF/X1-a), InDesign has to flatten any transparent areas in the layout.

While you can't flatten transparency within InDesign, you can see a preview of what will be flattened on a spread by using the Flattener Preview palette (**Window > Output > Flattener Preview**). Use the Flattener Preview to see what will happen to transparent elements and to prevent transparency-related problems during printing or exporting to PDF.

Blend modes

The Transparency palette offers a number of
different blend modes that you can apply to a
selected object. A blend mode defines how colors
in a selected object (the "blend" color) will interact
with the colors of underlying objects (the "base"
color). The default blend mode, Normal, is equivalent
to "no interaction" between the blend and the base
colors—the blend colors always replace the underlying
base colors. Applying any blend mode other than
Normal to a selection automatically introduces
transparency to the spread, even if its opacity is
left at 100%.

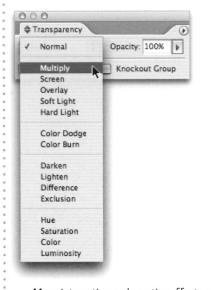

Many interesting and creative effects can be
achieved by experimenting with a selected object's
blend mode. If you also reduce the opacity of the
object—some blend modes applied to objects with
100% opacity result in overly harsh effects—even
more creative possibilities are available.

The next four pages contain a series of
illustrations showing what happens you apply each
of the 16 blend modes to elements in InDesign.
Each blend mode has been applied to the topmost
object (the blend color) in the following image pairs:
1) a gradient-filled shape at 100% opacity partially
overlapping a CMYK photograph; 2) the same
gradient-filled shape at 50% opacity overlapping
the same photograph; and 3) a text frame with
colored and black text (at 100% opacity) on top of
a gradient-filled shape.

Understanding blend modes

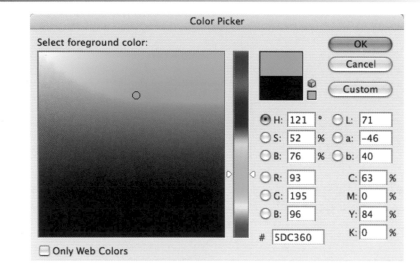

All of InDesign's blend
modes rely on some amount
of mathematical calculation,
involving the Hue,
Saturation, and Brightness
values of each pixel in the
blend color, and those of
the pixels underneath (in
the base color). While the
details of the math are
outside the scope of this
book, there are two related
considerations to keep
in mind.

Photoshop's Color Picker
provides an easy way to
understand the difference
between Hue, Saturation,
and Brightness. The

rainbow-colored vertical
bar contains Hues that the
user can choose. Each Hue
also has a certain Saturation
value (the horizontal axis of
the large colored box), and
a Brightness value (the
vertical axis of the box)
that the user chooses by
dragging the circle icon
inside the box.

First, use the correct
Transparency Blend Space
for the type of artwork
you're working with. Go
to Edit > Transparency
Blend Space and note that
the default is Document
CMYK. This is appropriate

for CMYK artwork, or files
that will be converted to
CMYK at output. If you're
creating something for
screen viewing only, choose
Document RGB. The two
Transparency Blend Spaces
create quite different
blended colors both on
screen and in final output,
because InDesign uses
different numbers for each
color mode in its blend
mode calculations.

Second, since the color
values for black and white
(or "Paper," in InDesign)
are equivalent to "absolute
0" or "absolute 1," their

presence in blend mode
math calculations sometimes
causes surprising results,
especially compared to other
colors in the same artwork.
We've included black and
white elements in the
artwork samples here to give
you an idea of how they're
affected by blend mode
changes. Similarly, applying
blend modes to solid colors
(such as the fills of the type
samples) can swing between
a small effect and a huge
effect because all the pixels
have the same color value
in the blend object.

Normal

The default blend mode for
any object in InDesign is
Normal, meaning its colors
don't affect the colors of
underlying objects. If an
object has no transparency
(100% opacity) and is set
to Normal blend mode, its
colors completely obscure
(knock out) the colors of

any objects underneath
it. If the object has some
transparency (less than
100% opacity), you'll be
able to "see through" it to
colored objects below, as
though you were looking
through a window or a lens
that's the same color as
the topmost blend object.

Multiply

The color values of the top and underlying objects are multiplied together, resulting in a darker color throughout the overlapping area, while maintaining the integrity of the colors themselves. Multiply (with black) is the default blend mode for shadows created with **Object > Drop Shadow**, because it mimics what shadows do in reality. Note how colors under the white areas of the gradient are unaffected—Multiply has no effect on white. This makes Multiply a good trick for creating the effect of a solid-to-none gradient.

Overlay

The Overlay mode is a combination of Multiply and Screen. Colors in the blend object that are darker than the base object are set to Multiply, and ones that are lighter are set to Screen. The end result is a marked increase in contrast in the underlying colors.

Hard Light

Hard Light is a stronger version of Soft Light. Like Soft Light, it's mainly concerned with the blend object's darkness and lightness, but like Overlay, it uses Multiply and Screen to create the final colors. The final result is similar to shining a harsh spotlight on the colors in the base object, using the luminosity of the blend object as the light source.

Screen

Screen mode can be thought of as the opposite of Multiply. Overlapping colors start out being multiplied together, but then the inverse of the result is applied. Because of this, Screen lightens the colors throughout the overlapping area while maintaining the integrity of the colors themselves. Screening a black color results in white.

Soft Light

Using Soft Light is like shining a diffused spotlight on the underlying colors, using the topmost object as the light source. Just as Overlay is a combination of Multiply and Screen, Soft Light is a combination of Darken and Lighten, which are more subtle blend modes. In a blend object set to Soft Light, colors with a luminosity (lightness value) greater than 50% lighten the colors in the base object. Dark colors in the blend object darken the colors in the base object.

Color Dodge

As with Screen, applying the Color Dodge mode to a blend object will always result in a lighter color. InDesign brightens the base color to reflect the blend color, heightening the contrast in the process.

Blend modes, continued

Color Burn

Applying Color Burn mode to a blend object will always result in a darker color. InDesign darkens the base color to reflect the blend color, decreasing contrast in the process.

Lighten

Just like Darken, Lighten does one-to-one pixel replacements. If a color in the blend object is lighter than the one beneath it, it stays; if it's not, the lighter color from the base object replaces it. Black elements turn white.

Exclusion

Exclusion uses the same math and methods as Difference, with one important exception: overlapping mid-range values stay in the same middle range. That means the end effect is usually lower in contrast than one created with Difference. Exclusion is often referred to as a watered-down Difference.

Darken

The Darken blend mode is interesting because InDesign doesn't do any math operations to come up with a result. Instead, it's a straightforward replacement of one color with another.

If a single pixel's color in the blend object is darker than the one beneath it, it stays; if it's not, the darker color from the base object replaces it. White elements turn black.

Difference

When you apply the Difference blend mode to a blend object, InDesign compares the brightness values of the overlapping colors and subtracts the color value of the darker pixels from the brighter pixels. If the two images are mostly mid-range color values, the end result is very dark, and often looks like a photo negative or an X-ray.

Hue

The Hue blend mode maintains the Hue (its color, basically) of the top blend object, but uses the Saturation (intensity) and Luminosity (brightness) of the base object's colors.

Saturation

This blend mode maintains the Saturation of the color values in the top blend object, but uses the Hue and Luminosity of the underlying colors.

Luminosity

The Luminosity blend mode maintains the Luminosity (brightness) of the top blend object but uses the Hue and Saturation of the underlying colors.

Color

Color applies the blend object's Hue and Saturation to the base object's Luminosity. Both the Color and Hue blend modes are useful for "colorizing" grayscale or monotone images underneath.

Applying transparency to grouped objects

1 By default, it makes no difference if you group items (**Object > Group**) with different opacities or blend modes applied to them.

Each item in a group interacts with (its transparency is affected by) the other overlapping items in the group, in addition to any non-grouped objects beneath.

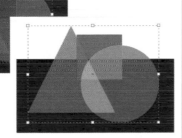

2 To stop the grouped items's opacity settings from affecting each other, while maintaining the way each individual item's opacity affects non-grouped items beneath, select the group and turn on the Knockout Group checkbox in the Transparency palette.

(If you don't see this option, select Show Options from the Transparency palette menu.) With Knockout Group checked, items in a group will knock out (completely obscure) each other, but they will overprint non-grouped items beneath according to their opacity.

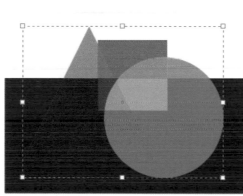

3 If items in the group have a blending mode (other than Normal) applied, you can isolate the interacting members of the group, preventing non-grouped items below the items from being affected. To do this, select the group and turn on the Isolate

Blending checkbox in the Transparency palette.

Each member of the group here has had both an opacity change and a blend mode applied, but neither Knockout Group nor Isolate Blending is turned on.

4 This is the same group with Isolate Blending turned on (Knockout Group is off—note how the background blue color is still affected by the Opacity settings of the group's objects).

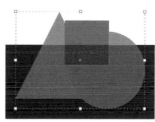

5 Finally, here's the same group with both Isolate Blending and Knockout Group turned on in the Transparency palette.

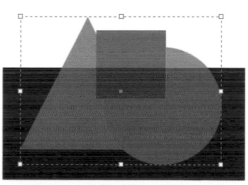

Drop shadows

Drop Shadows applied to InDesign page elements add a pleasing three-dimensional effect to a layout, because they make it look like the object is floating a little above the other page elements, or the page itself. The shadow is a raster element that becomes completely transparent at its outermost edges. Page elements that are overlapped by another element's shadow can still be seen through the shadow, just as in real life.

Adding drop shadows to text

Our premium line of postcards feature photography of beautiful, natural locales. *Shadows at Sunset* captures warm palettes of Mother Nature's rainbow as she falls asleep. Breathtaking vistas beckon in the *Mountain Highs* series. If you're looking for cool blues and a serene mindset, the *Mellow Reverie* series is your ticket. Another outstanding

1 All of InDesign's Transparency effects, including Drop Shadow, are frame-based. To apply a drop shadow to text, select the text frame with the Selection tool, and turn on the Drop Shadow checkbox in **Object > Drop Shadow**. All the text in the frame becomes shadowed yet is still fully editable with the Type tool.

Our premium line of postcards feature photography of beautiful, natural locales. *Shadows at Sunset* captures warm palettes of Mother Nature's rainbow as she falls asleep. Breathtaking vistas beckon in the *Mountain High* series. If you're looking for cool blues and a serene mindset, the *Mellow Reverie* series is your ticket. Another outstanding

2 The **Object > Drop Shadow** menu command is grayed out when you select text with the Type tool, so you'll have to use a workaround if you want only certain words in a frame to be shadowed, leaving the rest untouched.
   One method is to cut the text selection and paste it into its own frame, then paste the frame back into the text flow as an inline text frame. Select the inline frame with the Selection tool to apply the drop shadow. The text is still editable within its frame.

graphy of beautiful, s. *Shadows at Sunset* ca f Mother Nature's rainl

3 Another way is to convert text selected with the Type tool to outlines (**Type > Convert to Outlines**), though you lose the ability to edit the outlined text. InDesign automatically embeds the outlined text as a grouped inline image. You can then select the inline image with the Direct Selection tool and apply a drop shadow.
   Both of these methods are useful when applying other transparency effects to text selections as well.

Setting options in the Drop Shadow dialog box

1 Select one or more image frames, text frames, or lines with the Selection tool, choose **Object > Drop Shadow**, and turn on the Drop Shadow checkbox. If you turn on the Preview checkbox, you can see the effects of your settings in the Drop Shadow dialog box as you make them, without having to close it and open it again.

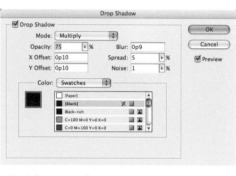

2 The default setting for a drop shadow applies a soft shadow at 75% opacity to the selection.

3 To allow more of the background elements to show through, reduce the shadow's opacity. This 30% opacity shadow may seem too light at first. The problem is that the Blur is still at the default measure of 0p5 (we're using picas, but the measurement will be in the units set in InDesign's preferences), and the Spread is still at zero percent. Blur and Spread work together to define the shadow's size (Blur) and softness (Spread).

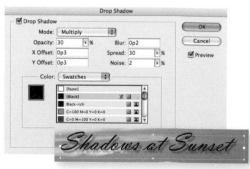

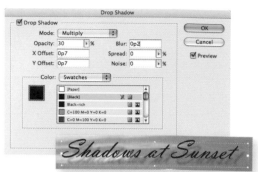

4 To tighten up the shadow, reducing the amount of space that the shadow has to fade out, reduce the Blur.

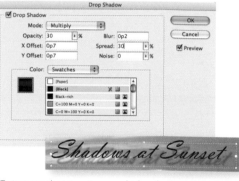

5 To increase the intensity of the shadow, increase the Spread percentage. The higher the Spread, the lower the Blur radius at the edges of the shadow.

6 To bring the shadow closer to the type, so the headline doesn't appear to float so high over the image, reduce the measures in the X Offset and Y Offset fields. These position the drop shadow relative to the selected object—positive numbers place the shadow to the right and below the object, negative numbers place the shadow to the left and above. Add a small percentage of Noise to add texture, and make the shadow appear more natural (less "computer-perfect").

Maintaining shadow consistency with an object style

Just as you can save a combination of text formatting options in a Paragraph or Character Style, you can save your custom Drop Shadow settings in an Object Style. Clicking on an Object Style to apply a shadow to a selection is much faster than editing every field of the Drop Shadow dialog box each time. It also ensures that your drop shadows are consistent throughout a spread, reinforcing the illusion of a single light source.

1 The easiest way to create an Object Style is to first create a source frame. Modify an example text frame or image frame with the appropriate menu and palette commands to get it to look the way you want. Our source is the final "Shadows at Sunset" frame from the previous example.

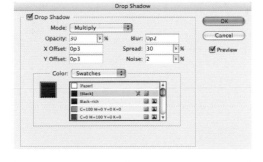

2 Then, with the shadowed frame selected, create a new Object Style: Alt/Option+click on the Create New Style icon at the bottom of the Object Style palette, or choose New Object Style from the Object Style palette menu, or double-click on the icon to the left of the Object Style drop-down menu in the Control palette.

The new style assumes the same settings as the selected object. Name the style and turn off all options (uncheck their boxes at the left) other than Drop Shadow & Feather, to restrict the style from

modifying anything other than a selected object's shadow. Of course, you can keep some of the other settings enabled if you want the style to modify those too. Click OK when you're done.

3 To apply your new Object Style, select one or more frames of the same type (text frames or graphic frames), and click the name of the style in the Object Style palette.

In this example, we've created two object styles: one that applies a custom drop shadow to the postcard images; and one that applies the drop shadow settings we created above to the postcard headlines.

4 Modifying the Drop Shadow settings in the Object Style allows you to quickly and consistently achieve different looks. Here we've changed the settings in the postcard shadows object style to a hard-edged shadow (100% Opacity and Spread, o Blur), and softened the shadow and increased the Offsets of the Shadow Text Object Style.

121

Applying drop shadows to vectors and clipping paths

1 InDesign applies drop shadows to the contours of a placed vector image or an embedded PostScript clipping path, as long as the frame has a fill color of None.

2 When the image frame is filled with a color, the shadow appears around the frame itself.

3 If the shadow appears around the frame boundaries even though the frame is filled with None (and you're sure the artwork doesn't contain an opaque background), it might be a display issue. Increase the Display Performance for both Vector Graphics and Transparency in InDesign's preferences.

4 If you're working with EPS files, you can ensure they have a high-resolution preview by opting to Rasterize the PostScript in Show Import Options when you place the file.

Feather

eathering an object means fading its edges so they make a subtle transition into complete transparency. Items behind the feathered object appear seamlessly composited with the image because the transparent edge pixels of the faded object allow background colors to show through. Compositing aside, feathering can also be used for special effects that stand on their own.

Tip

ACCURATE FEATHER PREVIEWS

For the most accurate screen previews of Feathering effects, make sure your Preferences for Display Performance (of Transparency, specifically) are set to High Quality.

Applying Feather settings

1 You can apply a feather to any object that you can select with InDesign's Selection tool. After a selection is made, choose **Object > Feather** and turn on the Feather checkbox. Turn on the Preview checkbox to see the effects of your Feather settings on the selection as you make them.

Feather Width is the distance between the object's current opacity and complete transparency, as measured from the edges of the image content inward. If the frame crops the perimeter of an image (as in the two photos below) or is filled with a background color, the Feather Width is measured from the edges of the frame inward.

2 The Corners options enable you to fine-tune how InDesign applies the transparency fade to the corners of your image. Sharp keeps the corners clearly defined; Rounded softens them, sometimes quite severely for very sharp corners. Diffused is the method you'll probably use most often, as it most closely mimics traditional Photoshop feathering. The Feather Width for each of these images of a campground lake is the same—45pt. The first lake photo is set to Diffuse, while the second is set to Sharp.

3 Noise breaks up the strictly linear fade to transparency by adding random pixel artifacts from the underlying colors throughout the transition. In the case of Feather, Noise is also useful for preventing banding, especially if the object being feathered is a solid color. A Noise percentage of between 2 and 5 is all that's usually needed. Apply larger amounts of Noise for a "dissolving" effect.

The original star-shaped frame on the left does not have a Feather applied. Each of the four duplicates to the right are feathered to various degrees.

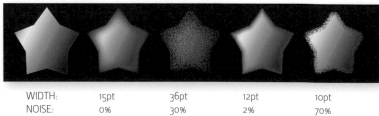

WIDTH:	15pt	36pt	12pt	10pt
NOISE:	0%	30%	2%	70%

Feathering text

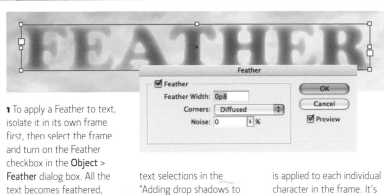

1 To apply a Feather to text, isolate it in its own frame first, then select the frame and turn on the Feather checkbox in the **Object > Feather** dialog box. All the text becomes feathered, yet remains fully editable. To feather a selection of text in a frame, leaving the remainder of the text in the frame unfeathered, follow the instructions for isolating

text selections in the "Adding drop shadows to text" section on page 120.

When you apply a Feather to a text frame with the default background fill of None (as in this example), the Feather Width measure

is applied to each individual character in the frame. It's best to use thick letterforms and small Feather Width settings to keep the text readable. Increase the Feather Width for a "ghostly" effect.

2 If the text frame has a background fill, the feathering is applied to the boundaries of the frame background and the edges of any characters that fall within the Feather Width measure, going inward. To apply the

feather evenly to all four sides of the text content, as shown here, select the text frame and choose Fit Frame to Content from the **Object > Fitting** menu.

If you like this effect but don't want a background

color behind the type, fill the frame with the Paper color from the Swatches palette. InDesign still counts the Paper fill color as an actual color, and so restricts its feathering to the edge of the frame itself.

3 To make the opaque white background drop out when it's on top of other objects, select the frame with the Selection tool and choose Multiply from the Transparency palette. Multiply makes white colors turn transparent.

Note that in this example, the text frame was enlarged and the text horizontally

centered within it, causing the Feather to only affect the top edge of the text characters.

4 Experiment with Noise and background fills to achieve other interesting Feather effects.

Feathering transparent art

As with text frames, Feather will affect the edges of image content (its non-transparent areas) as long as the frame itself has a fill of None.

1 Here, a Photoshop image with transparent areas (its background was hidden by a layer mask) has been placed in InDesign, partially overlapping an existing frame filled with a tan color. The image frame has an 8pt black stroke applied to it from the Control palette. A Feather was applied to the image with a Feather Width of 18pt—note how it also feathers the stroke—and its Corners were set to Sharp to maintain the integrity of the thin, angular ties and struts in the roller coaster.

2 This Illustrator image was placed on top of a frame filled with Black, and a simple Feather applied.

Fixing clipping paths with Feather

Clipping paths in placed images are by definition hard edged. You can soften the edges for a more natural transition to the background by applying a small feather to the object. The feather is applied to the edge of the image as defined by its clipping path.

1 If the clipping path wasn't perfectly drawn, or you've used **Object > Clipping Path > Detect Edges** to create a clipping path from within InDesign, then some of the silhouetted image's background may show through at the edges.

2 Applying a small amount of Feather fades these artifacts into transparency.

PAGES AND DOCUMENTS

Bridge

Adobe Bridge is a new addition to CS2. It's a powerful and sophisticated file browser and asset manager that provides a link between all of the Creative Suite programs. Bridge takes over from Photoshop's File Browser, while providing the same functions in InDesign and the other Creative Suite applications—and it can do a lot more besides. To launch Bridge from InDesign, click the Bridge button on the Control Palette.

Go to Bridge (Cmd–click for a maximised view, Cmd-Option–click to open a new Bridge window).

Tip

SNIPPETS

Snippets are groups of objects which can be dragged between InDesign and the Bridge. Snippets are a little like library objects, only better. To create a snippet, select multiple page elements, or a group, and drag them into the Bridge content window. To place snippets, drag and drop in the opposite direction. You'll find it easier to do this with the Bridge in compact mode—click the button on the top right. There's a more detailed look at Snippets on page 155.

126

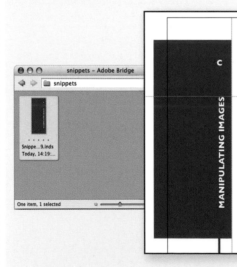

Using the Bridge Center

1 The Bridge Center provides access to recent files and folders; the Adobe Stock Photos service; color management settings, help, tips, and tricks; and an RSS feed of Adobe Studio articles, events, and tutorials. You can also save and load file groups—groups of documents created in different Creative Suite applications.

2 Click the Folders tab on the left to navigate the folder hierarchy on your hard drive. You can toggle between the four view options—Thumbnail, Filmstrip, Details, and Versions and Alternates—using the buttons in the bottom-right corner. Clicking on a document displays its preview and metadata or keywords. You can preview all pages in a PDF file and select one to place on an InDesign page using the buttons or page field at the bottom of the Preview window. Drag frequently used folders into the Favorites pane, or Right/Ctrl+click them and select Add to Favorites.

3 You can use Bridge to search for documents using criteria such as filename, date created, document kind, and description. Bridge also allows the searching of document metadata. Select Find from the Edit menu or press Ctrl/Cmd+F to open the Find dialog box. Select a location to search from the Look in drop-down menu, and check the Include All Subfolders box.

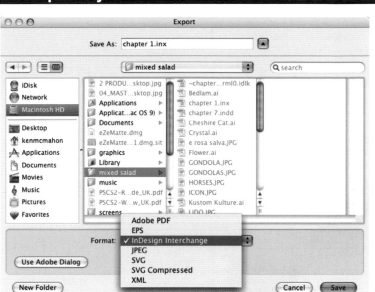

4 In the Criteria section, select All Metadata from the first drop-down menu, Contains from the second, and enter your search term in the Search field. Click the plus icon next to the Search field to add more search criteria. The Match drop-down is used to determine

if any (logic OR) or all (logic AND) of the search terms are required. InDesign includes font and color information in document metadata, so you can, for example, search for all InDesign files containing the color "Fire Dept Red," or the font Gill Sans Ultra Bold.

1 InDesign CS2 maintains backward compatibility with InDesign CS by means of the INX (InDesign Interchange) format. Obviously, this doesn't mean that InDesign CS will support new CS2 features such as Object styles and imported PSD files with layers. Page elements using these and other CS2 features are converted into an InDesign CS-compatible format. For example, Object styles are stripped out, but the individual attributes are applied—so the object's appearance is unchanged.

2 Why bother saving InDesign CS2 files in INX format if you don't intend to open them in InDesign CS? Well, INX files are much smaller—as little as one tenth the size of INDD files. So, if disk space is at a premium, or you intend to e-mail a file, export it as an INX file rather than saving as INDD.

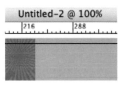

3 There are some minor drawbacks with INX. Files open as untitled documents, rather than with the original filename, and they also take longer to open than INDD files, so it's worth keeping an INDD backup.

4 To export an INX file, select **File > Export** or press Ctrl/Cmd+E. In the File Export dialog box, select InDesign Interchange from

the Format drop-down menu and click Save. You can, of course open an INX file back into InDesign CS2. In that case, all of the

InDesign CS2 features are retained—Object Styles, Anchored Objects, and footnotes are all intact.

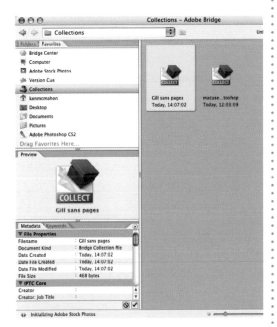

5 Saving search criteria as a collection enables you to repeat the same search without having to re-enter all the details. Click Save As Collection, and enter a name in the dialog box. To re-run the search, click on Collections in the Favorites

pane and double-click the collection you just saved. If you check the Start Search From Current Folder box, the search runs on the currently selected Folder rather than the folder specified in the original search.

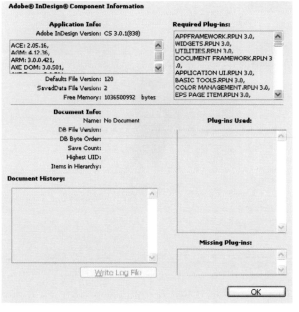

5 To open INX files in InDesign CS, you need to have installed the InDesign or InCopy CS 3.0.1 April 2005 update. To find out if the update is installed on a Mac, hold down the Command

key and select **InDesign > About InDesign**. On a Windows PC, hold down Control and select **Help > About InDesign**. If the update is installed, the line under the Application

Info heading should read "Adobe InDesign Version: CS 3.0.1(838)." If it doesn't, get the update from the downloads page on the Adobe website at www.adobe.com.

Workspaces

InDesign CS2 has so many palettes that if you displayed them all you wouldn't be able to see the document you were trying to work on. But many of those palettes are rarely used, and even those that are in frequent use are associated with specific tasks, so if you're doing something else, they don't need to be visible.

Collapsing and closing unused palettes helps reduce screen clutter, and you can avoid spending all your time on screen housekeeping by making use of workspaces—saved screen layouts that can be recalled from the Window > Workspace menu.

Default workspace

Display the default workspace by selecting Window > Workspace > [Default]. This collapses all but the Pages palette to the side of the screen, and displays the toolbox to the left and the Control palette at the top of the document window.

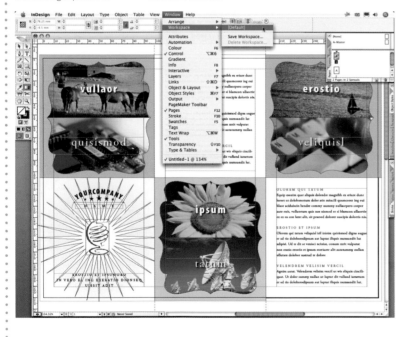

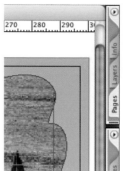

1 To create a workspace for text editing, first get rid of what you don't need from the Default workspace. Click the tab on the Pages palette group to collapse it, then Alt/Option+drag the Object Styles palette group to float it.

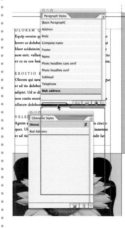

2 Drag the Paragraph Styles palette from its palette group and drop it elsewhere, so that it occupies its own palette. Do the same with the Character Styles palette, but drag it to the bottom of the Paragraph styles palette until a thick black line appears. The two palettes are now docked—linked together with both still visible (as opposed to the usual grouped arrangement where you can see only the palette at the front, with the rest displayed as tabs).

3 Depending on whether you make much use of the Object Styles and Swatches palettes while text editing, you can either turn them back into collapsed tabs by Alt/Option+dragging the palette group back to the tab bar at the edge of the screen, or close them. There are no hard and fast rules here, it's mainly down to personal preference.

4 Select Window > Text Wrap, or Ctrl/Cmd+Alt/Option+W to display the Text Wrap palette. Again, depending on personal preference and usage requirements, either leave it floating or collapse it by dragging it to the right or left side of the screen.

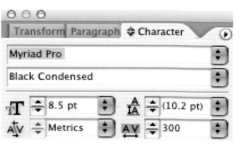

5 From the Type menu, select Character, or press Ctrl/Cmd+T to display the Character, Paragraph, and Transform palette group. This palette group duplicates a lot of the functions available on the Control palette, but you can easily toggle it on and off (along with the docked Paragraph Styles and Character Styles palettes) using the palette button on the Control palette. If you prefer, collapse it to a side tab underneath the Text Wrap palette (Alt/Option+drag to collapse the whole palette group, rather than individual palettes).

6 Display the Glyphs pane by selecting **Windows** > **Type & Tables** > **Glyphs** and, according to your preference, group it, collapse it, or leave it floating. Then Select **Window** > **Type & Tables** > **Table** and put the Table palette in a side tab somewhere convenient on the left or right of the screen.

7 Finally, go to **Window** > **Workspace** > **Save Workspace**, call the workspace "Text Editing," and click OK. Return to the Default workspace by selecting **Window** >

Workspace > **[Default]**. The Text Editing workspace now appears on the Workspace sub-menu. To recall it, select **Window** > **Workspace** > **Text Editing**.

Tip

AMENDING WORKSPACES

After working with a workspace for a time, you may decide to make adjustments. If, for example, you tend to use a small Swatches palette, or don't make much use of Object Styles, there would be room on the right to add one or more of the floating palettes to a collapsible tab. Resave amended workspaces with the same name as the original, and click OK to replace the existing one.

A workspace for drawing

Devising a workspace for drawing is, as always, a compromise between having the tools readily available and maximizing the work area. Here, the Stroke, Color, Gradient, and Transparency palettes are docked and floating. The Transform, Align, and Pathfinder palettes occupy one palette group on a collapsible tab on the left. On the right, the Navigator palette has been added to the Pages palette group, and the Swatches and Object styles palettes are on collapsible tabs.

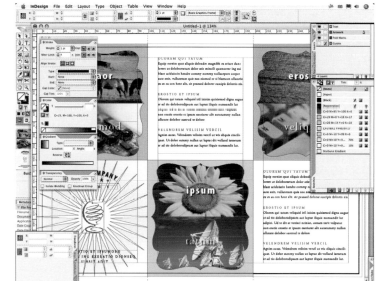

A workspace for print design

Create additional workspaces in the same manner by displaying and positioning the palettes required for the task in hand. This workspace for print design organizes the Flattener Preview, Separations Preview, Trap presets, and Attributes palettes into side tabs on the left of the screen. Other print-related palettes, including the Text Wrap, Stroke, Styles, Swatches, and Links palettes are similarly organized on the right.

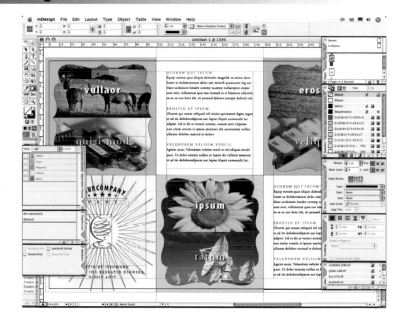

Tip

ASSIGNING KEYBOARD SHORTCUTS TO WORKSPACES

You can switch between workspaces more quickly by assigning keyboard shortcuts to them. Shortcuts can be defined for the first five workspaces on the Windows > Workspace menu. Select Edit > Keyboard Shortcuts and choose a set from the drop-down menu, or define a new one. Select Window Menu from the

Product Area Drop-down menu then scroll down to the bottom of the Commands list and click Workspace: Load 1st Workspace. Click in the New Shortcut field and press the shortcut keys (e.g. Ctrl+Shift+D), then click Assign. Define keyboard shortcuts for additional workspaces in the same way, and when you're done, click OK.

Document setup

The first step in creating a new InDesign CS2 publication is the New Document dialog box, which appears when you select File > New > Document (Ctrl/Cmd+N). This window is a combination of the Document setup and Margins and columns dialog boxes. The only option that isn't available once the document is created is the Master text frame checkbox, which adds a text frame to the A-Master page—though you can of course do this manually later.

Creating new presets

1 Enter all the settings in the New Document dialog as though you were creating a new document. Click Save Preset, name the preset, and click OK. The new preset is added to the Document Preset menu and automatically selected.

2 You can also create and edit document presets by selecting **File > Document Presets > Define**. The Document Preset dialog box lists existing presets and their settings. To edit an existing preset, click the Edit button. The Edit Document Preset window works in a very similar way to the New Document window. Even if you don't make much use of presets, it's worth editing the Default to reflect your most commonly used setup—changing the page size from A4 to Letter, for example.
To quickly create a new preset-based document, select **File > Document Presets** and choose the desired preset from the sub-menu.

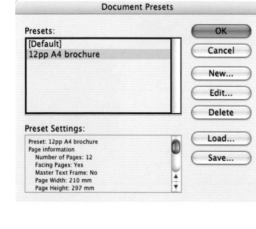

The New Document window

A Load a previously saved document preset.

B Enter the number of pages in the new document. Check Facing Pages for conventional left-right page spreads; uncheck it if you're producing single-page double-sided documents, concertina-folded DL leaflets, etc.

C Select from preset document sizes or enter custom width and height values. The units are those selected in Units & Increments preferences. The orientation buttons are interactive—if your custom width is bigger than the height, then the landscape button is selected. Click the deselected button to switch the dimensions.

D Enter page columns and gutter width here. These settings are applied to the A-Master page. The column settings will also apply to the Master Text Frame if that option is selected.

E Specify independent top, bottom, left, and right margins, or click the link button to make all the margins equal.

F Press the More Options button to enter bleed and slug settings. If necessary, you can change these later in the Document Setup dialog box. Click the link buttons to make the bleed and slug areas equal on all sides.

G Saving frequently used new document settings as a preset adds them to the Document Preset menu, allowing you to create new documents at a stroke.

H Click Cancel to exit the dialog without creating the new document. Alt/Option+click the button to reset everything to the defaults.

130

Changing document settings

1 Select **File > Document Setup** to make changes to page settings for an open document. The Document Setup dialog is virtually identical to the New Document Setup dialog, without the margins and columns settings.

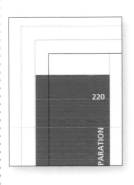

2 Reducing the number of pages will delete pages from the end of the document.

3 Click the More Options button to enter bleed and slug settings, which may not have been available at the time the document was created.

4 Bleed and slug areas are shown in the document window as red and blue rectangles. You can't create a bleed on the inside edges of facing pages.

Page sizes

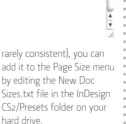

```
; NEW DOCUMENT SIZES FILE

; Version number:
1

; OVERVIEW
; This file enables you to define custom page sizes for documents. For
; more information on this feature, please refer to the product help
; documentation.

; INSTRUCTIONS
; Blank lines and lines in this file starting with a semicolon will be
; ignored.

; To add a custom page size, add the following text at the end this
; file:

; Preset Name    Width      Height

; For example, you can enter:
; Certificate    11"        9"
```

If you routinely use a custom page size, but don't want to define a preset using it (this may be the case if other settings, such as margins or columns, are rarely consistent), you can add it to the Page Size menu by editing the New Doc Sizes.txt file in the InDesign CS2/Presets folder on your hard drive.

Margins and Columns

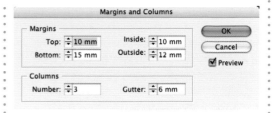

When you set up margins and columns for a new document, the settings are applied to the A-Master spread. Selecting **Layout > Margins and Columns** for an open document applies the changes to the pages selected in the Pages palette. This makes it possible to have different margin and column settings within the same document. For facing pages, margins are defined as inside and outside; otherwise, they are left and right.

Tip

CHANGING UNITS
The units displayed in the New Document dialog box are those chosen in the Units and Increments preferences. To change them, select InDesign > Preferences > Units & Increments with no documents open. You can enter alternate units by specifying them. For example, if the default units are millimeters and you want to specify 12 pica margins, type in 12p; for inches, type in 1in. The value you enter will be converted to the current default unit.

New Document

Document Preset: [Custom]	OK
Number of Pages: 1 ☑ Facing Pages ☐ Master Text Frame	Cancel
	Save Preset...
	Fewer Options

Page Size: A4
Width: 210 mm   Orientation:
Height: 297 mm

Columns
Number: 1   Gutter: 4.233 mm

Margins
Top: 50.8 mm   Inside: 12p
Bottom: 50.8 mm   Outside: 12.7 mm

Bleed and Slug

	Top	Bottom	Inside	Outside
Bleed:	0 mm	0 mm	0 mm	0 mm
Slug:	0 mm	0 mm	0 mm	0 mm

131

Managing pages

The Pages palette shows an icon-based view of all the pages in a document and any master pages that you have set up. Though you can use the scroll bars to move around within a document, the Pages palette provides a far more efficient means of navigation. This palette is also used to add and remove pages, rearrange page order, copy pages between documents, apply master pages, and to add page numbers and create sections.

The Pages palette also controls the document layout. Most publications start on a right-hand page and consist of double-page spreads, finishing on a left. The Pages palette can be used to create multiple-page spreads (called island spreads in InDesign) of up to ten pages. From the Pages palette you can configure InDesign to maintain island spreads, or to reflow them when pages are added or removed from the document.

The Pages palette is an indispensable tool, and you'll probably want to keep it displayed all the time, but it can be toggled on and off with the F12 key.

Default View

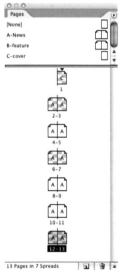

In its default view, the Pages palette shows master pages at the top with document pages below, but you can change its appearance by selecting Palette options from the Palette menu. The page icons carry the prefix letter of the master page on which they are based; if there is no letter, the [None] master is applied, which contains only margin guides. The checkerboard pattern indicates that spreads include transparent objects.

Page navigation

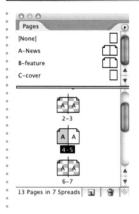

The simplest way to move around a document using the Pages palette is to double-click on a page. Several things happen when you do this: the page is displayed in the center of the document window; its icon is highlighted in the Pages palette, indicating that the page is selected; and the page numbers below the spread are also highlighted, indicating that this is the target spread.

Adding pages

1 To add a page, target the spread preceding the insertion point and click the Create new page button at the bottom right of the Pages palette. If you want to insert multiple pages or insert a page between pages of an existing spread, select Insert Pages from the Pages palette menu. The Insert Pages dialog box allows you to specify the number of pages, the insertion point, and the master page on which to base the new pages.

2 Another way to add pages is to drag a master page icon into the pages section of the palette, and drop it in the required location where the black insertion bar appears.

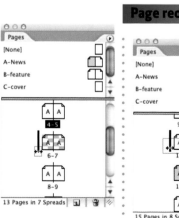

Deleting pages

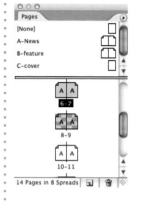

1 First, select the pages. Ctrl/Cmd+click to add non-contiguous pages to the selection, or Shift+click to select a block of pages.

2 Drag the pages to the Trash icon at the bottom right of the Pages palette, or simply click the Trash icon to delete them. If the deleted pages contain text boxes that are part of a linked sequence which includes undeleted pages, the text will reflow on those pages.

Page control and island spreads

Two items on the Pages palette menu—Keep Spread Together, and Allow Pages to Shuffle—control what happens when you insert, delete, and rearrange pages.

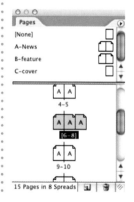

Allow Pages to Shuffle is the default setting, and preserves the double-page spread structure of the entire document. If turned off, it will allow the creation of island spreads and will preserve them when pages before and after them are added or removed.

When Keep Spread Together is applied to selected spreads, square brackets appear around the page numbers as shown.

Keep Spread Together determines what happens to specific spreads; Allow Pages to Shuffle determines what happens to pages in the rest of the document.

Page reordering

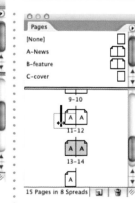

To reorder pages, simply select the pages you want to move, and drag and drop them in the new location.

You should exercise caution when moving pages in this way, as it can lead to unexpected reflows and pagination problems. If you do need to reorder pages within a document, move spreads, rather than single pages, wherever possible.

Copying pages between documents

1 Open both documents and drag the selected page icons from the Pages palette of the active document into the target document window.

2 The duplicated pages are added to the end of the target document.

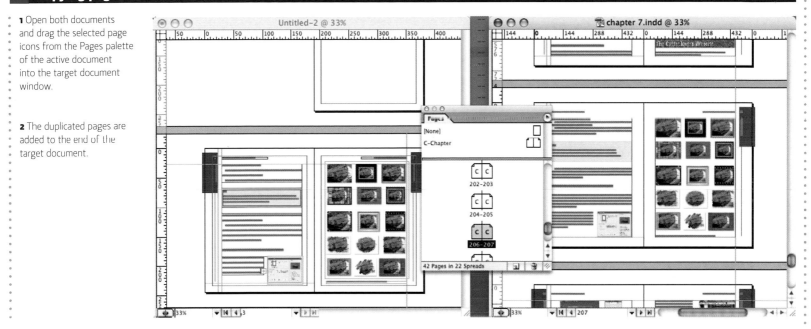

Duplicating pages

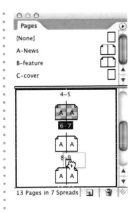

1 Select the page, or range of pages, and choose Duplicate Spread from the palette menu to add the duplicated pages to the end of the document. Dragging the pages onto the New Page button does the same thing. If you hold down the Alt/Option key, you can drag and duplicate selected pages to a new location in the Pages palette.

2 Whichever method you use, text threads from duplicated objects to other pages are broken, but the threads within the duplicated pages remain intact, as do those on the original pages.

Controlling master page items

| Insert Pages... |
| Move Pages... |
| New Master... |
| Duplicate Spread |
| Delete Spread |
| Select Unused Masters |
| Master Options... |
| Apply Master to Pages... |
| Save as Master |
| Override All Master Page Items ⌥⇧⌘L |
| Remove All Local Overrides |
| Detach All Objects from Master |
| Keep Spread Together |
| Hide Master Items |
| ✓ Allow Pages to Shuffle |
| Palette Options... |
| Numbering & Section Options... |
| Spread Flattening ▸ |

You can control the appearance and behavior of master page items from the Pages palette menu. Override All Master Page Items turns master page items into editable page items without breaking their association with the master page. Detach All Objects from Master breaks the association between overridden objects and their original master page items. Remove All Local Overrides returns modified master page objects to their original state. Obviously, this can't be done if you've already detached them. Each of these commands can be applied to individual objects as well as pages or spreads.

Tip

SELECTING AND TARGETING It's important to understand the difference between selected and targeted pages and spreads in the Pages palette. The page numbers of the target spread are reversed, and the page number of the target spread also appears in the page number field at the bottom left of the document window. The target spread may or may

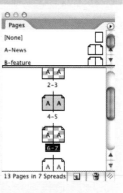

not be displayed in the document window—you'll know if it is, because for all but the target spread the rulers are grayed out.

To select a page, click its page icon. To select a spread, click the page numbers below it. To target a spread and display it in the document window, double-click the page numbers below it.

Selected spreads have reversed-out page icons. Here, pages 4-5 are selected, but 6-7 is the target spread (there can only be one target spread). The target spread is the one on which pasted and placed items appear. Select a spread, or range of spreads, to move delete or duplicate pages, or change page attributes such as master pages and master page overrides.

133

Page numbering

Automatic page numbering is the kind of feature you would expect to find in even the most basic page layout software. By adding Auto Page Number characters to master pages and inserting Next Page Number and Previous Page Number as special characters, you can drastically reduce the amount of work involved in paginating InDesign documents. InDesign CS2 provides even more advanced control, facilitating the automatic numbering of pages in long and complex documents.

It's possible to create independently numbered sections within a document, add a prefix and section marker text to page numbers and other page elements, and define a numbering style. Typically, numbering and section options are used to differentiate sections of a long document, such as introductions, inserts, and appendices.

Start Page Numbering at

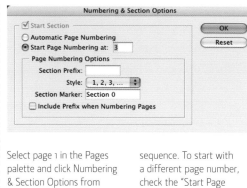

Select page 1 in the Pages palette and click Numbering & Section Options from the palette menu. With Automatic Page Numbering selected, the first page is page 1 and subsequent pages are numbered in sequence. To start with a different page number, check the "Start Page Numbering at" button and enter a value. Bear in mind that in a facing page document, right-hand pages are always odd.

New Section

You can begin a new section anywhere in a document. Select the page where you want the section to begin, choose Numbering & Section Options from the palette menu, and in the New Section dialog box enter the start page number of the new section.

Adding the Auto Page Number character

1 To add the automatic page number character to a master page, create a text box, Ctrl/Cmd+click the box, and select **Insert Special Character > Auto Page Number**. Or, from the keyboard, press Ctrl/Cmd+Alt/Option+Shift+N.

2 On master pages, the character appears as an A. On pages to which this master is applied, the page number will depend on the Numbering & Section Options.

Adding a section prefix

The section prefix—Sec:1—is automatically added for you, but you can overwrite it with anything you like, as long as it's no longer than five characters. Check the "Include Prefix when Numbering Pages" box to display the prefix before the automatic page number.

Adding a section marker

It's also possible to add a more descriptive section marker. You can use the section marker for a chapter title or other section description, such as Appendix, or Glossary. Either the section prefix, the Section marker, or both can be displayed in front of the page number. The Section marker is more flexible, though, and can be included in other page elements.

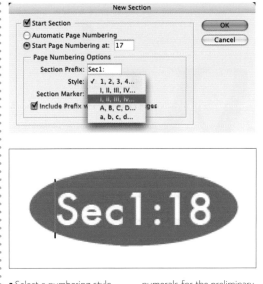

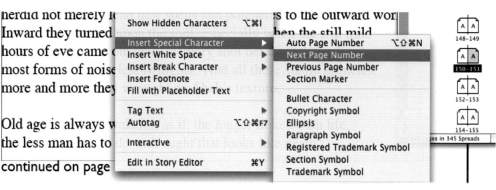

1 Select a numbering style from the drop-down menu. There are four style options available, from alphabetical to capital and lower case numerals. You might, for example, use roman numerals for the preliminary pages of a book.

When the "Include Prefix when Numbering Pages" box is checked, the prefix appears in front of the automatic page number.

2 If you want to include the section marker as well as, or instead of, the section prefix, add the section marker special character in front of the auto page number character on the master page. Right/Ctrl+click and select **Insert Special Character > Section Marker**.

This appears on the master page and all pages to which it is applied as "Section" until you define a section marker. If you intend to use both the prefix and marker, then include a space or another separator character at the end of the marker.

When added manually, continuation lines of the form "continued on page x" and "continued from page x" can lead to errors if they are overlooked when pagination changes are made.

InDesign provides two special characters—Next Page Number and Previous Page Number—that help to avoid this by automatically inserting the page number of corresponding linked text boxes.

2 Navigate to the page on which the story continues, and create another new text box at the beginning of the story continuation. Enter the "continued from page" text followed by the Previous Page Number special character. As before, ensure that the continuation frame touches or overlaps the story frame.

You may want to group the continuation and story frames to maintain their relative positions if the layout changes.

If the pagination changes or either section of the story moves, the continuation lines will automatically update to display the correct page number.

1 To use this feature, create a new text frame at the end of the story to be continued, type in "continued on page," Right/Ctrl+click, and select **Insert Special Character > Next Page Number**. Position the continuation frame so that it touches or overlaps the story, and the number of the continuation page (the page which contains the next threaded frame of the story) appears.

> continued from page 151
>
> Among sea-commanders, the old greybeards will oftenest leave their berths to visit the night-cloaked deck.
> It was so with Ahab; only that now, of late, he seemed so much to live in the open air, that truly speaking, his visits

135

Tip

USING A SECTION MARKER TO CREATE RUNNING HEADS

Most people create repeating elements such as running heads and folios on master pages, but in complex structured documents (technical manuals, for example), this might require the creation of many master pages—one for each section. One way around this is to create a single master page incorporating the section marker as a running head. Then all you need do is edit the section marker field in the Numbering and Section Options dialog box.

Navigation

To work productively in InDesign CS2, you need to know your way around. Layout work requires a constantly changing document view—one moment closely focussed on small detail, the next zoomed out to provide an overall view. In addition to moving around within a page or spread, you need to be able to move efficiently back and forth through documents.

InDesign CS2 provides a raft of navigation tools that make this task possible. The key to mastering them is to familiarize yourself with the keyboard shortcuts for the most commonly used navigation functions, such as zooming and page navigation.

The View menu

Overprint Preview	⌥⇧⌘Y
Proof Setup	▶
Proof Colors	
Zoom In	⌘=
Zoom Out	⌘−
Fit Page in Window	⌘0
Fit Spread in Window	⌥⌘0
Actual Size	⌘1
Entire Pasteboard	⌥⇧⌘0
Screen Mode	▶
Display Performance	▶
Structure	▶
Hide Hyperlinks	
Show Text Threads	⌥⌘Y
Show Frame Edges	⌘H
Hide Rulers	⌘R
Grids & Guides	▶
Story Editor	▶

The View menu contains a variety of zoom presets. Most experienced users, however, will use the many keyboard shortcuts that InDesign offers.

With the exception of Fit Page and Fit Spread, these View commands center on the currently selected object, or, if no object is selected, on the center of the current view.

InDesign CS2 also contains a very handy shortcut for quickly switching between zoom levels. By pressing Ctrl/Cmd+Alt/Option+2, the view is toggled between the previous and the current zoom level.

Fit page in window	**Ctrl/Cmd+0**
Fit spread in window	**Alt/Option+Ctrl/Cmd+0**
Actual size	**Ctrl/Cmd+1**
200 percent	**Ctrl/Cmd+2**
400 percent	**Ctrl/Cmd+4**
50 percent	**Ctrl/Cmd+5**
Zoom in	**Ctrl/Cmd+=**
Zoom out	**Ctrl/Cmd+−**

The Navigator palette

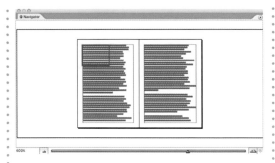

The often-ignored Navigator palette is a useful tool for quickly finding your way around a spread, particularly when working at high magnification. When your exact position on the page isn't obvious, a quick glance at the Navigator palette will tell you exactly where you are. Display the Navigator palette by selecting **Window > Object & Layout > Navigator**.

In default mode, the Navigator displays the active spread. The Red rectangle represents the current field of view. Grab it and move it around the thumbnail view to move around the spread—when you release the red rectangle, the new view is displayed in the main document window. Zoom in and out using either the slider or the buttons at the bottom of the palette. Alternatively, you can enter a value in the numeric magnification field.

View All Spreads

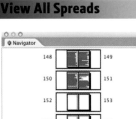

By selecting View All Spreads from the Navigator palette menu, you can move from spread to spread throughout the document.

The Zoom tool

You can of course change magnification by selecting the Zoom tool from the toolbox (or press the Z key), and clicking on the page. This zooms in to the next zoom preset (from 100% to 125%, then 150%, 200, 300, 400, etc.) centered on where you clicked. To zoom in on a specific part of the screen, click and drag to define the area you want to fill the screen. Zoom out by Alt/Option+clicking or dragging.

Keyboard zoom

As with the View menu, most experienced InDesign users prefer to use keyboard shortcuts rather than the Zoom tool. Ctrl/Cmd+Spacebar+click zooms in, and Ctrl/Cmd+Alt/Option+Spacebar+click zooms out. This shortcut can also be used when the Text tool is selected. When you've finished zooming, let go of the keyboard and you are returned to the tool you were using previously.

The Hand tool

You can move around a page, or spread, using the Hand tool (key H). As with the Zoom tool, there's a keyboard shortcut—press the Spacebar to activate the

Hand tool at any time other than when the Text tool is selected. With the Hand tool you simply click and hold to grab the page and drag it to a new location.

When you are in the middle of editing text, pressing the Spacebar will obviously just add unwanted spaces. In this situation, holding down the Alt/Option key

temporarily activates the Hand tool. When you let go of the key, you are returned to the Text tool and can continue editing where you left off.

Tip

NAVIGATION SHORTCUTS

As with most document navigation, the quickest way of getting from one page to another is using the keyboard shortcuts:

First page	Ctrl/Cmd+Shift+page up
Last page	Ctrl/Cmd+Shift+page down
Next page	Shift+page down
Previous page	Shift+page up
Next spread	Alt/Option+page down
Previous spread	Alt/Option+page up
Go back	Ctrl/Cmd+page up
Go forward	Ctrl/Cmd+page down

Document navigation

The Navigator palette, Zoom, and Hand tools work well for navigating within pages and spreads, but for moving from page to page, InDesign provides better tools. The first of these is the vertical scroll bar at the right-hand side of the screen. The currently displayed page number appears in the page box at the bottom left corner of

the document window, so you can quickly see where you are in the document.

You can also enter a page number directly into the page box. The keyboard shortcut for this is Ctrl/Cmd+J. To the right and left of the page box are previous and next page buttons and, either side of those, first and last page buttons.

Pop-up pages

Click on the downward pointing triangle next to the page box to display and select a page from a pop-up page list. The list holds all of the pages in order, with master pages appearing at the bottom.

The Pages palette

The Pages palette is the most commonly used method for navigating through long documents. You can see exactly where you are in relation to the rest of the document, and can easily carry out page-level editing, such as applying master pages to several pages simultaneously.

Go Back and Go Forward

Go Back and Go Forward are two of InDesign's most useful navigation commands. InDesign keeps an internal trail as you navigate through a document, and these commands allow you to travel back and forth through it in the same way as using the back and forward buttons of a web browser. For example, if you edit a table of contents entry on page 3, then go to a chapter title on page 76, followed by a section head on page 81, pressing Ctrl/Cmd+page up will take you back to page 76, then pressing it again will take you back to page 3.

137

aster pages or spreads are non-printing pages that provide repeating "background" elements which can be made to appear on every page of a publication.

InDesign CS2 master pages are very versatile. You can create multiple master spreads for a document, create master spreads based on other master spreads, copy them between documents, and edit master page elements on actual pages without breaking their link to the original master.

Layers

By default, master page elements appear behind document page elements in the same layout. So if you want master page elements to appear in front of document page elements, you'll need to place them in a higher layer.

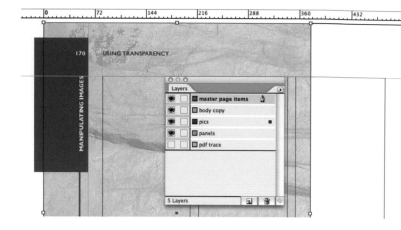

New Document

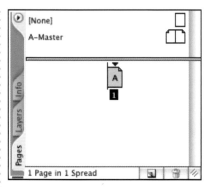

A new InDesign document is created with a default master page, or, if it's a facing-page layout, a master spread. Every master page or spread you create can have a prefix consisting of up to four letters followed

by the name. The default is called A-Master, and is displayed in the master page section of the Pages palette. The A-Master is automatically applied to the first page in a new document.

Applying masters

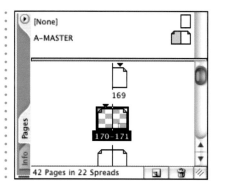

To apply master pages to new pages as you create them, drag the master spread into the document area in the Pages palette, or select Insert Pages from the Pages palette and choose the master from the drop-down menu in the Insert Pages dialog box.

To apply a master to existing pages, drag it over the page in the Pages

palette. Drop it when the page is highlighted with a thick black outline. To apply the master to a spread, drag and drop the master on the bottom edge of one of the spread pages, dropping it when the spread is highlighted. Alternatively, select the pages in the pages palette, and select Apply Master to Pages from the Pages palette menu.

Editing masters

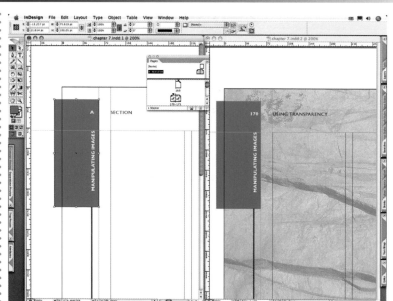

When you edit master page elements, the corresponding elements on all pages to which that master is applied also change. To see this in action, create a new view by selecting **Window > Arrange > New Window**, then **Window > Arrange > Tile**. Select the master spread in the left window and a document page based on the same master in the right-hand one. You will see that any changes made to the master are immediately updated on the document page and all other pages based on that master spread.

Editing master spreads

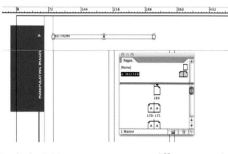

To edit the A-Master, double-click it. You can then change its margin and column settings by selecting **Layout > Margins and Columns**. Master pages can be worked on in exactly the same way as document pages—there

are no differences or other restrictions. Master pages also use layers in the same way as document pages, and you might find it helpful to arrange all of your master page elements in layers, or to put them all on one layer, for better organization.

138

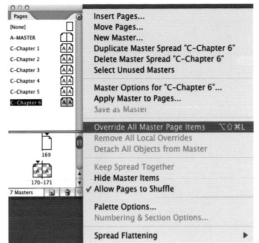

Often, you'll need several master pages that use the same layout and page elements, but with small differences. For example, a book might use the same style and page structure, but with different colors for each chapter. Or sections of a catalog may require different headings. Rather than creating different, unrelated master spreads for each, you can create nested "child" master spreads all based on the same "parent."

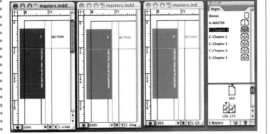

New Master

Prefix: C
Name: Chapter 6
Based on Master: A-MASTER
Number of Pages: 2

OK
Cancel

1 To create a master spread based on another master page, select New Master from the Pages palette and choose the "parent" master spread on which you want to base the new "child" master spread from

the "Based on Master" drop-down menu. The child master page icon in the Pages palette contains the prefix of the parent master. In this case the child master, C-Chapter 6, is based on A-Master.

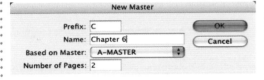

2 The new master spread—C-Chapter 6—contains all of the elements of the parent master spread—A-Master—on which it is based. You can add page elements, or edit existing ones. In this example, each chapter is based on A-Master, which contains a color-coded bleed panel holding the chapter

title and the Automatic Page Number special character. At the top of the page, also color coded, is the section heading; this is another special character—the Section Marker—and is replaced on the page by the text in the Section Marker field of the Numbering & Section Options dialog box.

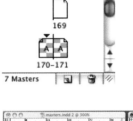

Pages menu:
Insert Pages...
Move Pages...
New Master...
Duplicate Master Spread "C-Chapter 6"
Delete Master Spread "C-Chapter 6"
Select Unused Masters

Master Options for "C-Chapter 6"...
Apply Master to Pages...
Save as Master

Override All Master Page Items
Remove All Local Overrides
Detach All Objects from Master

Keep Spread Together
Hide Master Items
✓ Allow Pages to Shuffle

Palette Options...
Numbering & Section Options...

Spread Flattening ▶

3 To edit master page elements, you must first override them. To do this, select Override All Master Page Items from the Pages palette menu. Now you can select the placeholder type and overwrite it with the

section name—in this case "Print Preparation."

Alternatively, you can Ctrl/Cmd+Shift+click on a master page item in a layout to override that item and make it editable.

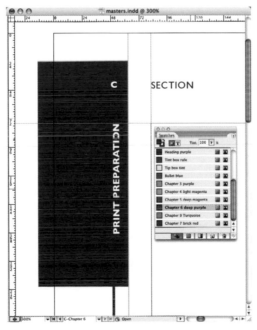

4 To change the color of the bleed panel, select it with the selection tool and choose a color from the Swatches palette—in this case "Chapter

6 deep purple." Because you chose Override All Master page Items, the color of the other elements can also be changed.

5 You can easily create additional child master pages in the same way. Here, we've created six child masters for our catalog, all based on A-Master, and in each instance overriding the master page items to include the appropriate section heading and color.

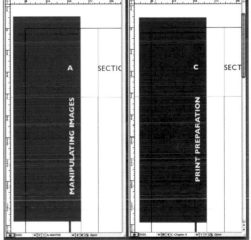

6 Should you need to make a change to an item that appears on all pages, for example, making a panel bleed off the top as well as the side of a page, you can do this on the original A-Master, and all of the child master spreads will

be automatically updated. If you have only a few chapters, this will save you a little time; however, in a long document with many chapters or sections, taking the time to set up nested master pages could save hours of laborious editing.

139

Master pages, continued

Typically, master pages are used to add folios, running heads, and other repeating page elements. They also define margin and column settings, as well as manually placed positional guides. The great advantage of master pages is that you can change the appearance of every page in a document with a single edit.

Master pages from document pages

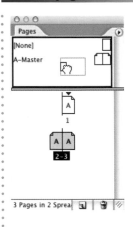

If you've neglected to create master pages—for example, if you are working from a design visual which needs to be adapted for production purposes—you can create a master spread from document pages. The easiest way to do this is to select the spread in the Pages palette and drag it into the master pages section. You will need to delete all the elements other than repeating master spread items—body copy text, for example, though placeholder text on master pages can be useful.

Hide Master Items

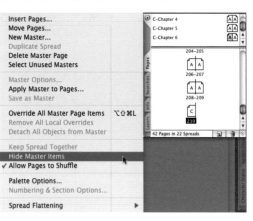

If master page items are getting in the way—if they appear on top of items you are trying to edit on a spread, for instance—select Hide Master Items from the Pages palette menu.

Hidden master items do not print, so don't forget to turn them back on by targeting the affected pages and choosing Show Master Items.

Global master page item visibility

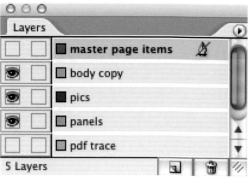

The Hide Master Items command only applies to the currently targeted spread. If you want to hide and show master items globally, the easiest way is to keep them all on a special layer. You can then toggle them on and off for the entire document using the Layers palette.

Threading

You can thread text boxes on master spreads in exactly the same way as on document spreads, but you can't thread outside of the spread. To thread text frames, click the out port of one frame, position the cursor over the next frame in the thread so that the thread icon appears, and click inside the text frame.

Tip

OVERRIDE OPTIONS

Initially, master spread items on a document spread are locked—you can't select, move, or edit them. But if you want to make some minor changes to an individual spread, you can do it by overriding either selected master page items or all of the master page items on the spread. To override all master page items, target a spread and choose Override All Master Page Items from the Pages palette menu. To override individual items, Ctrl/Cmd+Shift+click to select them, which then allows you to edit them.

Overridden attributes don't change when you update a master page. For example, if you override a master page folio and change the font color, then go to the master page and change the font color, the font color on the edited page will not change (though it will on other pages that haven't been overridden).

If you edit the font size, on the other hand, this will still have an effect—only specific overridden attributes are unaffected.

Overridden items still maintain a link with the master page, and you can revert to the master by selecting Remove All Local Overrides from the Pages Palette menu.

If you no longer want master page items to update when you edit a master page, you can detach them. This irreversibly breaks their link with the master page, and they behave like any other page item. You can only detach master page items which have been overridden.

Although you can't reinstate the link to a master spread, once you have detached master page items you can delete the detached items and reapply the master spread.

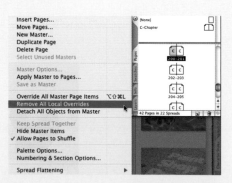

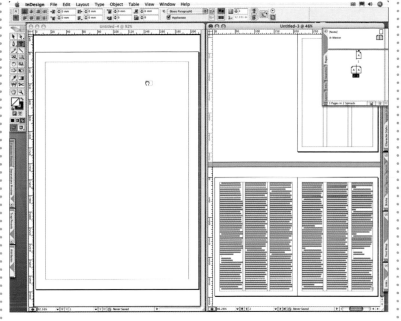

If you need to make changes to master page margin and column settings, you can save yourself a lot of time and effort by activating Layout Adjustment—a feature of InDesign that automatically redesigns pages whenever certain global changes, such as page size, are made.

1 Select Layout Adjustment from the Layout menu, and check Enable Layout Adjustment in the Layout Adjustment dialog box. For layout adjustment to work effectively, the page should be designed as tightly as possible to existing rulers and guides. InDesign will then try and keep the same relative positions and proportions of objects when it moves them. The Snap Zone defines how close an object must be to a column, margin guide, or page edge to snap to it during layout adjustment.

1 To copy a master spread from one document to another, open both the source and destination documents, and drag the master spread from the Pages palette of the source window to the target document window. You can also copy document pages in this way. When you copy document pages, their associated master pages are automatically copied as well.

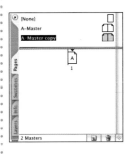

2 You need to be careful with master page naming when copying from one document to another. If you copy a master spread into a document with an existing master spread of the same name, the new master appears with the word "copy" appended (e.g. A-Master copy).

But if you copy document pages based on a master with the same name as a master in the new document, the new document master is applied to the imported pages. Unless you want this to happen, rename master spreads in the source document to avoid conflicts.

2 Target the master spread you want to adjust by double-clicking it in the Pages palette. Here, we'll change the gutter width by going to **Layout > Margins and Columns** and entering a new figure. In this example, the gutter width on the right-hand master has been changed from 6mm to 10mm. The text frames are then automatically resized and positioned to fit the new layout. You will, of course, need to attend to any text flow problems that may be caused by the narrower columns, but you won't need to individually resize and position multiple text frames on every page of the document.

Layers

InDesign's Layers allow you to group elements together and determine their stacking order—i.e., assign items to appear in front of or behind other items. Layers can be toggled on and off to isolate specific elements so you can more easily work on them, or to provide multiple variations of the same document.

Layer 1

When you create a new document, the Layers palette contains a single layer called Layer 1. Layers apply to the entire document, including master pages. Unlike Photoshop, Layer 1 isn't a background layer and doesn't have any unique properties—it's the same as any other layer.

Creating a new layer

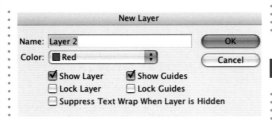

To create a new layer, click the New Layer button at the bottom of the Layers palette. If you hold down the Alt/Option key while doing this, the Layer New Layer dialog box (which is the same as the Layer Options dialog box) opens, which allows you to name the layer, change its color, and set other options. New layers appear at the top of the layer stack and anything on them appears in front of objects on lower layers.

Moving layers

To move a layer up or down the stack, drag it to the new location between two existing layers, or at the top or bottom of the stack. A thick black rule appears in the Layers palette indicating the position the layer will occupy when you drop it.

Layer Options

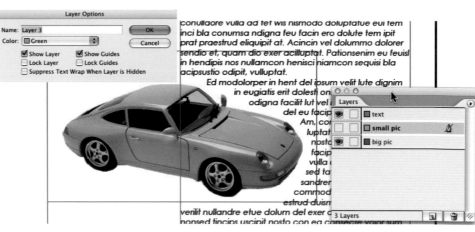

To open the Layer Options dialog for an existing layer, double-click it or select Layer Options from the Layers palette menu. Most of these choices can be made without going to the trouble of opening this dialog box, with the exception of the Suppress Text Wrap When Layer is Hidden checkbox.

If the Suppress Text Wrap When Layer is Hidden box is left unchecked, hidden layers with text wrap items will affect visible layers. This is often undesirable.

For example, if you're working on variations of a design, using layers to hold different layouts, then you don't want invisible objects to interfere with the layout on visible layers.

This example layout has two versions, one with a slightly larger picture. Suppress Text Wrap When Layer is Hidden is checked for both the "big pic" and "small pic" layers. When the big pic layer is hidden and the small pic layer turned on, the text wrap adapts to fit the smaller image, and vice versa.

Target layer

Clicking a layer makes it the Target Layer, indicated by the pen icon to the right of the layer name. Newly created text frames or graphics appear in the target layer, as do pasted items.

Layer visibility

To toggle layer visibility, click the eye icon to the left of the layer name. You can't select or edit anything on hidden layers, and they don't print. Hold down the Alt/Option key and click a layer's eye icon to turn it on and turn all the other layers off at the same time. Repeat to make all layers visible.

Selecting objects on layers

You can select objects on any layer at any time by clicking on them with the Selection tool. It's like having Photoshop's Auto Select Layer option on all the time. When you select an object, its layer becomes the target layer and a pen icon appears in the Layers palette to indicate this. A colored dot also appears, to indicate that the selected object is on this layer.

If you Shift+click to select objects on other layers, the target layer does not change, but colored dots appear in those layers to indicate the layer position of the newly selected items.

142

Moving objects between layers

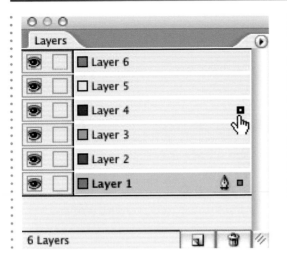

To move an object between layers, drag the colored dot from the target to the source layer in the Layers palette. Hold down the Alt/Option key while dragging if you want to copy items to another layer rather than move them. You can even move and copy items to locked layers by pressing the Ctrl/Cmd key to move, and Ctrl/Cmd+Alt/Option to copy.

Tip

STACKING ORDER

The order of layers in the Layers palette determines the visibility of objects on the page. Objects in higher layers appear "in front of" and obscure objects in lower layers which appear "behind" them. Layers also have their own internal stacking order.

Often it can be difficult to select the object you want because other things are in front of it, either within the layer stacking order or on higher layers. One way to get to the lower objects is to press Ctrl/Cmd+click to drill down through the stack of objects, selecting the next one down with each click.

InDesign also provides keyboard shortcuts that allow you to move through the stack of objects in these situations.

Next object below	**Alt/Option+Ctrl/Cmd+[**
Last object below	**Shift+Alt/Option+Ctrl/Cmd+[**
Next object above	**Alt/Option+Ctrl/Cmd+]**
Last object above	**Shift+Alt/Option+Ctrl/Cmd+]**

Moving layers to another document

> New Layer...
> Duplicate Layer "Layer 4"...
> Delete Layer "Layer 4"
>
> Layer Options for "Layer 4"...
>
> Hide Others
> Lock Others
>
> Paste Remembers Layers
>
> Merge Layers
> Delete Unused Layers
>
> Small Palette Rows

When you copy and paste an object from one document to another, the pasted object appears in the target layer. To copy the layer into the new document along with the object, first select Paste Remembers Layers from the Layers Palette in the source document. To copy a layer complete with its entire contents, Alt/Option+click the layer to select everything on it prior to copying.

Grouping layered objects

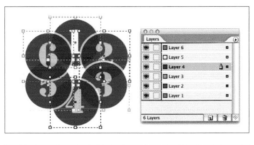

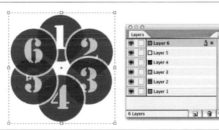

The quickest way to move several objects on different layers into one layer is to select them all and group them. All of the objects will move into the uppermost layer of the group, but their stacking order within the layer will remain the same. In the example here, Layer 1 objects will be on the bottom, Layer 3 in the middle, and Layer 6 on top.

Merging layers

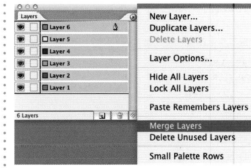

The Merge Layers command in the Layers palette fly-out menu combines several layers into the target layer and deletes all the original layers. Click the layer you want to keep to make it the target layer, and then Ctrl/Cmd+click to select the layers that you want to merge with the target layer. Now select Merge Layers from the Layers palette menu. Everything on the selected layers is moved to the target layer, and the merged layers are deleted from the Layers palette.

Guides and grids

Ruler guides and grids are non-printing horizontal and vertical rules that you can use in addition to column and margin guides to enable you to position and align elements on the page. InDesign's ruler guides are extremely versatile. They behave very much like other objects, and can be locked, hidden, moved, copied, and transformed.

Using ruler guides

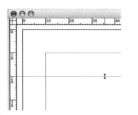

1 To position a ruler guide, you must first display the rulers. Press Ctrl/Cmd+R to toggle the rulers on and off. Click on the horizontal or vertical ruler, drag it onto the page, and release to place the guide in position.

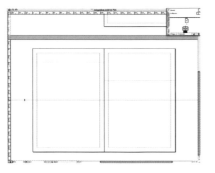

2 Releasing a ruler guide on the page creates a page guide which extends only to the page edges. Release the ruler guide on the pasteboard to create a spread guide which extends across a spread, and beyond

to the pasteboard. If you can't see the pasteboard, hold down the Ctrl/Cmd key when releasing to force a Spread guide. To snap Ruler Guides to the ruler measurements, hold down the Shift key while dragging.

3 To simultaneously place intersecting horizontal and vertical page guides, Ctrl/Cmd+click and drag from the ruler origin at the top left of the document window.

4 You can only place ruler guides on the targeted spread. If your ruler guides disappear when you release them, it may be because the visible spread is not the target spread. It could also be that you're attempting to place a guide on a locked or hidden layer.

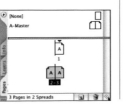

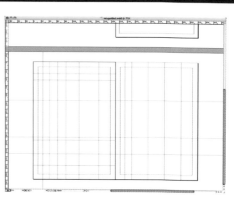

5 New ruler guides appear in the target layer. When selected, they appear in the layer color. All unselected guides appear in the default cyan. You can change this for all newly created guides or for existing selected guides by selecting **Layout > Ruler Guides** and changing the color.

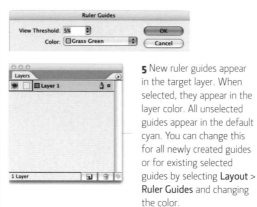

6 Although they are layer-based, ruler guides always appear by default in front of all other guides and objects. If they are obscuring your view, you can set them to appear behind other objects

(though they still appear in front of margin and column guides). To do this, check the Guides in Back box in the Guides & Pasteboard preferences.

7 You can move ruler guides, like other objects, by dragging and dropping them, or by selecting them and using the arrow keys to nudge them. To accurately position a guide, select it and enter a value in the X or Y field in the Control palette.

8 To delete a guide, select it and press backspace or delete. To delete all the ruler guides on a spread, first press Ctrl/Cmd+Alt/ Option+G to select all guides

(or use Ctrl/Cmd+A to select all if there's nothing else on the spread), then press delete. You can't drag guides, QuarkXPress-style, back onto a ruler to delete them.

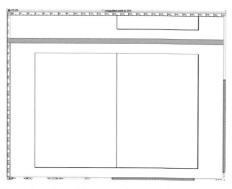

9 To toggle guide visibility, select **View > Grids & Guides > Hide Guides/Show Guides**, or press Ctrl/Cmd+;

(semicolon). This hides ruler, margin, and column guides throughout the document.

10 You can also hide the guides, along with the document grid and other non-printing items, by clicking the Preview mode button at the bottom of the toolbar.

144

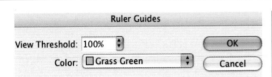

11 To prevent guides obscuring the layout at lower zoom magnifications, use the Threshold setting to define the view at which guides become visible. To do this for all newly created guides, first make sure that no guides are selected, then choose **Layout > Ruler Guides** and enter a value in the View Threshold field. The default of 5% is the minimum zoom magnification, and ensures that guides are always visible.

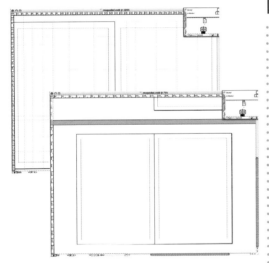

12 If you change it to 100%, guides will be visible at 100% magnification and above, but not below.

13 To lock all ruler guides, select **View > Grids & Guides > Lock Guides**, or press Ctrl/Cmd+Alt/Option+; (semicolon).

14 To lock the position of an individual guide, select it, Right/Ctrl+click it, and select Lock Position from the context menu, or press Ctrl/Cmd+L.

🔒 **15** If you try to reposition a locked guide, the cursor turns into a padlock icon. However, you can still copy it, move it to another layer, change the color, or change the view threshold.

Snap to guides

Probably the most useful thing about grids and guides is the ability to snap objects to them. Ruler guides and the document grid can act like magnets, pulling dragged objects towards them and holding them so you can position them accurately before dropping them. To activate Snap to Guides, press Ctrl/Cmd+Shift+; (semicolon) and for Snap to Document Grid, Ctrl/Cmd+Shift+' (apostrophe), or use the **View > Grids & Guides** menu.

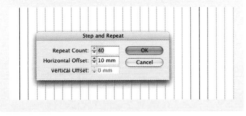

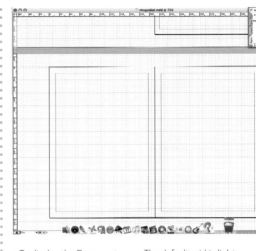

1 To display the Document Grid, select **View > Grids & Guides > Show Document Grid**, or press Ctrl/Cmd+' (apostrophe). The Grid is like a graph paper overlay.

The default grid is light gray with a grid line every inch, with eight subdivisions. If you're working in other units, you'll probably want to change this.

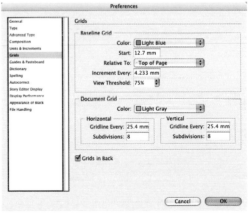

2 Like Guides, the Document Grid can be displayed on top of, or behind, everything else on the page. To change from the default setting, uncheck the Grids in Back box in the Grids preferences panel.

Books

An InDesign book is an associated collection of documents. Books are advantageous because they break longer documents into shorter, more manageable ones, and facilitate collaborative working. Styles and swatches can be shared and synchronized across all of the documents in a book to maintain consistency, and automatic book page numbering takes care of pagination.

The Books palette

To create a new book, select **File > New > Book** and give the file a name. Book files are saved with the extension INDB. When you save the file, the Books palette will open with the book file name in the tab. The Books palette is empty until you add documents to it.

Adding documents

To add a file to the book, click the Add Documents button at the bottom of the palette, then navigate to, and select, the document you want to add, and click Open. You can also drag and drop documents from Windows Explorer or the Finder onto the Books palette.

Deleting documents

To delete a file from the Books palette, select it and click the Remove Documents button. This only deletes the document from the book; it doesn't delete the document file from your hard drive.

Reordering documents

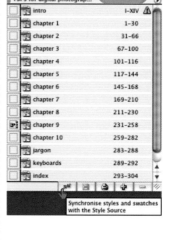

To change the order of documents, drag and drop them within the Books palette. If automatic pagination is turned on, the page numbers of all of the documents in the book will be revised.

Document Status

Icons in the Books palette indicate the current status of member documents.

Indicates an open document.

Indicates that the document is missing, or has been moved or renamed. Double-click it to find the missing document and replace it.

Indicates that someone else has the document open and is working on it.

Indicates that the document has been modified. This icon appears if you work on a document and resave it without the Books palette open. To update the book, double-click the document in the Books palette to open it, then close it again.

Synchronizing books

One of the functions of the Books palette is to maintain consistency across all of the documents in a book by synchronizing swatches and styles. One document is designated as the style source, and all other documents are updated with its swatches and styles.

1 To define a document as the style source, check the box to the left of the document in the Books palette to activate the style source icon.

2 Synchronize all documents in the book by clicking the synchronize button or selecting Synchronize book from the Books palette menu. If you only want to synchronize some documents, Shift or Ctrl/Cmd+click to select them, then click the Synchronize button or Synchronize Selected Documents from the palette menu.

Local styles

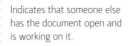

In the default setup, Synchronize copies all styles and swatches from the style source to other documents in the book. Styles and swatches with the same names are overwritten, but existing styles in documents being synchronized that don't appear in the style source are left intact. Therefore you can have local styles—for an index, preface, or glossary, for example.

146

Synchronize Options

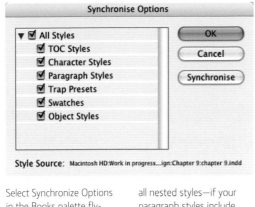

Select Synchronize Options in the Books palette fly-out menu to control which styles and swatches are copied. Be careful to copy

all nested styles—if your paragraph styles include character styles, both will need to be synchronized.

Automatic pagination

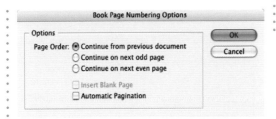

InDesign automatically repaginates book documents when you add or remove pages, reorder documents in the Books palette, or add or delete documents from the book.

To turn off automatic pagination, select Book Page Numbering Options from the Books palette menu and uncheck the Automatic Pagination box.

Tip

KEEPING TRACK OF PAGINATION

Changes such as repagination and synchronization, made to closed files, are irreversible—the files are opened, updated, and resaved in the background. If you are unsure about the effect of repagination or synchronization on documents, make sure they are open, so that you can close them without saving and discard the changes if something unexpected happens.

Numbering and Section Options

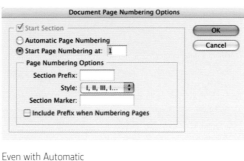

Even with Automatic Pagination turned on, InDesign respects document numbering and section options. You can review and edit these in the usual manner by selecting Numbering and Section Options from the Pages palette menu, or by selecting Document Page Numbering options from the Books palette menu—both open the same dialog box.

Printing books

You can print and export book documents to PDF without opening them. Select the documents in the Book palette, and choose Print Selected Documents or Export Selected Documents to PDF from the palette menu. If no documents are selected, the entire book will print or export.

Starting on a right-hand page

By default, InDesign starts the first page of a book document immediately following the last page of the previous one. If the final page of Chapter 3 is page 99, the first page of Chapter 4 will be page 100—a left-hand page.

For magazines, catalogs and the like, this is fine, but books often begin each chapter on a right-hand page.

1 InDesign will do this automatically for you if you check the Continue on next odd page radio button in the Book Page Numbering Options dialog box.

2 Check the Insert blank page box if you want InDesign to add a blank left-hand page to documents that end on a right-hand page.

Tables of contents

nDesign's Table of Contents feature takes the drudgery out of manually compiling a contents list. An automatically compiled table of contents is based on paragraph styles, so you can compile lists of anything—products, illustrations, footnotes, advertisers—as long as they have paragraph styles applied.

Creating a table of contents

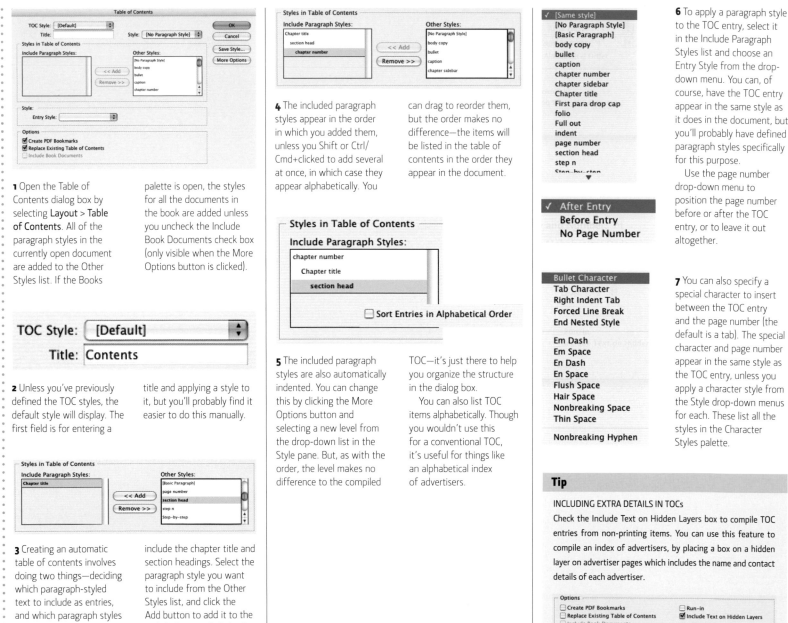

1 Open the Table of Contents dialog box by selecting **Layout > Table of Contents**. All of the paragraph styles in the currently open document are added to the Other Styles list. If the Books palette is open, the styles for all the documents in the book are added unless you uncheck the Include Book Documents check box (only visible when the More Options button is clicked).

2 Unless you've previously defined the TOC styles, the default style will display. The first field is for entering a title and applying a style to it, but you'll probably find it easier to do this manually.

3 Creating an automatic table of contents involves doing two things—deciding which paragraph-styled text to include as entries, and which paragraph styles to apply to those entries. In a book, you would typically include the chapter title and section headings. Select the paragraph style you want to include from the Other Styles list, and click the Add button to add it to the Include Paragraph Styles list.

4 The included paragraph styles appear in the order in which you added them, unless you Shift or Ctrl/Cmd+clicked to add several at once, in which case they appear alphabetically. You can drag to reorder them, but the order makes no difference—the items will be listed in the table of contents in the order they appear in the document.

5 The included paragraph styles are also automatically indented. You can change this by clicking the More Options button and selecting a new level from the drop-down list in the Style pane. But, as with the order, the level makes no difference to the compiled TOC—it's just there to help you organize the structure in the dialog box.

You can also list TOC items alphabetically. Though you wouldn't use this for a conventional TOC, it's useful for things like an alphabetical index of advertisers.

6 To apply a paragraph style to the TOC entry, select it in the Include Paragraph Styles list and choose an Entry Style from the drop-down menu. You can, of course, have the TOC entry appear in the same style as it does in the document, but you'll probably have defined paragraph styles specifically for this purpose.

Use the page number drop-down menu to position the page number before or after the TOC entry, or to leave it out altogether.

7 You can also specify a special character to insert between the TOC entry and the page number (the default is a tab). The special character and page number appear in the same style as the TOC entry, unless you apply a character style from the Style drop-down menus for each. These list all the styles in the Character Styles palette.

Tip

INCLUDING EXTRA DETAILS IN TOCs

Check the Include Text on Hidden Layers box to compile TOC entries from non-printing items. You can use this feature to compile an index of advertisers, by placing a box on a hidden layer on advertiser pages which includes the name and contact details of each advertiser.

148

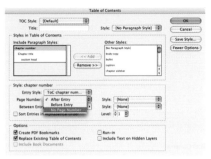

1 Here's how to produce a well-styled table of contents for any document organized in a main-heading/section-heading fashion, such as a book chapter. The easiest way is to first create a test TOC using the [Same Style]

option, and then restyle the entries and save them as the new TOC paragraph and character styles. Creating a test TOC will also tell you how many pages you will need to allow at the beginning of the document.

2 Define one paragraph style for each type of entry. In this case, three are required—one for the chapter number, one for the chapter title, and one for the section headings. Give these styles the same names as the paragraph styles of the entries, but with a recognizable prefix.

3 Now define the character styles for the leader characters and the page numbers. You can use a row of full points or another

leader character, but a nicely spaced character from a symbol font, like a Zapf Dingbat square bullet, can look a lot better.

4 In the Table of Contents dialog box, add the three TOC elements' paragraph styles to the Include

Paragraph Styles list. Click the More Options button, and reorder them and assign levels if you wish.

5 Select the chapter number and apply the TOC chapter number paragraph style from the Entry Style drop-

down menu. Select No Page Number from the Page Number drop-down.

6 Repeat the process for the chapter title, this time

applying the TOC chapter title style.

7 Do the same thing again for the section head, applying the TOC Section head style. Select After Entry in the Page Number drop down menu, and from the style drop-down menu opposite, select the TOC

page number character style. If the Between Entry and Number field isn't showing the tab character (^t), then select it from the drop-down list and select the TOC leader character style.

8 In the Options pane, check the Replace Existing Table of Contents box and, if you want them,

the Create PDF bookmarks box. Leave the other boxes unchecked.

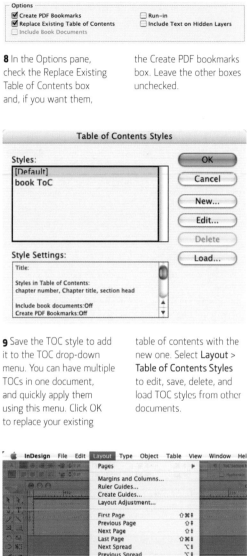

9 Save the TOC style to add it to the TOC drop-down menu. You can have multiple TOCs in one document, and quickly apply them using this menu. Click OK to replace your existing

table of contents with the new one. Select **Layout > Table of Contents Styles** to edit, save, delete, and load TOC styles from other documents.

10 Inevitably, as soon as you have created a TOC, changes to the document will render it inaccurate. To

update it, select Update Table of Contents from the Layout menu.

149

Unlike a table of contents, an index isn't something that can be created automatically. It requires knowledge of the document subject and contents, careful planning, and considered decision-making. InDesign makes this task easier by providing tools that help carry out the laborious task of categorizing, organizing, and keeping track of the location of indexed items on the page.

Creating an index

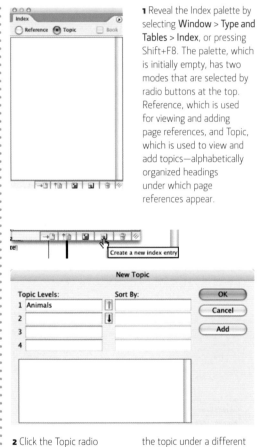

1 Reveal the Index palette by selecting **Window > Type and Tables > Index**, or pressing Shift+F8. The palette, which is initially empty, has two modes that are selected by radio buttons at the top. Reference, which is used for viewing and adding page references, and Topic, which is used to view and add topics—alphabetically organized headings under which page references appear.

2 Click the Topic radio button, followed by the Create New Index entry icon at the bottom of the palette.

In the New Topic dialog box, enter the topic name in the Level 1 field. To put the topic under a different alphabetic heading than its initial character—e.g. to have "10 Commandments" appear under T rather than at the beginning of the index, enter "ten" in the Sort By field.

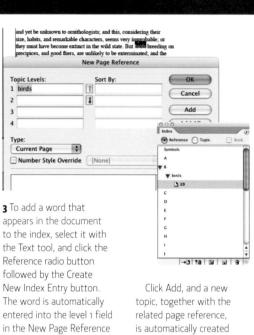

3 To add a word that appears in the document to the index, select it with the Text tool, and click the Reference radio button followed by the Create New Index Entry button. The word is automatically entered into the level 1 field in the New Page Reference dialog box.

Click Add, and a new topic, together with the related page reference, is automatically created in the Index palette.

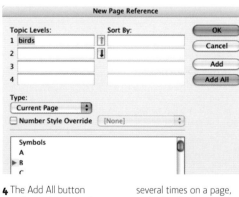

4 The Add All button searches a document for all occurrences of the index entry, and adds page references for them.

In most circumstances, you wouldn't want page references indexed in this fashion (if a word appears several times on a page, multiple references are generated), but it can be useful for some entries, including people and places. You can also use it to identify occurrences of a word before placing them within other topics.

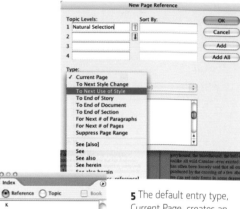

5 The default entry type, Current Page, creates an index entry including the page number on which that entry appears. Some topics may span several pages and, in this case, an entry like "Natural Selection 73–113" can be generated by making a selection from the Type drop-down menu in the New Page Reference dialog box.

The option you choose will depend on the structure and styling of the document, and this is another good argument for making consistent use of paragraph styles. To Next Style Change and the more specific To Next Use of Style (specified in the Style drop-down menu) are obvious candidates where a style change indicates the end of a content-based section. The six options at the end of the Type drop-down menu are for cross referencing, which is dealt with on pages 150–151.

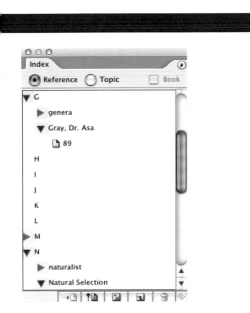

6 The quick way to add index entries is to use the keyboard shortcuts, which create an entry with the last-used settings in the New Page Reference dialog box. Press Ctrl/Cmd +Alt/Option+Shift+[(left square bracket) to add a standard index entry.

7 To locate an index entry in the text, select the page reference in the palette and click the Go to Selected Marker icon.

There's also a special shortcut purely for adding proper names to an index. If you add Dr. Asa Gray to an index in the standard form, it appears under D as Dr. Asa Gray. To add it to the G section in the conventional form—Gray, Dr. Asa—press Ctrl/Cmd+Alt/Option+Shift+] (right square bracket).

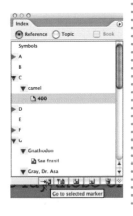

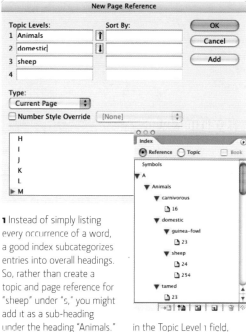

1 To edit a topic, or a page reference, double-click it in the Index palette to open the Topic Options dialog box or the Page Reference Options dialog box.

ry, and at my request D. *and Dr. Asa Gray those* *icipated. On the other ha*

2 You can delete an index entry by selecting it and clicking the trash icon. You can also delete an index entry by deleting its marker in the document. Index markers look like small colons with arrows beneath them.

To see the index markers, select **Type > Show Hidden Characters**. When you create an index entry from a selected word, the marker appears at the beginning of the word. To select the marker, position the cursor to the right of it and press Shift+left arrow, then press Backspace to delete it. When you delete the marker, the corresponding entry, including any subentries, are deleted from the Index palette.

1 Instead of simply listing every occurrence of a word, a good index subcategorizes entries into overall headings. So, rather than create a topic and page reference for "sheep" under "s," you might add it as a sub-heading under the heading "Animals."

In the New Page Reference dialog box, relegate the word "sheep" to Topic Level 3 by clicking the down arrow twice.

Create a first-level topic by typing the word "Animals" in the Topic Level 1 field, and a subcategory by typing the word "domestic" in the Topic Level 2 field.

Subcategorized second and third-level index entries are indented in the Index palette.

151

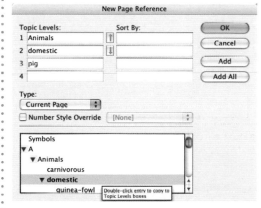

2 To add other references to the Animals/domestic subcategory, select the new word in the document, click the Create a New Index Entry button, and relegate the entry to Topic Level 3 as before. This time you can select the Level 1 and 2 entries from the list in the lower half of the dialog box.

Indexing, continued

Although it's the hardest part, compiling an index is only half the story. Once it's compiled, InDesign will automatically generate the index according to the style options you defined in the Generate Index dialog box. But first, in all but the simplest index, you'll need to create cross-references. Here's how to do it.

Generating indexes

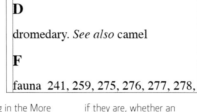

1 When you are ready to build the index, click the Generate Index button on the Index palette to open the Generate Index dialog box. This is quite a complex dialog box with a lot of options, but if you merely want to generate a standard-looking index, most of the options can safely be ignored by clicking the Fewer Options button.

2 It's usually worth generating a "proof," or test index, first, by clicking the OK button. Like the Table of Contents feature, Generate Index puts the index into a loaded text cursor that you can click into any page to flow the text there. The structure of the index mirrors the Index palette in Reference mode. Second and third level topics are indented, and multiple page references are separated by a comma.

☑ Replace Existing Index

3 Now that you have an Index, albeit in rough form, you can update it at any time by clicking the Generate index button.

InDesign assumes you will want to replace the existing index, so the Replace Existing Index checkbox is automatically checked.

☑ Include Index Section Headings
☐ Include Empty Index Sections

D

dromedary. *See also* camel

F

fauna 241, 259, 275, 276, 277, 278,

4 Everything in the More Options section of the Generate Index dialog box is concerned with the formatting and styling of the index. The first two checkboxes determine whether alphabetic section headings are included and, if they are, whether an empty section gets a heading or not.

The default setting displays headings only for sections with content. For example, this index has no "E" entries.

Gnathodon. *See* fossil

1 A common cross-referencing technique specifies an alternate existing topic and page reference for the index entry. In this instance, there would be no page reference for the cross-referenced entry.

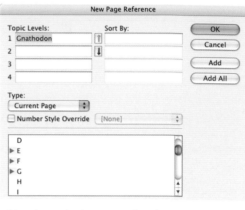

2 Select the word to be cross-referenced in the document and click the New Index Entry button on the Index palette. Note that the palette should be in Reference mode to do this, otherwise the New Topic dialog box will open.

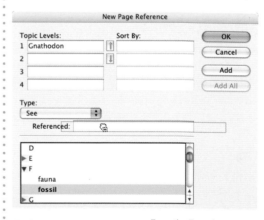

3 From the Type drop-down menu select See. A Referenced field appears below the Type menu, into which you can type the cross-reference topic. Better still, If you've already defined the topic, drag it from the panel below and drop it in the Referenced field. The cross-referenced entry is added to the Index palette.

152

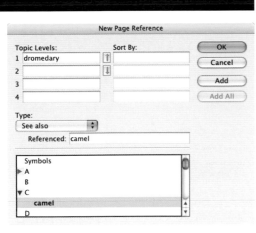

New Page Reference

Topic Levels:
1 dromedary
2
3
4

Sort By:

OK
Cancel
Add
Add All

Type:
See also

Referenced: camel

Symbols
► A
B
▼ C
   camel
D

---

4 To cross-reference related items that are not equivalent, select See Also from the Type drop-down menu. Whereas equivalent items do not usually have a page reference, related items do.

Current Page
To Next Style Change
To Next Use of Style
To End of Story
To End of Document
To End of Section
For Next # of Paragraphs
For Next # of Pages
Suppress Page Range

See [also]
See
✓ See also
See herein
See also herein
[Custom Cross–reference]

5 Other cross-reference type options include See Herein, which is a cross-reference within the topic. There's also a Custom Cross-reference, so you can include non-standard terms. See [also] creates a "See" cross-reference where there is no page reference, or a "See also" cross-reference for entries with an existing page reference.

Paragraph Styles

[Basic Paragraph]
chapter
Index Level 1
Index Level 2
Index Level 3
Index Section Head
Index Title

When you generate an index, InDesign automatically creates index-specific paragraph and character styles for the entries—Index Title, Index Section Head, Index Level 1, Index Level 2, Index Level 3, Index Cross-reference, and so on. Styles are only created for index entries, so if you don't have any Level 3 entries, the style won't be created.

Generate Index

Title: Index
Title Style: Index Title

☑ Replace Existing Index
☐ Include Book Documents   Book Name:
☐ Include Entries on Hidden Layers

Nested

☑ Include Index Section Headings
☐ Include Empty Index Sections

Level Styl   [Basic Paragraph]   Index Style
                    chapter
Level 1: ✓ Index Level 1   Section Heading: Index Section H...
Level 2:   Index Level 2   Page Number: [None]
Level 3:   Index Level 3   Cross-reference: Index Cross-ref...
Level 4:   Index Section Head   Cross-referenced Topic: [None]
            Index Title

Entry Separators
Following Topic: Between Page Numbers: .
Between Entries: ;   Before Cross-reference: .
Page Range: ^=   Entry End:

OK
Cancel
Fewer Options

1 Apply paragraph and character styles to index entries using the drop-down menus in the Level Style and Index Style panes of the Generate Index dialog box. There's one menu for each Index level, and each of them contains all of the styles in the Paragraph Styles palette. You can apply any existing paragraph styles to index entries, but the best option is to stick with the InDesign-created ones and edit them to change the appearance of the index.

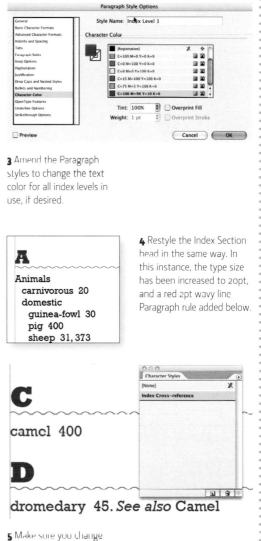

Animals
  carnivorous 20
  domestic
    guinea-fowl 30
    pig 400
    sheep 31,373
  tamed 30

2 The Index Level paragraph styles are all based on the [Basic Paragraph] style, which is 12pt Times. You can therefore change the entire index font by editing the Basic Paragraph style (providing you haven't used it for anything else).

Paragraph Style Options

General
Basic Character Formats
Advanced Character Formats
Indents and Spacing
Tabs
Paragraph Rules
Keep Options
Hyphenation
Justification
Drop Caps and Nested Styles
Bullets and Numbering
Character Color
OpenType Features
Underline Options
Strikethrough Options

Style Name: Index Level 3

Character Color

[Registration]
C=100 M=0 Y=0 K=0
C=0 M=100 Y=0 K=0
C=0 M=0 Y=100 K=0
C=15 M=100 Y=100 K=0
C=75 M=5 Y=100 K=0
C=100 M=90 Y=10 K=0

Tint: 100%   ☐ Overprint Fill
Weight: 1 pt   ☐ Overprint Stroke

☐ Preview   Cancel   OK

3 Amend the Paragraph styles to change the text color for all index levels in use, if desired.

Animals
  carnivorous 20
  domestic
    guinea-fowl 30
    pig 400
    sheep 31,373

4 Restyle the Index Section head in the same way. In this instance, the type size has been increased to 20pt, and a red 2pt wavy line Paragraph rule added below.

C
camel 400
D
dromedary 45. *See also* Camel

Character Styles
[None]
Index Cross–reference

5 Make sure you change all of the index styles to fit the overall design. Most are paragraph styles, but cross-references are character styles.

Tip

REDEFINING INDEX STYLES

An effective approach to altering styles is to restyle the entries on the page, then redefine the styles in the Paragraph Styles palette. For example, if you were changing the color of the index title, you'd highlight the title on the page, select a new text color from the Swatches palette, then select Redefine Style from the Paragraph Styles palette menu, or press Ctrl/Cmd+Alt/Option+Shift+R to update the Index Title style definition.

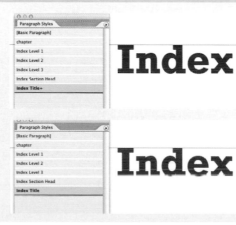

Object Library

The Object Library palette provides a convenient place to store frequently used logos, sidebars, pull-quotes, and other repeating items. The Object Library can store formatted text, and graphics and images complete with their attributes and link information. Snippets, a new InDesign CS2 feature, is a more sophisticated and flexible alternative to the Object Library, and uses Bridge to store and retrieve page items in the same way as other graphics.

Tip

BROKEN LINKS

Both Library INDL files and snippets are cross platform, and can be opened on other PCs and Macs running InDesign CS2. Where an object, or snippet has a text component you must ensure that the font is installed on the recipient system. If the font isn't present it will be substituted. Likewise, linked images and any associated graphics must be present in order to display and print. Missing graphics won't affect the thumbnail display in the Library palette, or Bridge, but when you place them you won't even get a low resolution placeholder, just a gray box. If graphics for Library objects and snippets are temporarily unavailable, you can use the Links palette to re-link them later.

Creating an Object Library

1 To create a new Object Library, select **File > New > Library** and enter a name and location for the library file in the dialog box. Click the Save button, and the Library palette is displayed with the name in the tab. You don't need to have a document open to create or open a Library, and there's no limit (other than system memory) on the number of libraries you can have open at once.

2 To add objects to the library, drag them from an open document and drop them on the Library palette. You can add individual or grouped objects in this way.

To add several related objects to the library, Shift+click to select them and drag and drop them onto the Library palette.

To add everything on a page (including guides) to the Library, press Ctrl/Cmd+Shift+A to make sure nothing is selected, and choose Add Items on Page from the Library palette fly-out menu. All of the items are then added as one library object. Select Add Items on Page as Separate Objects to add each object individually to the library.

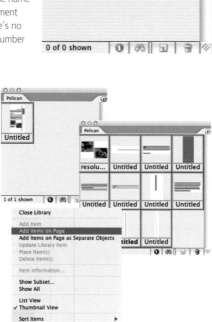

3 To copy objects from one Library palette to another, first drag one of the Library palette tabs from the palette group so that both palettes are visible. Select the item you want to copy, and drag and drop it from one palette onto the other.

4 If an object in the library is a placed graphic, its filename is displayed underneath the thumbnail, otherwise it's labeled Untitled. To display only the name, select List View from the palette menu.

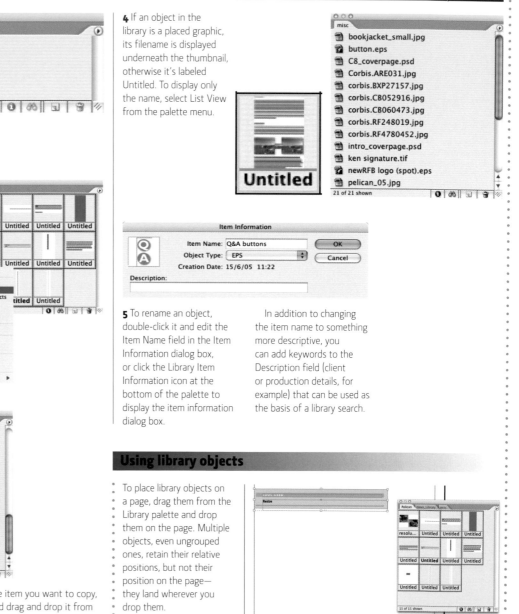

5 To rename an object, double-click it and edit the Item Name field in the Item Information dialog box, or click the Library Item Information icon at the bottom of the palette to display the item information dialog box.

In addition to changing the item name to something more descriptive, you can add keywords to the Description field (client or production details, for example) that can be used as the basis of a library search.

Using library objects

To place library objects on a page, drag them from the Library palette and drop them on the page. Multiple objects, even ungrouped ones, retain their relative positions, but not their position on the page—they land wherever you drop them.

154

1 Click the Show Library Subset icon to restrict the display to only those items that fulfill the criteria entered in the Show subset dialog. You can filter the Library on the basis of name, date, type, and description.

To only display images, select Object Type from the first drop-down menu, Equal from the second, and Image from the third.

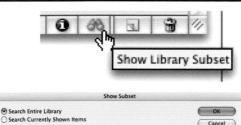

2 Click OK, and only image thumbnails are displayed in the Library palette. The number of visible items and the total number of Library items is displayed in the bottom-left corner of the palette.

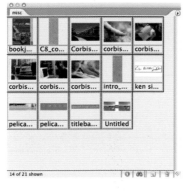

3 To search for keywords in the Description field, enter Description in the first drop-down menu, Contains in the second, and type the search term in the field on the right.

4 To search using multiple parameters, click the More Choices button. In this example, the subset shown will display only EPS files with the word "logo" in their Description field.

5 To display the entire contents of a library when only a subset is visible, select Show All from the palette menu.

Snippets are created in much the same way as objects, except that page items are dragged to the Bridge, rather than to the Library palette.

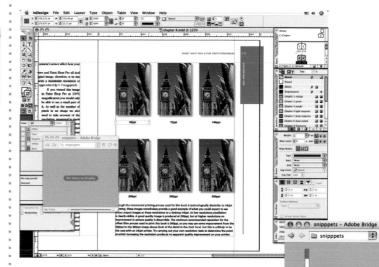

1 Click the Go to Bridge button on the Control palette, select the folder where you want to save the snippet, and switch to compact mode (see page 126) so you can see both the document page and Bridge.

Drag the object from the page and drop it on the Bridge window.

2 To place a snippet on the page, drag it from Bridge and drop it anywhere on the page. One big advantage snippets have over library objects is that they remember their original page location. This makes them excellent for sidebars, folios, and other position-critical page elements.

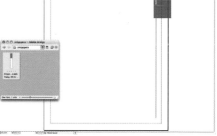

3 Another advantage snippets have over library objects is that they are saved individually in the folder specified in Bridge, with the extension INDS. This allows you to easily swap snippets with colleagues via a network server or e-mail.

155

INTERACTIVITY

Hyperlinks, anchors, and bookmarks
Rollover buttons
Button actions
Style tags

Hyperlinks, anchors, and bookmarks

Hyperlinks, anchors, and bookmarks are elements you can add to an InDesign document to provide interactive features in exported PDF files. Hyperlinks are also processed by Package for GoLive. Only PDF 1.5 (Acrobat 6) and later fully support interactive features, so make sure to select PDF 1.5 or later in the Export Adobe PDF dialog box.

Creating text anchors

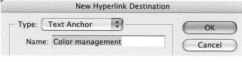

1 Another way to add hyperlinks is to first define a destination, then create a source and link to it. A hyperlink destination can consist of a page, a text anchor, or a URL. Using the Type tool, select the text where you want to create a hyperlink destination, and select New Hyperlink Destination from the Hyperlinks palette menu. The Type is automatically set to Text Anchor, and the selected text is automatically entered into the name field

in the New Hyperlink Destination dialog box.
Hyperlink destinations do not appear in the Hyperlinks palette.

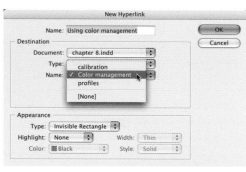

2 To link to the anchor, create a new hyperlink and select Text Anchor from the Type drop-down menu in the New Hyperlink dialog

box. Then, just select the anchor from the Name drop-down menu, which lists all of the text anchors in the document.

Using hyperlinks

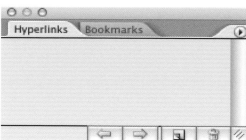

To add and manage hyperlinks in an InDesign document, display the Hyperlinks palette by selecting **Window > Interactive > Hyperlinks**.

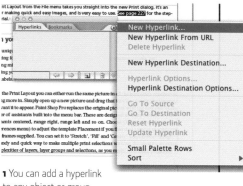

1 You can add a hyperlink to any object or group. To add a hyperlink to a block of text, select it with the Type tool, then select New Hyperlink from the Hyperlinks palette menu.

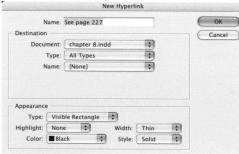

2 The hyperlink source in the New Hyperlink dialog box is automatically named after the selected text. The document drop-down menu displays the current document.

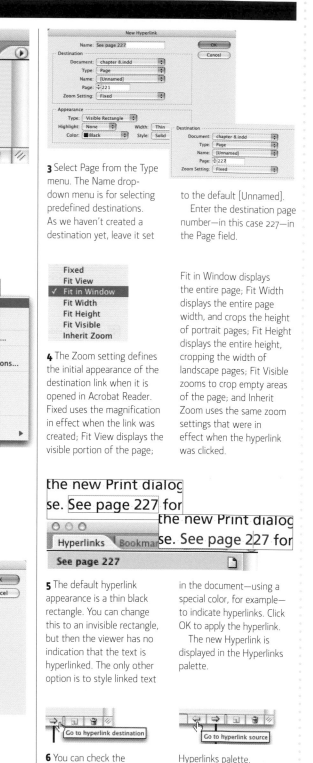

3 Select Page from the Type menu. The Name drop-down menu is for selecting predefined destinations. As we haven't created a destination yet, leave it set

to the default [Unnamed].
Enter the destination page number—in this case 227—in the Page field.

4 The Zoom setting defines the initial appearance of the destination link when it is opened in Acrobat Reader. Fixed uses the magnification in effect when the link was created; Fit View displays the visible portion of the page;

Fit in Window displays the entire page; Fit Width displays the entire page width, and crops the height of portrait pages; Fit Height displays the entire height, cropping the width of landscape pages; Fit Visible zooms to crop empty areas of the page; and Inherit Zoom uses the same zoom settings that were in effect when the hyperlink was clicked.

5 The default hyperlink appearance is a thin black rectangle. You can change this to an invisible rectangle, but then the viewer has no indication that the text is hyperlinked. The only other option is to style linked text

in the document—using a special color, for example—to indicate hyperlinks. Click OK to apply the hyperlink.
The new Hyperlink is displayed in the Hyperlinks palette.

6 You can check the hyperlink destination using the Go to Hyperlink Destination button at the bottom of the

Hyperlinks palette.
To return to the hyperlink source, click the Go to Hyperlink Source button.

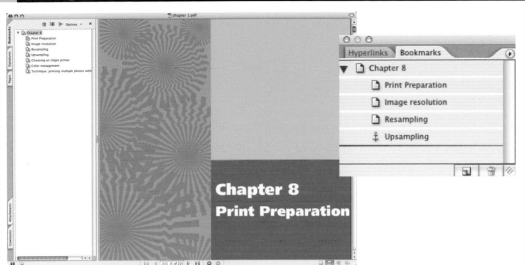

A bookmark is a special kind of link that appears in the Bookmarks tab in Acrobat or Acrobat Reader. When you create an automatic Table of Contents (see pages 148–149), you can elect to create bookmarks for the entries.

1 In the default workspace, the Bookmarks palette is grouped with the Hyperlinks palette. Select **Window > Interactive > Bookmarks** to display it, or, if the Hyperlinks palette group is visible, click the Bookmarks tab to bring it to the front.

2 To add a page bookmark, double-click the page in the Pages palette and select New Bookmark from the Bookmarks palette menu, or click the Create New Bookmark button at the bottom of the palette. Page and frame bookmarks

have a "page" icon in the Bookmarks palette.

To add a text anchor bookmark, select a frame or some text and click the Create New Bookmark icon. Text anchor bookmarks have an "anchor" icon in the Bookmarks palette.

3 If you use the Create New Bookmark button, the bookmark name appears highlighted and ready to overwrite in the Bookmarks palette.

In other instances, first select the bookmark in the

palette, then click its name and overwrite it. Don't be too quick, or your actions will be interpreted as a double-click. Alternatively, select Rename Bookmark from the palette menu.

4 If nothing is selected in the Bookmarks palette when you create a new bookmark, it is added to the bottom of the list. To create nested bookmarks—for subheadings within a

chapter, perhaps—first select the "heading" bookmark in the Bookmarks palette. Now, when you create a new bookmark, it is indented under the heading bookmark.

5 You can change the order of bookmarks by dragging and dropping them in the Bookmarks palette. Drop a bookmark on top of another bookmark to create a nested bookmark.

Select Sort Bookmarks from the Bookmarks palette menu to order bookmarks first by page number, then alphabetically within pages.

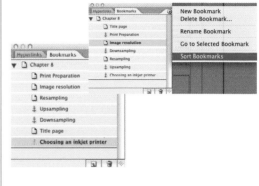

6 Double-click a bookmark in the Bookmarks palette to display it in the document window.

159

Tip

CREATING A URL HYPERLINK

To create a link to an outside URL, select the text you want to link from, and click New Hyperlink in the Hyperlinks palette menu. Choose URL from the Type drop-down menu, and enter the web address in the URL field.

To create a URL hyperlink directly from a URL in a text frame, select the URL with the Type tool, then choose New Hyperlink from URL in the Hyperlinks palette menu. The link is created and added to the Hyperlinks palette.

Rollover buttons

Interactive buttons that change appearance when your mouse rolls over them are a common web feature. You can also produce them in InDesign for export in interactive PDFs. Essentially the process involves creating two button states—an "up" state for when the button is doing nothing, and a "rollover" state for when the cursor is over the button.

Using the Button tool

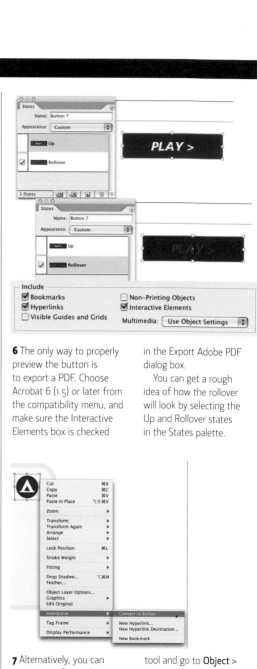

1 The simplest (though least often used) way to create a button is to use the Button tool. Select it from the Toolbar, or press B.

Click anywhere on the page to open the Button dialog box, and enter Width and Height values for the button. Alternatively, click and drag to create a button frame.

2 Type into the frame to create the button text (or paste into it, or place an image). The button frame is a container for the text frame or graphics frame within. You can edit the contents in the same way you would any other frame.

Set the type in the usual way, and apply a text style if you have one. In this instance, the text frame options have been used to center the text.

3 To view and edit button states, display the States palette by selecting **Window** > **Interactive** > **States**, and select the button with the Selection tool.

When you create a new button, it is in the default "up" state. To add additional states, select the button with the Selection tool, and click the Create New Optional State button at the bottom of the palette.

4 A button can have a maximum of three states—Up, Rollover, and Down. Up defines the button's default appearance, Rollover is what it looks like when the mouse pointer is positioned over any part of it, and Down is how the button appears as it is clicked. The Down state is often ignored, as it's only momentarily visible.

5 To change the color of the text when the cursor rolls over the button, select the Rollover state in the States palette, highlight the text with the Type tool, and change the fill color.

6 The only way to properly preview the button is to export a PDF. Choose Acrobat 6 (1.5) or later from the compatibility menu, and make sure the Interactive Elements box is checked in the Export Adobe PDF dialog box.

You can get a rough idea of how the rollover will look by selecting the Up and Rollover states in the States palette.

7 Alternatively, you can convert any frame, line, or grouped object into a button. First, create the object that you want to turn into a button, then click it with the Selection tool and go to **Object** > **Interactive** > **Convert to Button**, or Right/Ctrl+click it and select **Interactive** > **Convert to Button** from the context menu.

160

Here's how to create two-state rollover navigation buttons for an interactive PDF presentation. The "Next" and "Previous" buttons will appear on every page, and allow the user to navigate through the presentation even when the standard Acrobat controls are unavailable.

1 Create a rectangular text frame of about 28mm x 6mm on the master page by dragging with the Type tool. Enter "< Previous" in the text frame, and set it in 10pt, centered, all caps, in a bold sans serif face (this example is Frutiger 56 Italic). The type needs to be legible on the PDF page at 100% view, so if you can't see it on your InDesign page at 100%, it's not going to work. Increase the type's tracking if necessary to make it more readable on screen.

2 Fill and stroke the text frame with a suitable color scheme. Make the fill an 80% tint of a solid color swatch. We're going to add a drop shadow later, so make the stroke a darker color than the fill, and increase the width to 2pt. In the Stroke palette, align the stroke to the outside of the frame.

Corner Effects

Effect: Rounded	OK
Size: 1 mm	Cancel
	☑ Preview

3 Select **Object > Corner Effects** and add rounded corners with a 1mm radius.

4 Using the Direct Selection tool, and holding down the Shift key to constrain movement to the horizontal plane, drag the top edge of the text frame to the right to skew it by about 15 degrees.

5 Select the Type tool, triple-click the text to select it all, and baseline shift it until it is vertically centered. You can't vertically center it using the Text Frame Options dialog box, because it won't work once corner effects have been added to a frame or its shape has been edited.

Drop Shadow

☑ Drop Shadow

Mode: Multiply
Opacity: 50 %   Blur: 1.5 mm
X Offset: 1 mm   Spread: 0 %
Y Offset: 1 mm   Noise: 0 %

Color: Swatches

- [Paper]
- [Black]
- C=100 M=0 Y=0 K=0
- C=0 M=100 Y=0 K=0
- C=0 M=0 Y=100 K=0

OK
Cancel
☑ Preview

6 Select the frame with the Selection tool, and add a drop shadow. Set the opacity to 50%, the X and Y offsets to 1, and the blur to 1.5.

7 Right/Ctrl+click the text frame and select **Interactive > Convert to Button**. Click the Create New Optional State button in the States palette to add the rollover state.

8 Select the text frame with the Direct Selection tool, change the fill to 100% of the solid color, and change the stroke width to 2.5pt.

9 Still using the Direct Selection tool, double-click in the text frame, select the "<" character, and change its fill color to match the frame stroke.

10 Export to PDF to test the button. When you roll over the button, the background goes slightly darker, the red frame outline grows a little, and the "<" character changes color from black to red. Small visual clues are all that's needed to indicate that this is an interactive element.

11 Duplicate the button, and change the type (in both the Up and Rollover states) to read "NEXT >". Position the buttons on the master page.

Button actions

All buttons have a purpose; they do something when you roll over them, or click them. The Button Options dialog box allows you to assign behaviors—actions that buttons carry out in response to a mouse event. Even with the fairly limited set of behaviors available, InDesign's buttons provide scope for creating useful interactive PDFs.

Button names

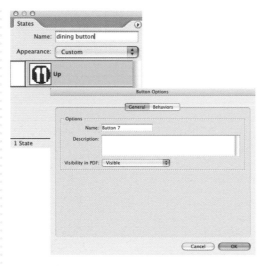

Name your buttons according to the behavior you've assigned to them. If there are several buttons on a page, and particularly if buttons interact with each other, you'll quickly lose track of what "button 1" refers to. Select the button and overwrite the default name in the States palette.

You can also rename the button in the Button Options dialog box. Select a button with the Selection tool, Right/Ctrl+click it and select Interactive > Button Options. Any text entered into the description panel will display in a balloon in the PDF file when the button is moused over.

Events

Click the Behaviors tab and select the Event drop-down menu. This lists the events that a button can respond to. Mouse Up, Down, Enter, and Exit are self-explanatory. On Focus is when the button is selected, and On Blur is when another button (or field) in the PDF is selected.

Behaviors

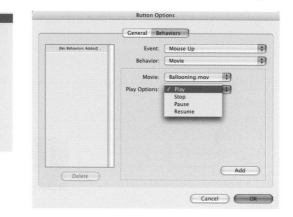

There are 15 options on the Behavior drop-down menu, most of which control navigation. All of these are useful for creating interactive PDFs that are configured to run full-screen or in a window without the Acrobat menu bar.

Select the Movie behavior to view the additional options available. These allow you to control the playback of any movie on the page using a button.

Activating a navigation button

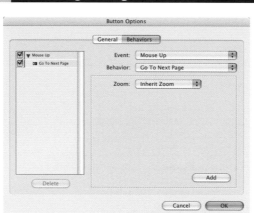

Here's how to activate the NEXT > navigation rollover button we created on page 161 so that it displays the next page when clicked.

1 Select the button on the master page, open the Button Options dialog box, and click the Behaviors tab. Select Mouse Up from the Event drop-down menu, and Go To Next Page from the Behaviors menu.

The Inherit Zoom setting means that the new page will display at the same magnification as the existing one. If you don't want this, select Fit in Window, or one of the other options, and click the Add button. The Mouse Up event appears in the list on the left, along with the associated behavior. Click OK and, if necessary, add another page to the document so there is a next page to go to when you test the button.

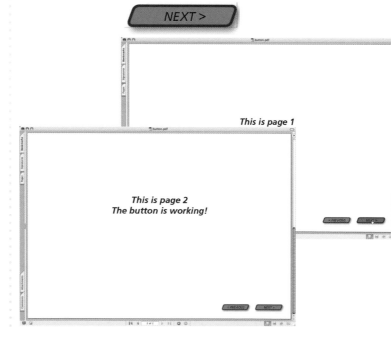

2 Export to PDF, not forgetting to check the Interactive Elements box, and test the button by clicking it to go to the next page.

Because the button is on a master page, there is nothing more to do (except to activate the "< Previous" button in the same way). The functioning button will appear on every page of the document.

Adding sounds to buttons

Here's how to add a short sound to a button that plays when you roll over it.

1 First, place the sound on the page in the same way you would a graphic. Sounds are represented by a speaker icon. Unless you want to see this icon in the PDF, leave it on the pasteboard.

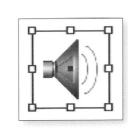

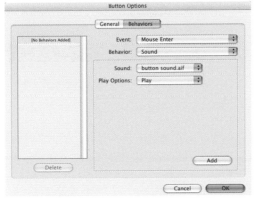

2 Choose the button with which you want to associate the sound. Open the Button options dialog box and click the Behaviors tab. Select Mouse Enter from the Event drop-down menu, and Sound from the Behavior drop-down menu.

3 Unless there are other sounds in the document, the placed sound file will appear in the Sound drop-down menu. You can use the Play Options menu to control the playback of sound files, but if you leave it in the play position, the

short sound effect will play once when the button is moused over.

4 Click the Add button to add the behavior, and it appears in the list on the left. Export the PDF and test the button. You may need to download a plug-in from the Adobe website to play certain files—in which case you will be informed by an alert box.

Creating interactive presentations

You can create rich, interactive presentations by using buttons merely to hide and reveal information on the page. Here's how to use buttons to display alternate images and text in an information panel.

1 First, create the required content. We have three layers:
a) a base layer containing the filled frame background;
b) a picture layer containing a knocked-back image in the same style frame as the background;
c) a top layer containing the buttons.

2 All the button icons should be defined as buttons by Right/ Ctrl+clicking them and selecting **Interactive > Convert to Button.**

3 Convert the picture to a button. The photo will appear when the picnic icon is moused over, so call it "picnic photo." Initially, the picnic photo will not be visible; it will appear when the picnic button is moused over, so select Hidden from the Visibility in PDF menu (It will still be visible in InDesign).

4 Select the picnic button, and open the Behaviors panel of the Button Options dialog box. Choose Mouse Enter from the Event menu, and Show/Hide Fields for Behavior.

5 Check the picnic photo box in the button list to make it visible when the picnic button is moused over, and click the Add button.

6 If you left it at that, the picnic photo would still be visible when you rolled off the button. To make it disappear again, select the Mouse Exit Event. The Show/Hide fields behavior should still be selected, so all you need to do is click the checkbox next to picnic photo until the hide icon (the eye with a line through it) is displayed.

7 Click the Add button to add the behavior to the list and click OK.
Export the file to PDF to check that everything is working. The panel should be empty until you mouse over the picnic button, when the knocked-back picnic photo will display. Move the pointer off the button and the photo disappears again.

8 Add Mouse Enter and Mouse Exit event behaviors to the other buttons, using different pictures to complete the panel. You can show and hide multiple fields to display text, or anything else in the panel, when a button is moused over.

Style tags

Style tags make it possible for those involved in the copy creation and editing stages of production to apply InDesign paragraph and character styles to text using a word processor or simple text editor. InDesign CS2's new style mapping feature means that Microsoft Word styles can be easily, flexibly, and automatically converted to InDesign styles.

Tagged text structure

```
<ParaStyle:small headline>Telegraph Wins <0x201C>Quark Award<0x201D>
<ParaStyle:standfirst>Quark-Sponsored UK Newspaper Design of the Year Award
goes to a Newspaper Published using Adobe InDesign and Adobe InCopy
Software.
<ParaStyle:bold first para>The Daily Telegraph, produced entirely in
```

```
Software.
<ParaStyle:bold first para>The Daily Telegraph, produced entirely in
Adobe<0x00AE> InDesign<0x00AE> and InCopy<0x00AE> software, has won the
prestigious UK Newspaper Design of the Year award for 2005, also known as
<0x201C>The Quark Award.<0x201D><0x00A0>
<ParaStyle:body copy>Quark Inc., provider of QuarkXPress software, sponsors
```

This text file contains four differently styled elements. The tag appears at the beginning of the text to which it applies. We've highlighted the intro and the first paragraph style here.

When placed in an InDesign document with paragraph style sheets corresponding to the tags, the styles are automatically applied.

Telegraph Wins "Quark Award"

Quark-Sponsored UK Newspaper Design of the Year Award goes to a Newspaper Published using Adobe InDesign and Adobe InCopy Software.

The Daily Telegraph, produced entirely in Adobe® InDesign® and InCopy® software, has won the prestigious UK Newspaper Design of the Year award for 2005, also known as "The Quark Award."

Quark Inc., provider of QuarkXPress software, sponsors the award that singles out the UK's best-designed newspaper.

Tip

LOCAL FORMATTING

When you preserve styles and formatting in imported Word text, local formatting—such as individual words with bold and italic styling applied—are maintained as local overrides.

In some workflows, it's necessary to strip all formatting from imported Word text using the Remove Styles and Formatting from Text and Tables option in the Microsoft Word Import Options dialog box. In these cases, it's still possible to preserve the italicizing and bolding if you check the Preserve Local Overrides box. Then, when you apply InDesign paragraph styles to text, local formatting is automatically preserved.

Formatting
◉ Remove Styles and Formatting from Text and Tables
☑ Preserve Local Overrides

Understanding tagged text

1 If you're unfamiliar with the formatting of style tags, you can view them by exporting a story from InDesign with paragraph styles applied. Use the Type tool to place an insertion point anywhere in the story, press Ctrl/Cmd+E, and click the Save button in the Export Dialog box to create a tagged text file.

Open the TXT file in a text editor such as TextEdit on the Mac, or Notepad on the PC.

```
<ASCII-MAC>
<Version:4><FeatureSet:InDesign-Roman><
purple:COLOR:CMYK:Process:0.64999997615
0,0,0,1><Bullet blue:COLOR:CMYK:Process
<DefineCharStyle:drop cap=<Nextstyle:dr
Ultra Black><cHorizontalScale:1.100000>
```

2 InDesign style tags are always enclosed by the < > characters. The first tags in the file denote the character coding and platform—in this case <ASCII-MAC>. This initial tag must be present, or the file won't be recognized as a tagged file—the copy will be imported into InDesign as plain text, complete with all the tags.

3 Next come all the style definitions. You don't need these if the InDesign document already has its own styles set up—they're only necessary to define new styles in the InDesign document. Generally speaking, you'll set up all the styles in InDesign and provide a list to copy editors so that they can format the text file as required.

```
ructing business because there are many i
he quality and resolution of the digita
aper used, and color managment and print
vided here you<0x2019>ll be able to cons
rom your printer.
::section head>Image resolution
```

4 The numbers you can see throughout the text are hexadecimal Unicode values for text characters. For example, the tag <0x2019> is the code for an apostrophe. You can enter any Unicode character in this way.

Using Microsoft Word styles

The main advantage of using a text editor to pre-style copy using tags is that writers and editors can provide layout-ready, tagged text without going anywhere near InDesign—all they need is a computer with a text editor.

If they are using Microsoft Word, however, the potential for prestyling text becomes even greater.

1 First, set up styles in Word and in InDesign. It's not strictly necessary to use identical names for the Word and InDesign styles, but it makes life a lot easier. This is the same news story used earlier, formatted in Word, with the four styles applied. The Word style definitions themselves don't matter, but it can be helpful for the writer or editor if they bear some resemblance to the final InDesign styles. Save the file in .doc format.

2 Place the file in InDesign in the usual way, checking Show Import Options in the Place dialog box. Check the button labeled Preserve Styles and Formatting from Text and Tables. If you have used the same style names, you will be presented with a warning. Here, the yellow warning triangle indicates that there are four style conflicts—that is, four style definitions in the Word and InDesign documents with the same names. This is, of course, exactly what we expected.

3 Previous versions of InDesign, though able to import Word documents with styles, didn't provide much control over what happened with style conflicts. In InDesign CS2, the Microsoft Word Import Options dialog box enables you to rename and keep the Word styles, replace them with the InDesign styles, or redefine the existing InDesign styles with the information from the Word styles.

4 Select Use InDesign Style Definition from both the Paragraph Style Conflicts and the Character Style Conflicts drop-down menus. Wherever the Word character or paragraph style names are the same as the InDesign names, the InDesign names will be used.

5 Click OK to place the text, which adopts the InDesign paragraph styling.

Mapping styles

Style mapping is required when the Word and InDesign styles don't have the same names. As long as the Word text elements are differentiated using styles, then InDesign styles can be mapped to them. For example, this document has been styled using the default Heading 1, Heading 2, Heading 3, and Normal styles.

1 Import the Word document with the Show Import Options box checked, and click the Preserve Styles and Formatting from Text and Tables button. If you leave the Import Styles Automatically button checked, InDesign will add the Word styles to the Paragraph Styles palette, and use them to style the text. In other words, it will look the same as it did in the Word document.

2 To map the Word styles to the correct InDesign paragraph styles, check the Customize Style Import radio button and click the Style Mapping button. The Style Mapping dialog box displays the used MS Word Styles on the left, and the InDesign styles they map to on the right.

3 From the drop-down menu opposite the Normal Word style, select the InDesign body copy style from the list of InDesign styles. Assign the other Word Styles to their corresponding InDesign styles in the same way, and click OK.

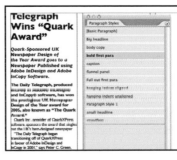

4 Click OK in the Microsoft Word Import Options dialog box, and place the text. If you've mapped the styles correctly, the copy will appear with the InDesign Styles applied. Style mapping is a little slower than automatic import of same-name styles, but it does mean that copy producers are able to supply pre-styled text without having to be aware of specific style names.

OUTPUT

Printing
Transparency flattening and separations
PDF for print
Preflighting and packaging

Printing

Printing your InDesign layout can be as simple as choosing File > Print and clicking OK, or it can involve careful tweaking of various options in the Print dialog box panels—either to solve a problem or to generate a specific type of printout. Most of the time your jobs will fall somewhere in between.

InDesign can print to PostScript (Level 2 and 3) printers and non-PostScript printers such as inkjets, as long as they have first been entered into your computer's operating system.

To start the printing process, choose File > Print, choose a custom Print Preset from File > Print Preset, or simply press Ctrl/Cmd+P. The Print dialog box opens and the first of its seven panels, General, is automatically selected.

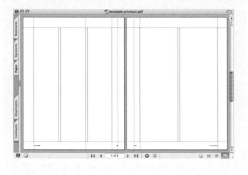

Tip

THE PREVIEW WINDOW

No matter which panel is active in the Print dialog box, the lower left corner will always contain a Preview window showing a proxy page (it has a large "P" on it). The proxy changes as you make modifications to the settings in the Print dialog box to let you know the results of your settings. If you change something that will cause pages to be cut off, for example, part of the proxy will "hang off" the white paper background. Fix the relevant setting, and the proxy redraws to show it will fit the paper. Keeping an eye on the proxy will help you avoid printing problems before they occur.

The General panel

Print

Print Preset: [Custom] **A**
Printer: C5300 **B**
PPD: OKI C5300(PS) **C**

General
Setup
Marks and Bleed
Output
Graphics
Color Management
Advanced
Summary

General

Copies: 1 ☐ Collate ☐ Reverse Order

Pages
Pages: ⦿ All
○ Range: 1–16
Sequence: All Pages
☐ Spreads
☐ Print Master Pages

D

Options
☐ Print Non-printing Objects **E**
☐ Print Blank Pages
☐ Print Visible Guides and Baseline Grids

(Page Setup...) (Printer...) (Save Preset...) (Cancel) (Print)

A Choose a Print Preset— if you have one already set up—from the drop-down menu at the top to quickly fill all the panels in the Print dialog box with settings you've previously saved.

B The printer you last used is preselected in the Printer drop-down menu. Click on the menu to choose a different printer on your network. You'll also see other virtual printers available here—for example, you could choose PostScript to "print" the layout to disk as a PostScript file. If you've installed Adobe Acrobat Pro (v6 or v7), you'll see Adobe PDF appear as an option in this menu.

PostScript® File

Adobe PDF
Adobe PDF 7.0
Bluetooth-Modem
✓ C5300
Internal Modem

C If printing to a PostScript device, the PPD (PostScript Printer Description) file should be selected here.

D Enter the number of copies you'd like to output, whether you want them collated or printed in reverse, and the page range. To output a single page from a multi-page document, enter its page number in the Range field (e.g. 5). Use hyphens and commas to specify other page ranges within a document (e.g. 2-5,17,20-22 would print pages 2, 3, 4, 5, 17, 20, 21, and 22).

E Tells InDesign to include page elements you've set to be non-printing via the Attributes palette. If you want to print items on hidden layers, you'll need to make those layers visible before opening the Print dialog box.

Tip

SAVING PRINT PRESETS

The more time you spend tweaking settings in different Print dialog box panels, the more you need to start saving your settings in Print Presets. That way, you just need to select the applicable Preset from the Print dialog box or from the File > Print Presets fly-out menu, and the settings associated with that Preset automatically populate all the panels in the Print dialog box.

The Setup panel

A Paper Size refers to the paper dimensions that your printer supports—Letter, Tabloid, A4, and so on. Only those sizes included in the printer's driver or PPD appear in the drop-down menu.

B If you choose a printer and PPD that offer continuous-roll printing, such as an imagesetter, you can set up Offset and Gap measures here.

C The page size is the size of a single page of your document—the Width and Height measurement you entered when you first set up the layout. This can be verified and modified in File > Document Setup.

D For non-critical in-house proofing, turning on Scale to Fit is all that's necessary to shrink an oversize design onto the paper printouts.

E You can use the Page Position drop-down menu to tell InDesign where to place the artwork relative to the paper. The default is the Upper Left corner of the paper. Other options are Centered Vertically, Centered Horizontally, and Centered (both Horizontally and Vertically).

F Turn on the Thumbnails checkbox and look at the page proxy in the Preview window to see the size at which the pages will appear. Choose the number of pages (or spreads) that you'd like to fit on each printed page from the drop-down menu, then click the Print button. All the content appears in the Thumbnail printouts, with page numbers automatically appearing above them.

G When tiling, InDesign prints out sections of each page at 100%—as much as can fit on the Paper size you specify. These will require manual re-assembly if you wish to display them as complete pages. The Preview window shows how each page will be divided, and where InDesign will overlap sections to aid in the reassembly. There are ways to customize the way InDesign divides the pages—use the Tiling method drop-down menu, the Overlap field, the Preview window, and the online Help as your guide.

The Marks and Bleed panel

To get Marks, Bleed, and Slug data to appear on the printouts, either the media needs to be large enough to contain the page at 100% plus the area needed for Marks and Bleeds, or you need to turn on Scale to Fit in the Setup panel to scale the page elements down.

A Crop Marks are thin horizontal and vertical rules that align with the page's trim boundaries, and appear at each of its four corners.

B Bleed Marks look just like Crop Marks, but are outset from them by the amount of the Bleed; they align with the Bleed Setting specified in the Bleed and Slug section of the dialog box.

C Registration Marks are small circular targets at the center sides of the page image that are used to align color-separated film plates (so they're not really needed for composite proofs).

D Turning on the checkbox for Color Bars adds small squares of CMYK and grayscale ink. Printers use these to help calibrate ink density on the press.

E When Page Information is enabled, a line of automatically generated text is added to the bottom of every printout between the Crop Marks, including the file name, the page number, and the date and time of the printout. The color plate name is also included when outputting color separations.

F The Type of Marks is standard and seldom changed in practice.

G By default, the Crop, Bleed, and Registration marks are all made with lines that are .25pt, which may be too light or too heavy for your purposes. You can increase the weight of the marks to .5pt, or decrease it to .125pt, in the Weight drop-down menu.

H To keep the marks further away from the page and its bleed, increase the Offset. Your print vendor may request a specific mark offset; this field is where you'd enter the measure.

I If you've specified a Bleed amount you can turn on Use Document Bleed Settings and the same measures will appear in the Bleed fields.

J You can also enter your Bleed measure manually. The measure tells InDesign how much of the Bleed to print on each side, and to crop out anything that extends beyond the measure. If you don't enter a Bleed here, InDesign crops any existing Bleeds to the trim edges in your printout.

K Unlike the Bleed settings, the Slug area has to be defined in the document; you can't enter measures here. Assuming you did define a Slug area in New Document or Document Setup, turning on the Include Slug Area checkbox will add that area to the printout.

Printing, continued

The first three panels in the Print dialog box, covered in the previous spread, deal with mechanical options: how many copies, in what arrangement, and at what scale. The next four panels, which we'll cover here, are concerned with the elements on the pages themselves: color output, graphics, fonts, inks, and transparency. (The eighth and last panel, Summary, simply lists all the options you selected in the previous seven panels.)

The Graphics panel

Tweak the Graphics panel defaults for the optimal combination of print quality and speed.

Ⓐ In Images, you can change the default Send Data method from Optimized Subsampling to All, so that InDesign doesn't downsample high-resolution images as it sends them to your printer. If your printer is low on memory and you have many high-res images, then you may want to change it back. Choose Proxy (a very low-resolution image) or None (images are replaced by gray boxes) for fast output of rough proofs when image quality isn't important.

Ⓑ In Fonts, change the default Download method from Complete to Subset. Complete downloads every glyph in every font used in the file (up to 2,000 glyphs per font, as per the default Font Downloading limit in Preferences > General) to the printer at the start of the job, which can slow down printing and overwhelm your printer's RAM. Subset sends just those characters used on a page to the printer as it sends each page's data. In either case, make sure that Download PPD fonts is checked so that the fonts on your hard drive are used even if the PPD says one or more of them are resident on your printer.

Ⓒ Choose the highest level of PostScript available in the drop-down menu (some printers can emulate more than one, and default to lower levels), and choose Binary instead of ASCII as the Data Format—binary files usually print faster. If the output is garbled, change the Data Format back to ASCII.

The Color Management panel

Ⓐ Leave the Print radio button set to Document if you just wish to print your InDesign document. The Proof button is used for simulating different printers. You can set the printer to simulate in the View > Proof Setup > Custom menu.

Ⓑ The Color Handling drop-down menu lets you specify whether color management should take place in InDesign or in the printer.

Ⓒ By default, the Color Management panel in InDesign is set to send the same CMYK color space data to your printer as that your document is based upon, resulting in a color managed workflow ... if you happen to be printing to a web offset press. This is because the default CMYK color space for the document, as defined in the Color Settings, is US Web Coated (SWOP) v2; and by default the Printer Profile is set to match the Document CMYK profile in the Color Management panel.
If you don't have a web press in your studio, but you did go to the trouble of creating and installing an ICC Profile for the color printer you do have, then choose its profile from the Printer Profile drop-down menu. If you don't have a custom printer profile, you can leave this set to Document CMYK—the colors it outputs will be "close enough."

Ⓓ When the Printer Profile is anything other than Document CMYK, the options for Preserve CMYK Numbers (on by default) and Simulate Paper Color (off by default) can be changed. Preserve CMYK Numbers maintains the color values of unmanaged CMYK images in your document (those saved without an embedded profile). This should normally be left turned on. Be prepared for a shock, though, if you turn on Simulate Paper Color, because the color can be heavily modified as InDesign tries to show you how the design might look on cheap newsprint, for example.

The Output panel

```
                    Print

Print Preset:  [Custom]                              ❶   Composite Leave Unchanged
                                                     ❷   Composite Gray
    Printer:   C5300                                 ❸   Composite RGB
       PPD:    OKI C5300(PS)                    ❹ ✓  Composite CMYK
                                                     ┌─ Separations
┌──────────────────┐   Output                   ❺   └─ In-RIP Separations
│ General          │
│ Setup            │   🅐 Color:    Separations  ▼        ☐ Text as Black 🅑
│ Marks and Bleed  │   🅒 Trapping: Application Built-In ▼
│ Output           │   🅓 Flip:     None         ▼        ☐ Negative
│ Graphics         │   🅔 Screening: 150 lpi / 1200 dpi ▼
│ Color Management │
│ Advanced         │   ┌─ Inks ──────────────────────────────┐
│ Summary          │   │ 🖨 Ink              Frequency  Angle │
└──────────────────┘   │ 🖨 ▪ Process Cyan      154      124  │
                       │ 🖨 ▪ Process Magenta   154       56  │
┌──────────────┐       │ 🖨 ▫ Process Yellow     70       32  │   🅕
│              │       │ 🖨 ▪ Process Black     150       90  │
│      ┌─────┐ │       │ 🖨 ▪ PANTONE 541 C     150       45  │
│      │  P  │ │       │ 🖨 ▪ PANTONE 540 C     150       45  │
│      └─────┘ │       └──────────────────────────────────────┘
│              │
└──────────────┘       Frequency: 150    lpi    ☐ Simulate Overprint
                       Angle:     45      °   🅖   ( Ink Manager... ) 🅗

( Page Setup... )  ( Printer... )  ( Save Preset... )  ( Cancel )  ( Print )
```

🅐 The four choices for composite color output differ mainly in what they do with the color values in your document. Except for imported vector or EPS artwork (unless they interact with transparency), any color conversion performed by InDesign only affects imported raster images and colors applied to native InDesign elements. Disable any color management features that your printer driver may be running, so the color doesn't get converted twice.

1) Composite Leave Unchanged should only be used when all of your elements have been color-managed for a particular output device, and you want InDesign to output the original color values precisely. In this mode, InDesign ignores the CMYK color space selected in the Color Settings. If RGB colors are present, InDesign sends those RGB values to the printer—it doesn't convert them to CMYK (your color printer will do this internally).

2) Composite Gray converts all color (except RGB or Lab colors in placed PDF or EPS files, which are locked to InDesign) to grayscale equivalents. It's useful to see how a color printout will look on a black-and-white copier, or to save on toner for in-house proofs.

3) Composite RGB converts all color to the RGB color space, and sends that data to your printer. Some printers, such as inkjets and film recorders, produce optimal color when they receive RGB data.

4) The default color output method, Composite CMYK, is the best all-purpose setting for printing CMYK color proofs and color separations on PostScript printers. It supports CMYK and spot color plates, and converts any RGB or Lab colors to their CMYK equivalents, even if Color Management is turned off.

5) Choose one of the two Separations output methods to print color separations. Doing so will output one page per process or spot color for each page in the chosen range. Separations always print with black ink because they're meant for making printing plates from film separations. If your printer doesn't support PostScript, you won't be able to choose a Separated output option. If your PostScript printer doesn't support In-RIP separations (the separating is done in the printer's RIP, not by InDesign), that option will be grayed out.

171

Use the Output panel to specify how you'd like InDesign to send color output to the device you're printing to—either as composites or as color separations—and which method for either type of output you'd like it to use.

🅑 Turning on the Text as Black checkbox converts colored type to 100% Black in any of the Composite modes. Text that's filled with the [Paper] color is left untouched.

🅒 Trapping is Off by default, even when you choose Separations. To include trapping, choose Application Built-In or Adobe In-RIP if your printer supports it.

🅓 The Flip drop-down menu (its options are None, Horizontal, Vertical, and Horizontal & Vertical), along with the Negative checkbox, is used when outputting separations to film or direct-to-plate.

🅔 The Screening options enable you to choose between the different Linescreen (lines per inch, or lpi) and Resolution (dots per inch, or dpi) modes your printer supports.

🅕 The area labeled Inks at the bottom of the Output panel lists all the Process inks (Cyan, Magenta, Yellow, and Black), even if they're not used in the layout. Similarly, all spot colors from the Swatches palette are listed. RGB and Lab colors used in the document are never listed, because they're converted to CMYK (by InDesign or by your printer's RIP) on the fly during the printing process.

When you're printing composites, the individual inks are locked—you can't turn them on or off, or change their Frequency or Angle. All that's available is the Simulate Overprint option (to roughly proof overprinting fills and strokes), and the Ink Manager. Remember that you can use the Ink Manager to convert all your spots to process, or to alias one ink to another.

Unlike Composites, when you're printing Separations you do have control over which inks are output. You can leave them all selected (the small printer icon to the left of each ink name indicates that you want that ink to print) and not worry about wasting paper, since InDesign will only output an ink separation for a page if it's needed.

To tell InDesign not to output a particular ink, even if it is used, click the printer icon to the left of the ink's name so the icon disappears. (Click the empty square again to turn the ink back on.)

🅖 When you've chosen separated output, you can also select an ink and change its default Frequency (lpi) and Angle, as defined by the PostScript printer's PPD.

There's seldom a need to change the default Frequency and Angle except in one particular situation: when two or more Spot colors will be applied to the same area, as in a Gradient from one Spot to another, or when they're both included in a Mixed Ink swatch. If you leave every spot ink at InDesign's default Frequency of 150 and Angle of 45 degrees, the results will be muddy because they'll print right on top of each other. Change the Angle, at least, for each additional Spot color to a unique measure (check with your print vendor for their recommendation) before preparing pre-separated output.

🅗 See page 106 for more information on the Ink Manager.

The Advanced panel

The Advanced panel of the Print dialog is refreshingly simple. There are only two options to deal with: OPI and the Transparency Flattener.

🅐 If you're working in a network where an OPI image server is swapping low-res images for high-res images when you print or export a file, turn on the checkbox for OPI Image Replacement and disable any image formats that aren't managed by the OPI server. Otherwise, if you're not working in such an environment you can ignore this section, as OPI is turned off by default.

🅑 If your network printer has a decent amount of memory, you should change the default for the Transparency Flattener preset from Medium Resolution to High Resolution. High Resolution requires more processing, but delivers results closer to what a commercial printer will provide.

Transparency flattening and separations

One of InDesign's most exciting design-level features is its rich support for transparency. Any object can have its opacity reduced from 100% to whatever level fits your design concept, and a range of blending modes provides Photoshop-level control over the way the elements interact on the page. You can also import images with transparent areas—for example, native Photoshop graphics with soft cutouts and translucent layers.

Transparency controls open up a world of creative possibilities. However, a problem arises with reproducing the effects outside InDesign, either by saving to a PDF file or outputting directly to a high-quality printer. PostScript, the page description language behind the PDF format and virtually all professional printing, doesn't support true object transparency at all.

The way around this is for InDesign to generate a "flattened" version of the layout on output, by slicing up, filling, and assembling the different elements and, if necessary, rendering effects as bitmaps to replicate the visual effects of the transparency. This only happens when a layout contains transparency settings or objects, but remember that this includes any soft shadows and feathered edges created in InDesign. When required, flattening happens automatically at three different points in a layout: printing, creating a PDF file (unless you want to preserve transparency), or exporting to EPS format.

Flattening with PostScript printers

When printing to PostScript devices such as prepress imagesetters, digital presses and most laser printers, the flattening settings in the Print dialog's Advanced panel are used.

Flattening when exporting to PDF

Use the Advanced panel of the Export PDF Presets dialog to set flattening controls for PDF production presets. If the Transparency Flattener menu is disabled, set the Compatibility level to Acrobat 4. Technically, flattening isn't an absolute requirement for PDF files, as Acrobat 5.0 and above can handle transparency through extensions of the underlying PDF code. However, if you're creating PDF files for press work, it is usually best to use the flattening options. Part of the PDF/X production settings includes flattening as standard.

Flattening when exporting to EPS

When exporting to an EPS file, the Advanced tab in the Export EPS dialog contains the flattening settings.

Flattening with non-PostScript printers

If you're printing to a non-PostScript device, such as an inkjet printer, the Transparency Flattener presets aren't available. Instead, choose the Output panel in the Print dialog and enable Simulate Overprint. The results will replicate what you see on the display when you select View > Overprint Preview. This is usually an acceptable way to generate desktop proofs from a non-PostScript printer, although you should always double-check the print against the on-screen layout for any anomalies.

The transparency behavior is slightly different when working in RGB mode than in CMYK. To switch from one to the other, go to Edit > Transparency Blend Space, and select the options which suit your layout's final destination. Normally this will be Document CMYK for print work.

Transparency Flattener Presets

There are three presets provided for transparency flattening. These define the resolution for any rendering that's applied, and this directly affects the output quality and the amount of in-printer processing that is required. When making quick prints, and outputting to PDF for onscreen checking, Low Resolution is generally the best option. This renders line artwork at 288ppi and other imagery at 144ppi. For desktop proofing and print-on-demand output, Medium Resolution is a better choice. This renders line art and continuous

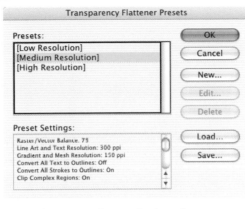

tone graphics respectively at the more laser printer-oriented 300ppi and 150ppi resolutions. For the highest quality output with prepress equipment, the High

Resolution flattener preset should be selected. This generates line art at 1200ppi, ensuring smooth results at commercial print levels.

Tip

CHECKING FOR TRANSPARENCY Flattening involves referencing the high-resolution originals of any imported documents, so run your layout through a quick preflight check to catch any problems and to see pages with "non-transparent objects." Images which are flagged as missing won't be able to be flattened properly. This can be an issue in OPI workflows, where low-resolution placement images are replaced with press-ready versions on output, and where DCS (desktop color separation) graphics are used.

For a simpler way to see if transparency is used in your document, look at the Pages palette. This shows pages with transparency by giving them the standard Photoshop-derived gray checkerboard background.

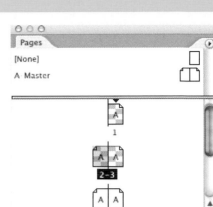

Using the Flattener Preview palette

The Flattener Preview palette is invaluable for finding the specific items that will be affected by flattening before sending a layout off to print.

None

Rasterized Complex Regions
Transparent Objects
All Affected Objects
Affected Graphics
Outlined Strokes
Outlined Text
Raster-fill Text and Strokes
✓ All Rasterized Regions

1 When you pick a highlight option in its popup list, the layout is rendered in gray tints, and any relevant areas in the layout which will be flattened will be highlighted with a color.

2 If you have very specific requirements for how flattening will be handled, you can create your own Flattener presets. Choose Transparency Flattener Presets from the Flattener Preview palette's popup menu (or choose Edit > Transparency Flattener Presets) and click New in the this dialog. Your custom presets will be available wherever the flattener preset choices are shown.

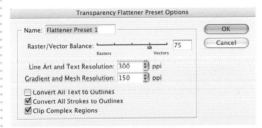

Previewing separations

1 Previewing how a layout will be split up as separations is equally useful. Choose Window > Output > Separations Preview to open the Separations Preview palette. Now choose Separations from its View popup menu, then click to hide or show the different inks in its window. Your layout will be rendered with just the inks you choose, so you can see how the layout will be produced, ink by ink, on the press. If you hide all but one ink, then the page will be rendered in black—very helpful when checking how paler inks such as process yellow or a light spot color are used.

2 Choose Ink Limit from the View popup menu. When you move your cursor over an area on the page, the percentage of each ink that will be applied at that point is shown in the palette, with the total ink amount for process colors listed in the CMYK row. Ask your printer what the maximum ink coverage should be and put that into the Ink Limit field at the top of this palette. Areas that exceed this will be highlighted.

You can carry on editing your layout with separation previewing enabled, and with the flattening preview turned on if you like, but this is normally best reserved for examining how the layout will be processed and recreated, rather than switched on as standard while you work.

PDF for print

PDF is a reliable, robust format for delivering artwork for printing—but only if the files are prepared properly for the type of output you plan to use. InDesign provides you with all you need, but you have to make a number of choices before you'll achieve the best results. There are many options available when building PDF files, so you can fine-tune the production process to tailor the output precisely to your requirements.

New PDF Export Preset dialog

InDesign CS2 ships with five ready-made PDF export presets, named after their most appropriate use. Choose File > Adobe PDF Presets and pick from the list of alternatives. When you export to PDF from here, it will be generated with the settings you chose. Most of the time, this is all you need to do to get perfect PDF files.

If you'd like to define new presets, or simply to examine the existing ones, choose File > Adobe PDF Presets > Define, and select a preset in the dialog. The Preset Settings Summary shows all the different options for the current preset. To look in greater detail, and to build a new one from any existing preset, click New. You'll start with the options taken from the selected preset.

The print presets, along with their recommended usage, are described below:

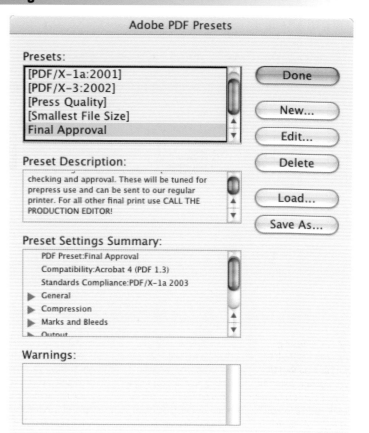

• High Quality Print is best for desktop printers and basic studio and office proofers. Until you're ready to output for high-quality production, this is normally the best choice. The PDF files you get will be a reasonable size, but without compromised quality. Images with output pixel resolutions higher than 450ppi will be resampled to 300ppi to keep the file size from becoming too large.

• Press Quality is a good general-purpose press-oriented option. It is very similar to High Quality Print, but converts colors with embedded profiles to the specified destination color profile if they're different.

• Smallest File Size is a good choice for delivering PDF files for use on screen, whether it's for quick layout approval, or creating on-screen documentation. Large images are downsampled to 100ppi and compressed fairly heavily, and colors are converted to the sRGB color space.

The other two presets are PDF/X-1a and PDF/X-3. PDF/X isn't a different file format, it is the term for PDF files created to specific prepress ISO standards for predictable, reliable graphic content delivery. These export options provide two specific industry-approved ranges of output settings, which are intended to provide precisely what is needed by an imagesetter or digital press that is prepared for PDF/X standards.

• PDF/X-1a is designed to generate basic prepress-ready documents without any extras. This supports CMYK and spot color output (and nothing else), targeted to a specific output device.

• PDF/X-3 covers similar ground to PDF/X-1a, but also adds color management workflow support, and the ability to specify restricted halftone settings to everything found in the PDF/X-1a standard.

PDF/X isn't the be-all and end-all for prepress production. The even newer pass4press prepress output standard adds to the PDF/X approach. This is a set of guidelines which cover the full gamut of preflighting, proofing, and delivery. This encompasses far more than can be covered by PDF production settings, but you'll find complete information including recommended PDF creation settings at www.pass4press.com.

New PDF Export Preset dialog

New PDF Export Preset

Preset Name: Final Approval

Standard: PDF/X-1a:2003   Compatibility: Acrobat 4 (PDF 1.3)

General
Compression
Marks and Bleeds
Output
Advanced
Summary

Summary

Description: Use this to generate PDFs for final production checking and approval. These will be tuned for prepress use and can be sent to our regular printer. For all other final print use CALL THE PRODUCTION EDITOR!

Options:
PDF Preset:Adobe PDF Preset 1
Compatibility:Acrobat 4 (PDF 1.3)
Standards Compliance:PDF/X-1a 2003
▶ General
▶ Compression
▼ Marks and Bleeds
    Crop Marks: On
    Bleed Marks: On
    Registration Marks: On
    Color Bars: On
    Page Information: On
    Page Mark Type: Default
    Weight: 0.25 pt

Warnings:

Save Summary...

Cancel   OK

If none of the existing presets quite fits the bill, Choose **File > Adobe PDF Presets > Define**, select the preset that's closest to your requirements (the New PDF Export Preset dialog will open with these settings),

and click New. Now go through the headings on the left of the window, making your choices in the panel on the right. You can add a custom description in the General section to alert users to important

points. One of the main reasons why you might want to make your own PDF export preset is to include registration and crop marks, as these aren't included in any of the ready-made settings.

Image cropping in PDF

Print

Print Preset: [Custom]

Printer: PostScript® File

PPD: Device Independent

General
Setup
Marks and Bleed
Output
Graphics
Color Management
Advanced
Summary

Advanced

OPI
☑ OPI Image Replacement
Omit For OPI: ☐ EPS ☐ PDF ☐ Bitmap Images

Transparency Flattener
Preset: [Medium Resolution]
☐ Ignore Spread Overrides

P

Page Setup...   Printer...   Save Preset...   Cancel   Save

All the standard presets create PDF files that can be opened in Acrobat 5.0 or later, except for the PDF/X settings which cater for Acrobat 4.0 and above. InDesign doesn't cater to older versions of Acrobat,

but this is unlikely to matter as new versions of Acrobat Reader are freely available to download. Each preset is set to crop image data to its frame edges. This is useful for removing data not needed for viewing

or printing, but it means that last-minute changes to image cropping can't be done without using the original InDesign layout. If you make your own presets, you can turn this off, but it will lead to larger file sizes.

Converting color

New PDF Export Preset

Preset Name: Adobe PDF Preset 1

Standard: None   Compatibility: Acrobat 5 (PDF 1.4)

General
Compression
Marks and Bleeds
Output
Advanced
Summary

Output

Color
Color Conversion: Convert to Destination (Prese...
Destination: Europe ISO Coated FOGRA27
Profile Inclusion Policy: Include Destination Profile

☐ Simulate Overprint   Ink Manager...

PDF/X
Output Intent Profile Name: N/A
Output Condition Name: N/A
Output Condition Identifier: N/A
Registry Name: N/A

Description
Colors will be converted to the destination profile space only if they have embedded profiles that differ from the destination profile (or if they are RGB colors and the destination profile is CMYK, or vice versa). Color objects without embedded profiles and native objects (such as line art or type) are not converted, so that color numbers are preserved.

Cancel   OK

In the Output section of the New PDF Export Preset dialog, you can force colors to be converted to the destination's color space, or to leave them unchanged, so that the final PDF file will be produced only using the color space that you want.

If you convert colors, it is generally best to choose Convert to Destination

(Preserve Numbers) to avoid color shifts in native colors and graphics without embedded profiles.

Converting during PDF export isn't necessarily the best approach, though. If the final output device can adequately handle color conversions, then leaving things unchanged means that your PDF file

will contain the widest possible color gamut. If you're not sure about this, converting inappropriate colors to the device color space will avoid potential disasters. However, for full control, this is best done beforehand in your color lists and source images.

Preflighting and packaging

Preflighting is the process of checking a document for any potential problems, much as a pilot will run through a system of checks before taking a plane down the runway. This is usually performed just before sending a job to print, to ensure that all of its components are available. If an image is missing or is in the wrong format, a font is disabled, or a color is defined in the wrong color space, your job won't print properly.

Running preflight checks

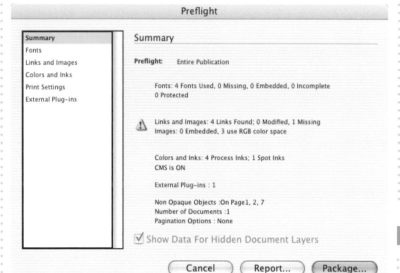

Choose **File > Preflight** to run your current document through InDesign's built-in preflight process. If problems are found, you'll see a small alert icon next to the relevant section in the brief summary.

Preflighting isn't just for when you're preparing for publishing, however. It can be useful at any stage for confirming that all is as it should be. Whenever you share InDesign layouts with anyone else—and especially if work has been done on different computers—it's advisable to run a quick preflight check.

The standard preflight report will show information on absolutely every aspect of your document, whether it is a problem or not.

If you're faced with a long, unwieldy list, click the Show Problems Only checkbox. Anything which isn't a problem will be omitted from the lists, leaving you free to get on with dealing with the troublemakers in isolation.

Preflighting fonts

Select Fonts in the Preflight dialog to see a detailed report on every font used by your layout document. This includes the fonts used in EPS and PDF files that have been placed into the pages, in addition to those set directly in text frames. It is very easy to forget about fonts in imported graphics in the rush of sending a job to print, so always use the Preflight process to check. If any font is listed as missing or incomplete (a PostScript font with missing screen or printer font files), select the offending item and click Find Font. The resulting InDesign Find Font dialog can help you track down and, if necessary, replace a problematic typeface in your layout.

Preflighting images

All graphics in InDesign can be either embedded directly in the layout itself, or, more usually, linked to external files. The Links and Images section of the Preflight report lists all linked files, showing the filename, the type of graphic, the page where it can be found, its status, and, if appropriate, whether it has an ICC color profile. Select an image that has been modified since it was imported and you'll be able to update its in-page image. If the item has been renamed or moved, you can relink it. The Repair All button walks through the list, fixing things as it goes and prompting you for help if necessary.

From here, assuming you've fixed any issues which could cause trouble, you can click the Package button to create a copy of your document and all its resources, ready to send off for production—or to send off to someone else for further work.

1 When you're ready to send a layout to be printed, you may prefer to send a copy of your InDesign layout and all its associated images and fonts to the printer rather than producing a PDF. This allows more last-minute editing to be done if needed, so your printer or prepress operator may prefer this to a PDF. It is also a sensible option if you're a freelancer delivering layouts to a client, or if you're not sure which options to use for PDF production. InDesign's Package feature gathers together all the elements used in your layout, from fonts to linked images, and also generates a text file with detailed output instructions. Choose **File > Package** to start the process.

2 The first thing that happens is a quick preflight check (see page 176) to see whether there are any problems with the file itself, or the fonts, images, or colors that you've used. If you're told that possible problems were detected, you should choose to view the information in detail to see whether it is a real cause for concern.

3 The Printing Instructions form will be produced along with the layout files and used as reference by whomever prints your work. At the very least, you should enter your name, contact number, and any relevant instructions for outputting the files.

4 Finally, choose which items will be included with your packaged version of the layout. InDesign defaults to copying all linked images into a "Links" folder, and adjusting the link paths in the layout. It also copies the fonts used in the layout. Note that the Package option will not include fonts based on Chinese, Japanese, or Korean character sets. It will, however, include other non-Roman sets.

5 You'll also see a notice about not breaching your font license by sending it along with your layout, but that's left up to you. To avoid breaking the law, you should check the details of your usage rights for each font, but the most common requirement is that the printer must have their own copy of those fonts. This doesn't mean that you don't need to include those typefaces, however. Some fonts have different metrics (character spacing settings) depending on when and by which foundry they were produced, so using different versions of the same typeface can, in theory, alter line breaks and spacing in a layout.

177

INDESIGN FOR QUARKXPRESS USERS

Find a feature

Keyboard shortcuts

Palettes and dialogs

Getting up to speed with InDesign can be frustrating for experienced QuarkXPress users if there's no cross-reference guide to hand. Not knowing where to find essential features in a hurry is one of the main reasons why many designers put off making the switch. The following pages show where to find a number of vital controls, settings, and features in InDesign, and explain the differences between the two packages.

The selection tools

First of all, the basics: InDesign's direct equivalent to the QuarkXPress Item Selection tool is the Selection tool—the solid arrow in the Toolbar. Use this to select and manipulate objects such as graphic and text boxes on the page. The Direct Selection and Text tools are similar to the Content selection tool in QuarkXPress, selecting and working directly with the contents of objects.

The difference between the Selection tool and the other tools can seem subtle, but it is an important one to remember. For example, when using the Direct Selection tool, the Transform controls will affect the box contents, and when using the Selection tool they will affect the box itself. The Type and Path Type tools—T and Shift+T respectively—are the typographic equivalent of the Direct Selection tool, used for editing text in text frames and on paths.

There's also the Position tool, the alternative to Direct Selection. This repositions images within frames without moving the frames.

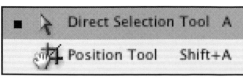

Text and graphic frames

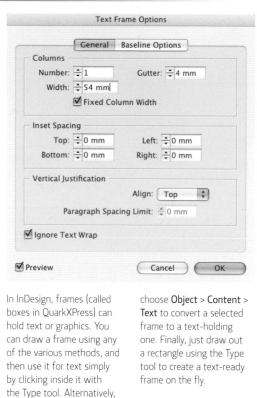

In InDesign, frames (called boxes in QuarkXPress) can hold text or graphics. You can draw a frame using any of the various methods, and then use it for text simply by clicking inside it with the Type tool. Alternatively, choose **Object > Content > Text** to convert a selected frame to a text-holding one. Finally, just draw out a rectangle using the Type tool to create a text-ready frame on the fly.

Editing master page items

If you want to work with items that belong to a master page, you can't select them in the normal manner; InDesign protects them from accidental editing. To gain control over these items, just hold down Ctrl/Cmd+Shift and click.

Default text styles

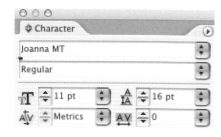

The default typeface, style, size, and so on that apply to new text boxes are determined by the settings in the Control or Character palette. Change these when you have the Type tool selected but no text box active, and your settings will apply to subsequent text boxes automatically. Of course, this just controls how the type settings work in a particular instance, rather than defining a stylesheet—so for proper, professional control over your type, you should create specific styles instead.

Measurements and Control

InDesign's Control palette, the bar which normally runs above your document window, is the equivalent of the Measurements palette in QuarkXPress. This changes its appearance according to what's selected, so in addition to the ubiquitous width, height, and location fields, you'll find type formatting options when working with text; a range of fitting options for frames and their content, rotation and skew settings; and many more. For the full complement of options for different tasks, you should turn to the appropriate dedicated palette. The Stroke palette, for example, offers over half a dozen more line-related features than the Control palette. Nevertheless, it's worth looking here first for the essentials.

Tip

PICTURE BOXES

Moving an image around in a picture box in InDesign reveals a little more than you might be used to in QuarkXPress. The picture box boundaries will crop the image in the same way, but when you use the Direct Selection tool—the closest equivalent to the QuarkXPress content tool in this context— you'll see a brown outline showing you the outer bounds of the image within the frame. This is surprisingly useful, as it shows how much leeway you have when repositioning the graphic within the box. While you use the Direct Selection tool, this outline is displayed for any selected box that contains a placed image. Deselect or switch tools to hide the border again.

180

Linking text frames

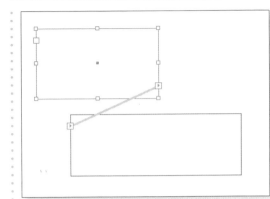

The QuarkXPress process of chaining text boxes together using the Link tool is simpler and more subtle in InDesign. Select a frame and look for the in and out ports, small boxes attached to the selection edge. If there's overmatter (too much text to fit in the frame), the out port on the right will show up in red with a plus sign inside; otherwise it'll be blue and empty. Click this out port and then click anywhere in another frame to flow the text thread from the first box to the second. Alternatively, just click and drag to make a new text box, which is linked in automatically.

Applying type styles

InDesign doesn't let you apply bold, italic, and other styles to type in the same way QuarkXPress does. This is because if the style doesn't actually exist in the typeface family, you'll get unexpected results when you send your job to print. The Style menu in the Control palette and the Character palette only shows the styles available in the current typeface, preventing you from inadvertently applying a pseudo-bold style to a roman-only typeface.

H&J settings

InDesign doesn't have a separate H&J (hyphenation and justification) feature like QuarkXPress. Instead, these settings are provided as part of the paragraph controls. In the Paragraph palette, click the fly-out menu button and choose Justification or Hyphenation to get at these controls. You'll find the options here to be quite familiar, although the slider for choosing better spacing or fewer hyphens is a useful innovation. Both these windows are dialogs rather than palettes, but, as with many of InDesign's dialogs, there's a Preview checkbox which lets you see your changes on the page before you click OK.

181

Tip

SETTING OVERPRINT

Setting something to overprint in InDesign is rather different than doing it in QuarkXPress. Rather than defining an ink as overprinting, this is assigned on an object-by-object basis. If you want certain elements to overprint, choose Window > Attributes to open the Attributes palette, select the element you want to overprint, then click the appropriate Attributes palette checkbox. To ensure that things are working as expected, choose Window > Output > Separations Preview and use that to hide different inks in the layout. Text will overprint by default, but only if it is set with the default [Black] ink. Any other ink, including custom blacks, will be knocked out unless you specifically set the text to overprint using the Attributes palette.

Another way to set text using inks other than the default black so that they overprint is to use the More Options button in the Find/Change palette (Edit > Find/Change). Click the first Format button to choose which text format attribute to look for (choose Character Color and select your color), then click the second Format button in the Find/Change palette, pick the same character color setting, but click the Overprint Fill checkbox. This palette is also where you can set any item to be non-printing, whatever its fills and strokes may be.

Find a feature, continued

Leading controls

InDesign applies leading to type as a character-level attribute, rather than to whole paragraphs at once. This is much more flexible than the QuarkXPress approach, but it can take time to become accustomed to this difference. If you really prefer the QuarkXPress paragraph-level leading method, go to the InDesign Preferences window, choose the Type panel, and pick Apply Leading to Entire Paragraph. Now it will behave in the simpler whole-paragraph manner when applying leading.

Text wrapping

Text runaround settings in InDesign normally include text on top of the item with text wrap settings in addition to the text beneath it. This can be very useful, but it can also be disconcerting if you're used to the QuarkXPress "wrap beneath only" method. To make InDesign behave more like QuarkXPress in this respect, go to the Composition panel in InDesign's Preferences and choose Text Wrap Only Affects Text Beneath.

Applying fill and stroke colors

Assigning color to fills and strokes can be done from both the Swatches and the Color palettes, with Swatches being closest to the Colors palette in QuarkXPress. You may find that you apply color to a stroke when you meant to use it for the fill, and vice versa; make sure that the correct fill or stroke box is foremost when you select a swatch color. The three places this fill/stroke pair of boxes appears are the Swatches palette, the Color palette, and the Toolbar, and clicking one of those puts the focus on it in all three places. If you've assigned a fill color to the stroke, or the other way around, clicking on the flipper arrows by the top-right corner of the fill/stroke swatch controls reassigns the colors.

If you have fill and stroke settings that you'd like to apply to other items, the Eyedropper tool makes this fast and easy. To load the Eyedropper tool, click on the object that has the desired settings. Its cursor icon will change to show it is ready; now click one at a time on every other item you'd like to be the same. When you're done, or if you'd like to unload the tool to start again, click on an empty part of the page or pasteboard.

Tip

SETTING STROKES

Setting strokes in InDesign is far easier than in QuarkXPress. Rather than using a modal dialog that has to be dismissed each time, you have the Stroke palette (Window > Stroke). This controls all basic stroke attributes—weight, stroke alignment, line type, and so on—except for color, which is set using the Swatches palette (Window > Swatches). As with InDesign's many other palettes, this is very useful as an object settings inspection method, in addition to setting parameters; click on an item and glance at the Stroke palette to see how it is set up.

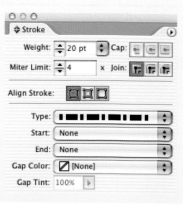

Runarounds

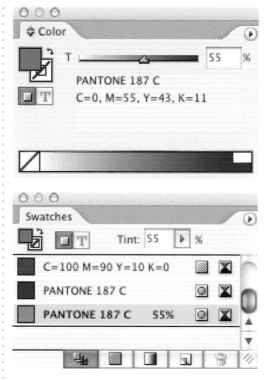

Tints and transparency

Similar to the tint control in QuarkXPress, tints in InDesign are assigned from the Color palette using the standard Tint slider or the associated percentage setting box. But there's more: if you want to save a particular tint as a separate swatch, drag its color chip from the Color palette into the Swatches palette list. Its color values will be shown along with the tint percentage setting.

The transparency feature is one of the reasons why InDesign has caught the attention of so many designers. Use the Transparency palette to control this. There you will find a percentage slider, and a Photoshop-like list of blending mode settings from Overlay to Luminosity. The Knockout Group option makes items in a group behave as one unit, rather than individually.

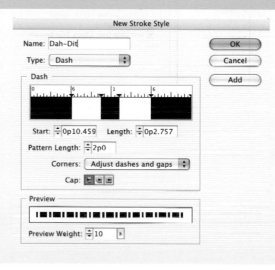

Text wrap, or runarounds, are set in InDesign using the Text Wrap palette, found in **Window > Text Wrap**. Select an object and choose the type of text wrap you'd like the object to have: wrap around the bounding box or the object shape, jump past the whole object, or jump to the next text column. The measurement fields in this palette let you set the amount of offset that's applied, including negative offset to allow

the text to encroach on the object's border, and an option to invert the wrap. Choose **Object > Text Frame Options** and click Ignore Text Wrap to disable wrapping for a text box. One big difference between InDesign and QuarkXPress is that text wrap normally applies to text items on top of the object as well as below it. See Text wrapping on page 182 for more on this subject.

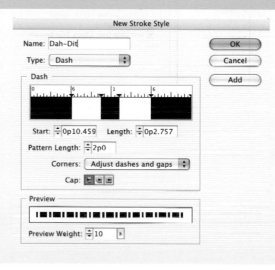

Tip

CREATING CUSTOM RULES

If you like using custom rules, InDesign lets you design your own within your layouts. In the Stroke palette, click the menu button and choose Stroke Styles. Then click New to open the New Stroke Style dialog. Here, you can draw out the profile of your custom line, whether it is a stripe, dotted, or dashed line. Click and drag the arrowhead markers on existing elements, and then click and drag in the stroke creation area to add new elements to the line style. Other options let you choose how the stroke behaves in corners, and how long each repetition of the pattern is on the page. You can't edit any of the ready-made strokes, but your custom strokes can be edited later.

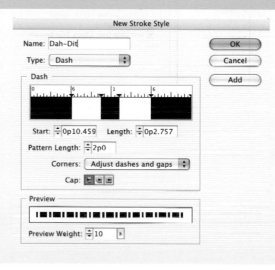

183

Keyboard shortcuts

Every experienced QuarkXPress user will know and use dozens of keyboard shortcuts, jumping from one set of controls to another at high speed. The good news with InDesign is that this hard-won knowledge is directly transferable. Some, but not all, of InDesign's keyboard shortcuts match those in QuarkXPress. You can change any keyboard shortcut you like, but it is well worth approaching this with a degree of caution.

There are two schools of thought when it comes to customizing keyboard shortcuts. One holds that you should shape your production environment to suit your needs and experience, so if you're more comfortable with the QuarkXPress set of keyboard shortcuts, then you should use those. The other contends that you're simply avoiding making the switch to this new, modern layout environment, and your longer-term productivity will suffer as a result. In fact, there's no single right answer. If you're a jobbing designer or production worker, you may need to be able to fit in with the setup of several different studios, so learning the native InDesign shortcuts is a wise move. These will also match many of those in Adobe Illustrator and Photoshop, which can be an advantage. On the other hand, if you don't switch contracts and studios on a regular basis, then customizing the controls to suit your own process can be just as sensible.

184

Edit keyboard shortcuts

To change InDesign's keyboard shortcuts, choose **Edit > Keyboard Shortcuts**. This dialog lists three ready-made sets of shortcuts: Default, Shortcuts for PageMaker 7.0, and Shortcuts for QuarkXPress 4.0. To switch to the tried-and-trusted QuarkXPress range of shortcuts, choose that from the Set menu and click OK. All commands that have a clear equivalent in InDesign will behave as you'd expect.

Custom shortcut sets

Before you spend too much time customizing the Default set, be aware that there's no simple way to revert to the original settings. It is much wiser to create a new custom set and build on that. Click the New Set button, pick the set upon which it is to be based, give it a name, and then add the shortcuts you prefer.

If you plan to modify more than a small handful of shortcuts, plan ahead by making notes of the shortcuts you'd like to include and the items that already use them, in addition to any new shortcuts you might want to create.

With related commands, it is best to try and use related sets of shortcuts. For example, the standard InDesign commands for Fit Page in Window and Fit Spread in Window use Ctrl/Cmd+o and Ctrl/Cmd+Alt/Option+o, and Entire Pasteboard is Ctrl/Cmd+Alt/Option+Shift+o. This kind of grouping makes it much easier to remember whole sets of commands at once. Consider the different modifier keys as well as the characters you use, and try to keep things as consistent as possible.

Shortcuts area

To customize a shortcut in a set, find the command or item by browsing the Product Area menu and scrolling through the list. Select the command, click in the New Shortcut field, then type the key combination that you'd like to use. The application will flag it if it is already assigned to something else (but it won't tell you in which area it is located). You can click the Assign button to add the shortcut to the chosen command. If it is already in use with another command, it will be removed from there automatically, so pay attention as you experiment. If there was a previous shortcut for this command, it will still be listed in the Current Shortcuts, so select it and click Remove. Alternatively, leave it in place to allow both shortcuts to work.

Toolbar shortcuts

Always remember that some of InDesign's tool-selecting shortcuts and behaviors work differently depending on whether or not you're in text-editing mode. As long as you're not clicked into a text box, you can switch tools by typing the appropriate key; just hover over the tool's icon for a few seconds to see its shortcut in a pop-up tooltip label. Every tool in the Toolbar has its own shortcut key, and most of these make basic mnemonic sense. For example, the Pen tool is selected by typing P, the Text tool by typing T, and so on. Others are chosen more for general location convenience, but it doesn't take long to learn the ones that matter to you the most.

If you're editing text, these are obviously not going to work as shortcuts. Hold down the Ctrl/Cmd key and click anywhere to step out of text editing mode, or press Ctrl/Cmd+Shift+A to deselect everything.

There's a similar issue with the Page Grabber tool, used to drag the page around within the window. The normal shortcut for this tool is the Spacebar, but if you're editing text, hold down the Alt/Option key instead. The obligation to use different keys for such an important feature depending on the editing mode is one of the few aspects of InDesign that can become a little tiresome, but you'll get used to it.

Shortcuts

The table below lists all of the keyboard shortcuts in QuarkXPress that perform a different function in InDesign, and gives their alternative InDesign shortcut.

If you're trying to learn the InDesign key commands, but keep hitting Ctrl/Cmd+E to get a picture, this table will tell you what you should be pressing.

	QuarkXPress shortcut	InDesign alternative
General Preferences	Ctrl/Cmd+Y	Ctrl/Cmd+K
Duplicate Item	Ctrl/Cmd+D	Ctrl/Cmd+Alt/Opt+Shift+D
Check Spelling	Ctrl/Cmd+L	Ctrl/Cmd+I
Document Setup	Ctrl/Cmd+Alt/Opt+Shift+P	Ctrl/Cmd+Alt/Opt+P
Export	Ctrl/Cmd+Alt/Opt+E	Ctrl/Cmd+E
New Library	Ctrl/Cmd+Alt/Opt+N	none defined
Place	Ctrl/Cmd+E	Ctrl/Cmd+D
Save As	Ctrl/Cmd+Alt/Opt+S	Ctrl/Cmd+Shift+S
Go to First Page	Ctrl+Shift+A	Ctrl/Cmd+Shift+Page Up
Go to Last Page	Ctrl+Shift+D	Ctrl/Cmd+Shift+Page Down
Go to Next Page	Ctrl+Shift+L	Shift+Page Down
Go to Previous Page	Ctrl+Shift+K	Shift+Page Up
Decrease Item Size/Scale by 5%	Ctrl/Cmd+Alt/Opt+Shift+	Ctrl/Cmd+Alt/Opt+
Increase Item Size/Scale by 5%	Ctrl/Cmd+Alt/Opt+Shift+	Ctrl/Cmd+Alt/Opt+
Nudge Item Down 1/10	Alt/Opt+Down Arrow	Ctrl/Cmd+Shift+Down Arrow
Nudge Item Left 1/10	Alt/Opt+Left Arrow	Ctrl/Cmd+Shift+Left Arrow
Nudge Item Right 1/10	Alt/Opt+Right Arrow	Ctrl/Cmd+Shift+Right Arrow
Nudge Item Up 1/10	Alt/Opt+Up Arrow	Ctrl/Cmd+Shift+Up Arrow
Arrange—Bring Forward	Alt/Opt+F5	Ctrl/Cmd+]
Arrange—Bring to Front	F5	Ctrl/Cmd+Shift+]
Arrange—Send Backward	Alt/Opt+Shift+F5	Ctrl/Cmd+[
Arrange—Send to Back	Shift+F5	Ctrl/Cmd+Shift+[
Clipping Path	Ctrl/Cmd+Opt+T	Ctrl/Cmd+Alt/Opt+Shift+K
Center Content	Ctrl/Cmd+Shift+M	Ctrl/Cmd+Shift+E
Fit Content Proportionally	Ctrl/Cmd+Alt/Opt+Shift+F	Ctrl/Cmd+Alt/Opt+Shift+E
Fit Content to Frame	Ctrl/Cmd+Shift+F	Ctrl/Cmd+Alt/Opt+E
Lock/Unlock position	F6	Ctrl/Cmd+L or Ctrl/Cmd+Alt/Opt+L
Ungroup	Ctrl/Cmd+U	Ctrl/Cmd+Shift+G
Close All Windows	Ctrl/Cmd+Alt/Opt+W	Ctrl/Cmd+Alt/Opt+Shift+W
Make Text Selection Subscript	Ctrl/Cmd+Shift+-	Ctrl/Cmd+Alt/Opt+Shift+=
Open Rules Options	Ctrl/Cmd+Shift+N	Ctrl/Cmd+Alt/Opt+J
Force Justify Text	Ctrl/Cmd+Alt/Opt+Shift+J	Ctrl/Cmd+Shift+F
Make Text Selection Plain	Ctrl/Cmd+Shift+P	Ctrl/Cmd+Shift+Y
Decrease Baseline Shift	Ctrl/Cmd+Alt/Opt+Shift+-	Alt/Opt+Shift+Down Arrow
Decrease Horizontal Scale	Ctrl/Cmd+Alt/Opt+[	none defined
Decrease Horizontal Scale x5	Ctrl/Cmd+[	none defined
Decrease Kerning/Tracking	Ctrl/Cmd+Alt/Opt+Shift+[	Alt/Opt+Left Arrow
Decrease Kerning/Tracking x5	Ctrl/Cmd+Shift+[	Ctrl/Cmd+Alt/Opt+Left Arrow
Decrease Leading	Ctrl/Cmd+Alt/Opt+Shift+;	Alt/Opt+Up Arrow

	QuarkXPress shortcut	InDesign alternative
Decrease Leading x5	Ctrl/Cmd+Shift+;	Ctrl/Cmd+Alt/Opt+Up Arrow
Increase Baseline Shift	Ctrl/Cmd+Alt/Opt+Shift+=	Alt/Opt+Shift+Up Arrow
Increase Horizontal Scale	Ctrl/Cmd+Alt/Opt+]	none defined
Increase Horizontal Scale x5	Ctrl/Cmd+]	none defined
Increase Kerning/Tracking	Ctrl/Cmd+Alt/Opt+Shift+]	Alt/Opt+Right Arrow
Increase Kerning/Tracking x5	Ctrl/Cmd+Shift+]	Ctrl/Cmd+Alt/Opt+Right Arrow
Increase Leading	Ctrl/Cmd+Alt/Opt+Shift+'	Alt/Opt+Down Arrow
Increase Leading x5	Ctrl/Cmd+Shift+	Ctrl/Cmd+Alt/Opt+Down Arrow
Move to Beginning of Story	Ctrl/Cmd+Alt/Opt+Up Arrow	Ctrl/Cmd+Home
Move to End of Story	Ctrl/Cmd+Alt/Opt+Down Arrow	Ctrl/Cmd+End
Move to Start of Line	Ctrl/Cmd+Alt/Opt+Left Arrow	Home
Move to End of Line	Ctrl/Cmd+Alt/Opt+Right Arrow	End
Select to Beginning of Story	Ctrl/Cmd+Alt/Opt+Shift+Up Arrow	Ctrl/Cmd+Shift+Home
Select to End of Story	Ctrl/Cmd+Alt/Opt+Shift+Down Arrow	Ctrl/Cmd+Shift+End
Open Character Palette	Ctrl/Cmd+Shift+D	Ctrl/Cmd+T
Insert Auto Page Number	Ctrl/Cmd+3	Ctrl/Cmd+Alt/Opt+Shift+N
Insert Next Page Number	Ctrl/Cmd+2	none defined
Insert Previous Page Number	Ctrl/Cmd+4	none defined
Insert En Space	Ctrl/Cmd+Alt/Opt+5	Ctrl/Cmd+Shift+N
Insert Nonbreaking Space	Ctrl/Cmd+5	Ctrl/Cmd+Alt/Opt+X
Open Paragraph Palette	Ctrl/Cmd+Shift+F	Ctrl/Cmd+Alt/Opt+T
Show Hidden Characters	Ctrl/Cmd+I	Ctrl/Cmd+Alt/Opt+I
Change Text Size	Ctrl/Cmd+Shift+\	none defined
View Entire Pasteboard	Ctrl/Cmd+Alt/Opt+0	Ctrl/Cmd+Alt/Opt+Shift+0
Show/Hide Guides	F7	Ctrl/Cmd+;
Show/Hide Baseline Grid	Alt/Opt+F7	Ctrl/Cmd+Alt/Opt+'
Snap to Guides	Shift+F7	Ctrl/Cmd+Shift+;
Enter Zoom Percentage	Ctrl+V	Ctrl/Cmd+Alt/Opt+5
Force Screen Redraw	Ctrl/Cmd+Alt/Opt+.	Shift+F5
Suppress Overrides (View Optimized)	Ctrl/Cmd+.	Shift+Escape
Open Align Options	Ctrl/Cmd+,	Shift+F7
Show/Hide Control Palette	F9	Ctrl/Cmd+Alt/Opt+6
Open Index Options	Ctrl/Cmd+Alt/Opt+I	Shift+F8
Open Picture Usage/Links	Alt/Opt+F13	Ctrl/Cmd+Shift+D
Open Pages Palette	F10	F12
Open Stroke Options	Ctrl/Cmd+B	F10
Open Colors/Swatches Palette	F12	F5
Open Text Wrap Options	Ctrl/Cmd+T	Ctrl/Cmd+Alt/Opt+W
Show/Hide Toolbar	F8	none defined

Most of InDesign's features can be found in its palettes. This puts almost everything just a couple of clicks away, and doesn't block access to the layout while you try out settings. However, it does mean that you have to get used to having dozens of different palette windows to deal with. Fortunately, there are a number of tricks that can make a great deal of difference.

The Control palette

First of all, the Control palette, which normally appears as a bar above the document window, shows the essentials for most basic object and type formatting tasks. It is the nearest equivalent to the QuarkXPress Measurements palette, and although you can drag it out to act as a regular floating window, it is best used as a docked bar; document windows won't resize to go underneath it in this mode. If you prefer, you can move it elsewhere by clicking and dragging the vertical bar on the left. To dock it again, grab the vertical drag bar just in the window's left side (not the window title bar itself) and drag it to the left edge of the display, either at the top or bottom. It is generally more useful at the top—particularly on the Macintosh, where the Dock's position is normally at the base of the screen— but you're free to choose.

The Toolbar

InDesign's Toolbar is normally the standard Adobe two-column layout, but you can switch to the more QuarkXPress-like single vertical bar, or a horizontal row, by double-clicking its title bar. The single vertical bar can be very useful when you maximize the document window to fill the screen, as it only covers part of the rulers rather than obscuring a part of your layout.

Most palettes (but not all) have their own keyboard shortcuts for hiding and showing. If a palette is part of a group, the whole group will show, with the palette whose shortcut you entered at the front. If you enter the keyboard shortcut for a palette that's already open, it will close, so if your workspace is cluttered you can use this to see where a palette is located. You can also tab between fields in a palette once it is active, so with a little practice, you can race through palette settings at top speed.

186

Tip

LANGUAGES

The Spelling palette (Edit > Spelling > Check Spelling) is simple to operate, but you may have reason to use something other than the default language of "English: USA." This can't be changed here; instead, go to the Dictionary option in the InDesign preferences, and pick your preferred language for checking spelling. The list is impressive, including U.S. legal and medical dictionaries, as well as U.K. English, Italian, three dialects of German, and so on.

Bulgarian
Catalan
Croatian
Czech
Danish
Dutch
English: Canadian
✓ English: UK
English: USA
English: USA Legal
English: USA Medical
Estonian
Finnish
French
French: Canadian
German: Reformed
German: Swiss
German: Traditional
Greek
Hungarian
Italian

Entering values in fields

When dealing with numbers in the many different fields in these palettes, you can use basic math operations as well as typing numbers in directly. You're also free to mix measurement systems, so if you'd like to position something 70mm + 10pt from the top of the page, just type that into the appropriate field and press the Return key. The result will be shown in the unit of measure you have set for the document. You can't do more complex math in one step, such as 70mm + (3.5 * 11pt). Those calculations must be done step by step.

Docking palettes

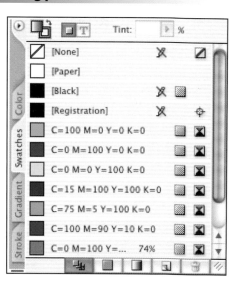

Palettes can be free-floating or docked to the side of the display. When they are docked, they slide open and closed at a click, staying neatly out of the way as vertically minimized tabs when closed. This helps keep features at hand without taking up too much space on your screen. To dock a palette, drag it by its tab to either side of the display, and to undock it, just drag it out again. InDesign starts off with all the docked palettes placed on the right, but it can make just as much sense to place some of them on the left. You could use this approach to split the docked items into two main categories, so you always reach in one direction for certain controls.

Palette modes

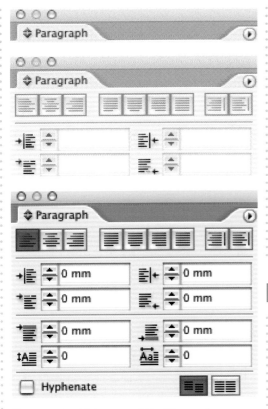

If you want to minimize a floating palette, just click its grow button (the green button in the Mac, or the horizontal bar on the right in Windows) or double-click the window's title bar. Try

clicking this more than once; some palettes cycle between three different sizes. Alternatively, click the "double arrow" symbol next to the palette's title to switch modes.

Palette groups

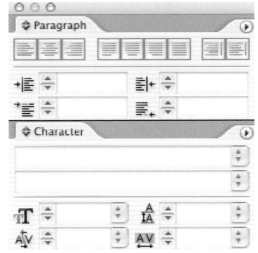

As well as managing palette windows by resizing and docking them, you can combine different palettes within a single window. When you show one of these, the others in its group come with it as clickable tabs. Some palettes are combined already, but you can make your own combinations to suit how you prefer to work. Drag a palette by its title tab onto another one to combine it, and drag it out by its tab to remove it from a group.

Going even further, you can stick windows together

by dragging one by its title tab onto the base of another palette. Don't let go until the base of the second window is highlighted. Now you've combined two palettes so they move and hide as one, but in a way that lets you see both sets of controls at the same time. Finally, if your palettes are cluttering up the screen, press the Tab key (assuming you're not editing text) to hide them all, or press Shift+Tab to hide everything but the Toolbar, and press the shortcut once more to reveal everything again.

Save Workspace

Once you've arranged everything to your liking, go to **Window > Workspace > Save Workspace** and save the entire arrangement—including which items are open and which closed—so you can recall it at any time. You could even use multiple workspace arrangements, one set up for creative design work and another optimized for final production. See pages 128–129 for more on this.

Dialog windows

InDesign does use dialog windows when necessary, but the majority of them have a Preview checkbox so you can see the results of any changes to settings

without having to click OK first. You can use basic math and mix measurement systems in appropriate fields here, too, just as in InDesign's palettes.

See pages 128–129 for more on this.

Tip

QUICK APPLY

The Quick Apply window appears when you choose Edit > Quick Apply or type Ctrl/Cmd+Return. This lists any existing styles that are appropriate to the selection—character and paragraph styles for text, and object styles for anything else. You can apply styles quickly here, and if your styles list is too long to browse comfortably, just type some of the letters from the name for any styles you want to see. Styles without those letters in their name (in any order) will be hidden, leaving you with just the ones you want. For example, type "ed2" to find a style called "Header style 2."

To apply a style, press Return. To apply a paragraph style and remove existing overriding paragraph style settings, press Alt/Option+Return, and press Alt/Option+Shift+Return to override

character styles as well. Use Shift+Return to apply a style and leave the Quick Apply window open.

- [ ] **Filled artwork box**
- [ ] **Mapping**
- [ ] **Teaser**
- [ ] **[Basic Graphics Frame]**
- [ ] **[Basic Text Frame]**
- [ ] **[None]**

Index

INDEX

Acknowledgments

Keith Martin would like to thank his wife for being understanding about his deadlines.

Anne-Marie Concepción would like to thank her friend and fellow InDesign geek, David Blatner, for helping her truly master this program; her "Number Two" at Seneca Design, Sherri Austin, for keeping the decks cleared and the dogs at bay while she was working on her chapters; and whoever wrote the Adobe white papers on printing and transparency, which were an invaluable resource to her (and highly recommended to any InDesign user—you can download the PDFs from the Adobe web site).

Cutting board image used on pages 116–119
©2005 JupiterImages Corporation™